Mommy's Little Girl

*Casey Anthony and Her Daughter
Caylee's Tragic Fate*

DIANE FANNING

St. Martin's Paperbacks

To Caylee Marie Anthony

ACKNOWLEDGMENTS

I honestly don't know how Danielle Tavernier of the State Attorney's Office managed to keep up with all the media requests for this case. Not only were the number of queries extraordinary, but the volume of documents, video and audio recordings and photographs was staggering. Thank you, Danielle, for always being courteous, professional and prompt with your responses. You deserve a medal.

I truly appreciate Rick Cuza[1], Jesse Grund, Richard Grund and Jackie Mattlin for sharing their personal experiences. And thanks to the many others who spoke with me but requested anonymity.

Thanks to Carlos Padilla and Fox 35's Shannon Butler for their helpfulness and to Dan Philips of Mission Investigations for his assistance.

I extend endless appreciation to Matt Phelps, Kathryn Casey and Sue Russell for their friendship and support as I worked on this book.

Thanks to Charlie Spicer for giving me this opportunity, to Yaniv Soha for his input and advice and to Jane Dystel, my guiding light.

And as always, I couldn't have done it without my own 24/7 cheerleader, Wayne Fanning—thanks for always being here.

---

[1] The last name of Cindy Anthony's birth family has been changed throughout the book to protect their privacy.

AUTHOR'S NOTE

This is a true story, though some names have been changed.

This book is based on a careful review of more than 6000 pages of transcripts of police interviews, police reports and other official documents, as well as audiotaped and videotaped conversations and interviews, and information gathered from on-site research and personal interviews. However, the author conducted no interviews with Casey, Cindy, George, or Lee Anthony.

THE DISCLOSURE

"Repetition does not transform
a lie into the truth."

—Franklin Roosevelt

CHAPTER 1

George Anthony stopped by the post office to pick up a certified letter just before noon on July 15, 2008. White hair flowed straight back from his forehead, leaving a pronounced widow's peak. Still-dark eyebrows predominated his face, making his eyes appear sunken over his sharp nose.

Considering the way the mail was sent, and his recent financial problems, George thought it was bound to be bad news inside the envelope. He was right. It was a notification from Johnson's Wrecker Service. It made no sense. According to the company, they had possession of his family Pontiac. His daughter Casey drove this car, and she was in Jacksonville. He didn't understand how the 1998 Pontiac Sunfire had ended up in an impound lot in Orlando.

He called his wife Cindy. She was equally puzzled by the situation. George headed to the Narcoossee Road address to ask questions and pick up the car. At the front counter, Nicole Lett surprised him when she said that Johnson's Wreckers had towed the Pontiac at the end of June at the request of Amscot, a payday loan company, on the corner of East Colonial Drive and North Goldenrod Road in Orlando. To retrieve the vehicle, he needed to show proof of ownership and pay $466.78 in cash for the towing and storage charges.

George called Cindy again. Then he called Amscot and asked why they'd ordered the car removed from their lot. They told him the car had sat in the spot for three days before they'd called Johnson's Wreckers. They thought it had been abandoned.

Cindy and George met at home, picked up the title, stopped at the bank to withdraw $500 and, two hours after George's first visit, returned to the towing company.

The couple walked up to the counter and greeted Nicole. Cindy, in a cute, short blonde cut with youthful bangs, was in obvious ire. She demanded an explanation of the company's process for sending a certified letter, expressing her annoyance at the number of days that had passed before they received notification in the mail. "We thought the car was in Jacksonville. How were we supposed to know it was here?"

Nicole attempted to explain the situation, but Cindy wasn't listening. She launched instead into a long complaint about having to pay the high charges, particularly the $35 administrative fee for sending the certified letter. She also balked at paying all of the accumulated storage charges, blaming the company for the notification delay.

Nicole was used to dealing with disgruntled customers. No one was ever pleased to come to the lot to recover their car, and usually, they took it out on her. The difference with this couple was their surprise and confusion. They could not understand why the car was here instead of up north where their daughter said she'd driven it. They fretted vocally about not seeing her or their granddaughter for a month or more. Nicole had no answers to that question. She called her supervisor, Simon Burch, to address their other concerns.

When he approached the counter, Cindy asked, "Why is the bill so expensive? Why did it take eleven days to notify me that you had my car?"

"Per Florida statutes, on the fourth day, we're required by law to send out a certified letter to the registered owner of the vehicle. Our computer system automatically generates those letters," he answered. He spread out a calendar and together they looked at the dates. "Four days after

your car arrived was the Fourth of July. Due to the holiday and the weekend that followed, that's probably why it
took so long for the letter to get to you. We can't control
the post office."

"Okay," Cindy said. "I understand, and I appreciate it."
She then turned to George and they exchanged terse comments. She obviously was still dissatisfied and a bit disgruntled that George was not taking a strong stand. She
turned back to Simon and asked for a discount.

"I'm sorry, ma'am. I'm not at liberty to do that. You
know, unfortunately, this is a business. It's not a particularly pleasant job sometimes, but it is a business, you know,
that's in business to make money, and we don't give dis-
counts."

Unhappy, but seeing no other alternative, Cindy agreed
to pay. Nicole filled out the paperwork, got verification of
ownership on line, accepted payment and issued a receipt. Simon asked, "Do you have the keys?"

George said he did.

"Okay, no problem, then. I'll come around and get you."

As Simon and George walked to the vehicle in the pour-
ing rain, George apologized for his wife's aggressive manner. "We'll probably get divorced over this. The daughter is
telling us crap, a bunch of lies."

"I'm sorry about your situation," Simon sympathized.

"I just need to see my granddaughter. You know, she
won't let us see our granddaughter," George complained.

"I'm sorry about your situation, sir. You know, I'm
sorry your car got impounded, but this is what it is,"
Simon said.

When they got within three feet of the white Pontiac,
George smelled a distinctive unpleasant odor. He'd once
worked in law enforcement. He knew that smell, and it
filled him with dread. He thought of his daughter and
granddaughter. *Please don't let this be what I think it is.*
He walked around to the driver's side and inserted the
key. He noticed his granddaughter's car seat in the back
and pulled open the door.

"Whoa, does that stink!" Simon exclaimed. The stench reminded him of another car that had been impounded recently. Before they towed it, the vehicle had sat for five days—with the body of a man who'd committed suicide inside.

George sat down in the driver's seat and reached over to the other side, opening the passenger's door to ventilate the car. As he breathed in the odor, his horror increased. He turned the key in the ignition to start it, but then he paused. *No, George*, he told himself. *If there's something wrong, you got to find out now. You can't take it away.*

"Will you please walk around to the back of the car and look inside this with me?" George asked. *Please don't let this be my Caylee.*

"Well, here, let me. Give me the keys and we'll open the trunk up. There's something like garbage in here."

"Yeah," was all George could find to reply.

When the trunk opened, flies buzzed out, and both men rocked back on their heels from the pungent odor. "Puff!" George exclaimed. "That's rotten!"

Simon knew with certainty that rotting garbage did not smell like that, but he kept those thoughts to himself.

The men saw an imperfectly round, basketball-sized stain in the middle of the trunk. To the left, by the tail-light, was a trash bag. "Let's just make sure there is garbage in here," Simon said. He pulled the bag toward the edge of the trunk, surprised by its light weight. Unfastening the tie, he spread open the top. They both peered down at papers, dryer lint, Arm & Hammer laundry detergent, a pizza box and other assorted trash.

"Well, here, I'll take care of this. I'll get rid of it for you," Simon said. He walked toward the front of the car, where a Dumpster sat on the other side of the fence. He heaved the bag over. While Simon disposed of the trash, George stepped into a corner, hunched over and heaved up his most recent meal.

George pulled himself together, slid into the front seat and tried to start the car again, but he couldn't get the engine to turn over. Simon looked over George's shoulder at the control panel and saw that the gas gauge pointed to empty. "Oh, it's out of gas," he said.

"Okay," George said. "Well, I brought gas with me."

Together they walked back to George's car. George re-iterated his complaints about his daughter's lies along the way. He pulled a small, round, battered metal gas can with chipped paint out of the trunk. On the way back to the Pontiac, George apologized again for his wife's attitude.

"I totally understand, dude," Simon said. "We get it all the time. It's no big deal."

With a gallon of gas in its tank, the car started right up. George drove it out of the fenced lot to the front of the business, where he got out and approached Simon again. George offered his hand and said, "Thank you. I'm sorry."

Simon shook his hand and said, "Yeah, no problem. No problem. Have a good day now." He turned away and went inside as George approached Cindy's car.

"This car stinks so bad," he told his wife, "I don't know how I can drive it home."

He wanted to roll the windows all the way down, but the rainfall made that impossible. With the windows cracked less than an inch, he could not get enough fresh air, and gagged all the way home. He pulled the Pontiac into the garage.

Cindy walked in and came to an abrupt stop. "Jesus Christ!" she shouted. "What died?"

CHAPTER 2

George stood in silence, not daring to voice his darkest fears.

"George, it was the pizza, right?" Cindy asked in a voice tinged with desperation.

"Yeah," George lied, "it was the pizza."

Nonetheless, the sight of Caylee's car seat in the back, along with her white backpack, adorned with brown monkeys, and her very favorite baby doll, cinched up Cindy's anxiety another notch. The couple removed the battery from the car to foil any plans their daughter Casey might have to remove the vehicle from the garage. They thought about going through the car in search of answers, but Cindy saw the rising level of anger in her husband and knew they both needed to be at work. "I'll take care of everything with Casey," she told her agitated husband. Cindy left home to finish her day as a managing nurse at Gentiva Health Services in Winter Park. George reported for security duty at the Premiere Cinema in the Fashion Square Mall.

When Cindy returned home, she walked straight to the garage. She thought it very odd that Casey had left a purse in the car. She picked it up and found a piece of paper beneath it with the phone number for Amy Huizenga scrawled on it. Cindy had never met Amy, but knew she was her daughter's friend. She stopped her inspection of the car to call.

Cindy caught Amy at The Florida Mall where she was

hanging out with her friend J.P., who was shopping for a cell phone. "Amy, this is Mrs. Anthony, Casey's mom. Have you seen Casey in the last few days?"

"Well, Mrs. Anthony, she picked me up at the airport a few hours ago. I just got back from Puerto Rico."

"Really? How did she pick you up?"

"I had lent her my car for the last week because her car was in the shop."

"Do you have your car now?" Cindy asked.

"No, I'm at the mall with a friend."

"Well where is your car? Does Casey still have it?"

"No, I dropped her off at Tony Lazzaro's. I believe that's where she's at. My car is at my apartment."

"How long will you be there? When do you think you'll get back to the apartment? I'd like to meet up with you and talk to you."

"I don't know," Amy said. "We might be here for a little while."

"Amy, I don't know where Casey is, and I don't know if Caylee's with her or not. I'm a little concerned. Do you think I could come pick you up? 'Cause I'm not that far. We live close to the airport. It would take me twenty minutes, maybe half an hour."

When Amy paused, Cindy explained about the car in the impound lot and said that she needed Amy's help. "If we don't find Casey, she'll end up in jail," Cindy pleaded, sounding as if she were on the verge of tears. If she didn't locate her granddaughter soon, someone would certainly call the police.

Amy hesitated. "I could meet you somewhere, but I need to make a phone call first." She disconnected the line and thought about the panic in Cindy's voice, the strained tone of an emotional parent who was concerned and not sure what to do. Cindy's willingness to drive all the way to the mall compelled Amy to help her. She called J.P.'s cell and asked him how much longer he thought he'd be in line, waiting to get the new iPhone.

"An hour or more," he said.

Amy told him she was getting another ride. She returned Cindy's call and agreed to the pick-up.

Amy was the visually opposite of her petite, olive-complected friend Casey—half-a-foot taller, with blonde hair and an athletic build. On the ride over to Tony's apartment to find Casey, Cindy related every detail of the impounded car story, from receiving the initial letter to bringing the vehicle home from the wrecker company. "The car smelled like something died in it," Cindy confided. "We were terrified that either Caylee or Casey was stuffed in the trunk until we got it open."

"Oh, yeah," Amy said. "Casey told me she had run something over with her car."

"Really? Well, we didn't know that."

Amy decided not to expand on the story. Actually Casey had said that her dad ran something over with the car, but she knew Casey often lied.

Cindy continued her story about the smell in the trunk of the car. "The impound lot didn't have the keys, so they couldn't open the trunk. When we opened the trunk, there were pizza boxes with maggots inside. We're assuming that's what the smell was," Cindy said.

Amy didn't contradict Cindy, but she was certain that Casey had told her the smell came from the engine.

Cindy continued, "But I'm worried about Caylee. I haven't talked to her. I haven't seen her for over a month. Casey keeps telling me, 'She's fine. She's with the nanny.' But I'm worried. I think Casey is an unfit mother. She parties all the time. If this goes on much longer, I'll sue for custody of Caylee if it comes to that. Do you know where Casey works?"

"Universal?"

"I'm not even sure she has a job," Cindy said, and then outlined Casey's history of stealing money from her parents. "She even stole money from her eighty-year-old grandmother by using the routing number on a birthday check."

"I loaned her eighty dollars to get the car towed," Amy said. Then she told Cindy about another mystery. According to Casey, Amy had sleepwalking problems. Casey said that recently Amy, in a semi-conscious state, had pulled out a wad of bills, counted it out—$400 altogether—and tucked it away for safe keeping. Amy believed the story because of an incident a couple of weeks earlier. "I don't remember doing it. I don't know why I did it, but I woke up in a different pair of pants." Amy tore the house apart looking for the cash, but never found it. She thought she must have hidden it a little too well.

"No, honey," Cindy said. "That money is gone. You'll never see it again."

Amy wondered how deep Casey's lies went. "Has Mr. Anthony been sick at all lately, or been in the hospital?"

"No, not at all," Cindy answered.

So the story of the stroke was a lie. "Alright, this is a little personal, but I need to know how far this thing goes. Are you and your husband having any, you know, marital trouble right now?"

"No, not at all."

Casey's story of her father's two-year affair was a lie then, too, Amy thought. "Are you selling your house to Casey?"

"That was never even a thought in my mind." Cindy went on to explain that she'd once considered Casey's request to buy the house, but her daughter could not afford the mortgage.

Amy led Cindy up the stairs to Tony's apartment. Cindy hung back in a corner, out of view. When Amy knocked, a voice shouted, "Come in."

Amy opened the door, saw Casey, and motioned her over. She then turned to Cindy and urged her closer. When the two came together, Amy remained trapped in a corner while they squabbled.

Beneath slick, dark chin-length hair, Casey's face radiated sweetness, warmth and a fun-loving nature when she smiled. But at moments like this, when she was angered, all of that washed away in a cold deluge, making her look hard, harsh and unforgiving. "What are you doing here?" Casey snapped at her mother.

"Where is Caylee?" Cindy demanded to know.

"She's fine. She's with the nanny," Casey said without any attempt to disguise her irritation.

"You're going to take me to her right now," Cindy insisted.

"You don't need to see her."

Amy wriggled out of the corner and went a ways down the stairs to get out of the line of fire while she waited for her ride home.

"I have to see her and make sure she's okay," Cindy pleaded.

"She's with the nanny. She's good. We needed some space." Casey's angry tone increased with every word she spoke.

Twenty-two-year-old Casey displayed an attitude that reminded Amy of a petulant sixteen-year-old girl caught violating curfew and lashing out at her mother.

Cindy's voice hardened. "I want to see my granddaughter. I want to be selfish. You are taking me to see Caylee now."

Cindy remained unrelenting on the subject. Finally, after half an hour, Casey gave in. "Fine," she said. "We'll drop off Amy and we'll talk."

"We can talk, but you're taking me to Caylee. I want to see my granddaughter."

Casey stormed back into the apartment. Unaware of the conversation outside of the apartment, Anthony and his roommate were surprised by the intensity of her angry entrance. Cindy waited in the doorway. "Get your things," Cindy shouted as Casey rushed away. "You're coming with me."

"Okay, but I'm coming back," Casey snapped.

"No," Cindy insisted. "Get all of your things."

"No, I'm coming back," Casey retorted.

While Casey gathered a few items from the bedroom,

Cindy stood rigidly at the door. Tony felt awkward, having never met Casey's mother, but he tried to be courteous. "Hello," he said. "You can come in."

Cindy stepped inside and said, "I hope you're rich, because Casey's going to take all your money and leave you high and dry."

Anthony and his roommate stared at her blankly, not knowing how to respond. Casey stomped back into the living room and shouted, "Shut up!" at her mother. Without another word, she walked outside and Cindy followed.

As they drove, Cindy continued to badger Casey for answers. Casey was not at all forthcoming. Amy squirmed in the back seat. The mother–daughter war of wills made her very uncomfortable.

Cindy continued to pepper her daughter with questions. "The car smells like shit. We were terrified. We thought something happened to you and Caylee. What happened in that car?"

Casey gave no response.

"Why did you lead Amy on about buying the house?" Cindy continued.

Amy cringed. She wanted to be left out of it. *Just take me home. Drop me off. I found Casey, my job is done.*

Casey didn't answer that query either. She gazed straight ahead, outside of the car. Her face was hard and cold, with no evidence of remorse, no hint of apology.

When they pulled to the curb to drop her off, Amy suppressed a huge sigh of relief. As she stepped out of the car, Cindy said, "I'll let you know what happens. I'll let you know if Caylee's okay."

For a while, Cindy drove around, begging and insisting that Casey take her to Caylee. Her daughter, however, resisted, claiming Caylee would be asleep and she didn't want to bother her.

Exasperated with her daughter, Cindy called her husband's cell and left a message. "Hey, George, call me as quick as you can."

George called her back ten or fifteen minutes later, at

about 8:15, but the call was routed to voicemail. "Hey, I just wanted to let you know I'm here. What's going on? Is everything okay?" When he hadn't heard from her fifteen minutes later, he tried the home phone and got no answer there either. He called his son, Lee, who lived a couple of blocks away. "It's a long story, but Casey's in a lot of trouble. We don't know where Caylee's at. I'm worried about your mother. Get down there. Beat feet. Get to Mom."

CHAPTER 3

Casey's older brother Lee pulled up to the house five minutes after talking to his father. The coarse blackness of his facial hair gave him a nearly perpetual 5 o'clock shadow beneath the ridge of his heavy brow and dominant eyebrows. As usual he entered through the garage, where he found himself repelled by the smell. He saw the white Pontiac his sister drove—the trunk was open, the windows rolled down.

He went into the house, but no one was at home, raising his sense of alarm. He called his mother's cell. Meanwhile, Cindy had given up on getting any cooperation from her daughter and called the sheriff's department, where she was told to go home and call them back from there. To Lee she said, "I'm thirty seconds away from pulling in. I've got your sister in the car."

"Okay," Lee said and went outside to meet them as they pulled into the driveway. He saw the strain on their faces as they stepped out of the car. Casey snapped at her mother, "You know you won't even listen to me, so why do I even bother!" She stomped off inside.

"Mom, what's going on?" Lee asked.

"Your sister knows where Caylee is, and she won't take me to her. I'm going to call the police, and you need to talk to your sister."

Lee left his mother in the living room and went down the hall to his sister's bedroom. He stood in the doorway while Casey sat on the side of the bed. He hoped he could delay the call to the police by getting information from her. "Where is Caylee?"

"I know where Caylee is. She's with the nanny. She's sleeping. I don't want to take her out of what's been normal for her lately. We can get her in the morning," Casey insisted.

Cindy stalked down the hall talking about her concern over the state of the car and complaining that Casey had lied about being out of town. "Okay," she said. "If you weren't where you were, how do I know that Caylee is where you say she's been?"

Lee offered what he hoped was an acceptable compromise: "I will go. Tell me where I can go to see Caylee myself. I'll go for five minutes. I'll do it your way. I'll just go and just make sure that she's okay." He then offered to take along his roommate to verify what he saw.

Cindy interrupted, "That is unacceptable. I want her here. I want her home. I don't want just to see her. I want to hold her. I want her to be here." She walked away in frustration.

"Mom won't allow that to happen," Casey told Lee, confirming her mother's statement.

Lee continued to try to reason with his sister. At nearly six feet tall, he towered over his younger sister. "What's going on? What's the deal? Why are you going to allow Mom to get the police involved in this?"

"I don't want to disrupt her life, because from here on out, Caylee's life will never be the same."

"Could you take Mom and me to Caylee tomorrow?" Lee asked, seeking a compromise between his mother and sister.

"Mom has thrown it in my face many times before that I'm an unfit mother, and, you know, maybe she's right, and maybe I am."

Lee didn't want to get distracted by side issues. He wanted to solve the problem of the moment. "Why won't you allow us to see Caylee?"

"Maybe I'm a spiteful bitch," Casey snarled.

"Well, I don't get it. What's in it for you? Why are you letting the police get involved in this? This doesn't make any sense to me."

"Look, maybe this should have been done a long time ago. I've stolen money from Mom. I've been a bad daughter. I've stolen money from you. I've been untrustworthy. And maybe I have been a . . . a . . . a, you know, a bad mother, daughter and sister, you know? So this should have been done a long time ago."

Lee asked again about seeing Caylee, and Casey continued in her obstinate refusal.

At last he threw up his hands and turned to his mother. "Fine, call the cops, because I'm with you. I want her to prove it, if she won't allow us to go."

Cindy stepped outside with the phone and punched in 9-1-1. "I have someone here who I need to be arrested in my home," Cindy told the operator.

"They are there right now?"

"And I have a possible missing child," Cindy said with a sob. "I have a three-year-old who has been missing for a month."

"A three-year-old? Have you reported that?"

"I'm trying to do that now," Cindy snapped.

"Okay, what did the person do that you need arrested?"

"My daughter."

"For what?"

"For stealing an auto and stealing money," Cindy explained. "I already spoke to someone who said they would patch me through to the Orlando sheriff's department and have a deputy here. I was in the car and I was going to drive her to the police station and no one is open. They said they would bring a deputy to my home when I got home to call them."

"So, she stole your vehicle?"

"Yeah."

"When did she do that?"

"On the thirtieth. I just got back from the impound. I'd

like to speak to an officer. Can you have someone come out to my house?"

"Okay. Okay, I've got to ask these questions so I can put them in the call, okay?"

"Okay."

"The thirtieth of June?" the operator confirmed.

"Yeah."

"Okay, how old is your daughter?"

"Twenty-two."

"Okay what's her name?"

"My name?"

"Her name."

"Her name? Casey Anthony. C-A-S-E-Y."

"And your name?"

"Cynthia Anthony."

After getting Cindy's telephone number, the dispatcher continued. "And you said you have the vehicle back."

"Yes. And I have the, uhm, statement."

"Casey's there right now?"

"Yes, I got her. I finally found her after a month. She's been missing for a month. I found her, but we can't find my granddaughter."

"Okay. How tall is Casey?"

"Five foot one-and-a-half."

"Thin, medium or heavy build?"

"Thin."

"What color hair?"

"Brown."

"What color shirt is she wearing?"

"White."

"What color pants?"

"Oh, they're shorts," Cindy said. "But they're plaid. They're like pink and teal and light black plaid."

"Does she have any weapons on her?"

"No."

"Is Casey not telling you where her daughter is?"

"Correct."

"Alright, we'll have a deputy out to you as soon as one's available."

"Thank you," Cindy said as she walked into the house and loudly declared, "The cops are on the way. She's going to have to prove it now." She turned around and went back outside.

Lee walked down the hall to his sister's room. "Casey, here's what I don't get. What's in this for you? Mom, as much as she doesn't like that you're running up her credit bills and all this stuff, she's never called the police. She's never even threatened to call the police. So why would you let all these other things be the reason why you get in trouble? I don't get it. What's your motivation right now? I just don't understand. You've got to understand what's going to happen when the officer arrives. So, let's go through this right now, because I don't understand what you're going to do there."

Casey did not respond.

Lee continued, "The officer is going to say, you know, 'Good evening, Ms. Anthony. Where's your daughter?' That's exactly what he's going to say. And what are you going to say?"

"She's with the nanny. She's sleeping," Casey said.

Lee continued in the role of policeman. "Great, Ms. Anthony. I'm so happy to hear that. That's going to be a relief for everybody. So hop in the car. Your mom's going to follow. Let's go get her." A shocked expression crossed Casey's face. Lee shrugged his shoulders. "What's it going to be, Casey? What are you going to say?"

Casey slumped and burst into tears. "Lee, you want to know the truth? I haven't seen Caylee in thirty-one days." She threw her hands over her face and repeated the sentence.

"Where have you been?" Lee whispered, afraid his mother would overhear. "When and where is the last time you've seen her?"

"She was kidnapped," Casey sobbed.

Cindy heard the furtive conversation and knew something was up. She exploded through the doorway and
demanded, "What have you done? Why are you crying?
What's going on?"

Casey raised her head and turned tear-stained eyes to
her mother. "I don't know where Caylee is."

CHAPTER 4

Cindy shouted, "Who took her? Who took her?"

"Uhm, the nanny did. She was kidnapped, Mom," Casey cried.

Cindy slammed her fist on the bed. "We could have found her a month ago. Why did you wait?"

Casey's tears dried as if they'd never been shed, and her eyes turned as cold and sharp as shattered crystals. Lee ran from the room and into the kitchen to get a pad of paper and a pen. He wanted to get information from his sister so that he could search for Caylee. When he returned to the bedroom, Cindy held a telephone to her ear while she talked to her daughter. "We'll have a court order to get her. If that's how you want to play, we'll do it, and you'll never . . ."

"That's not how I want to play," Casey objected.

"Well, then you have . . ."

Casey cut her off. "Give me one more day."

"No, I'm not giving you another day. I've given you a month . . ."

The operator interrupted. "9-1-1, what's your emergency?"

"I called a little bit ago," Cindy said. "The deputy sheriff's not here. I found out my granddaughter has been taken. She's been missing for a month. Her mother finally admitted she's been missing." While she talked, Cindy walked up the hall, out of the house and into the garage.

"Okay. What's the address you're calling from?"

Ignoring her question, Cindy said, "We're talking about a three-year-old little girl. My daughter finally admitted that the baby-sitter stole her. I need to find her."

"Your daughter admitted that the baby is where?"

"That the baby-sitter took her a month ago. That my daughter's been looking for her. I told you my daughter was missing for a month. I just found her today. But I can't find my granddaughter. She just admitted to me that she's been trying to find her herself. There's something wrong," Cindy's voice strained with emotion. "I found my daughter's car today and it smells like there's been a dead body in the damn car."

"Okay. What is the three-year-old's name?"

"Caylee. C-A-Y-L-E-E Anthony."

"Caylee Anthony?"

"Yes."

"Okay. Is she white, black or Hispanic?"

"She's white."

"How long has she been missing for?"

"I have not seen her since the seventh of June," Cindy wailed as she watched from the open garage door as George returned from work and pulled into the driveway.

"What is her date of birth?"

"Um. Eight . . . Eight/Nine/two thousand . . . Oh God, she's three. She's . . . Two-thousand-*five*." Cindy turned to her husband. "George, Caylee's missing."

"What?"

"Caylee's missing. Casey says she [the nanny] took her a month ago," Cindy shrieked.

The dispatcher interrupted. "Okay. I need, um. I understand. Can you just calm down for me for just a minute? I need to know what's going on. Okay?"

Cindy mumbled and the operator continued, "Is your daughter there?"

"I'm on the phone with them," Cindy told George.

"Is your daughter there?" the dispatcher repeated.

"Yes."

"Can I speak with her? Do you mind if I speak with her? Thank you."

Cindy talked to George as she walked into the house and down the hall to Casey's room. "I called them two hours ago, and they haven't gotten here. Casey finally admitted that [Zenaida, the nanny] took her a month ago and [Casey] has been trying to find her."

Not sure of what was going on, the dispatcher attempted to get Cindy's attention. "Ma'am? Ma'am?"

Cindy reached the bedroom where her son was jotting down notes. She told her daughter, "It's the Orange County sheriff's department. They want to talk to you. Answer their questions."

Casey grabbed the phone and greeted the operator.

"Hi. What can you tell me about what's going on, a little bit?" the dispatcher asked.

"I'm sorry," Casey said, not understanding the awkwardly posed question.

"Can you tell me a little bit what's going on?"

"My daughter's been missing for the last thirty-one days."

"And you know who has her?"

"I know who has her. I've tried to contact her. I actually received a phone call today. Now, from a number that is no longer in service. I did get to speak to my daughter for about a moment. About a minute."

"Okay. Did you guys call and report a vehicle stolen?"

"Uhm. Yes, my mom did."

"Okay. So is the vehicle stolen, too?"

"No," Casey said. "This is my vehicle."

"What vehicle was stolen?"

"Um, it's a 'ninety-eight Pontiac Sunfire."

"Okay. I have deputies on the way to you right now for that. So now your three-year-old daughter is missing? Caylee Anthony?"

"Yes," Casey answered without any apparent emotion.

"White female?"

"Yes. White female."

"Three years old? Eight/nine/two thousand five is her date of birth?"

"Yes."

"And you last saw her a month ago?"

"Thirty-one days, been thirty-one days."

"Who has her? Do you have a name?"

"Her name is Zenaida Fernandez-Gonzales."

"Who is that?" the dispatcher asked. "Baby-sitter?"

"She's been my nanny for about a year-and-a-half. Almost two years."

"Why are you calling now? Why didn't you call thirty-one days ago?"

"I've been looking for her and have gone through other resources to try to find her, which was stupid."

CHAPTER 5

After learning about Casey's habitual theft, Amy grew concerned about her own bank account. She went on line to check her balance. She'd thought she had a little more than $600 remaining. The bank thought otherwise: Her balance was zero.

She made a conscious effort to avoid panic and to still the automatic response that was making her hyperventilate. The last time she'd seen her checkbook, it was in the car. Casey had driven her car.

She sent her roommate, Rico Morales, down to look in her vehicle while she called the Bank of America. As she explained the situation, Rico came back upstairs with the bad news. Her checkbook was not in the car. The bank told her that nothing could be done that night.

Curious about the unfolding situation, Tony Lazzaro sent a text message to Casey. He heard the tone from Casey's cell and realized that she hadn't taken the phone with her. He dumped out the contents of Casey's different bags. Inside one of them, he found the cell phone and a checkbook belonging to Amy Huizenga.

He scrolled through Casey's contact information until he located Amy's number. Amy was glad he'd found her checkbook, but she warned him that he and his roommate needed to check their bank accounts, because Casey had stolen money from hers.

Tony folded and repacked Casey's clothing in the duffle bag, still confused about what was happening with Casey.

Deputy Ryan Eberlin, the first officer to arrive at the Anthony home on Hopespring Drive, met Lee Anthony outside. Lee ran through the situation he'd discovered at home and the backstory about the suspected kidnapper. He agreed to provide a written statement.

Eberlin then spoke to Cindy Anthony. She explained that she had requested the return of the car and a visit with her granddaughter three weeks ago. Casey had told her she couldn't return the car, since she was in Jacksonville. Although she'd harbored suspicions about Casey's stories for a month, Cindy had believed her daughter until they got the notice that the car had been towed in Orlando. George spoke to Eberlin next, confirming the statements of his wife and son.

While Eberlin spoke to Lee's parents, he sat out in the garage with his sister. The atrocious stench from the car drove him back into the house. When he returned, he asked his sister about the smell.

"Well, it actually started around Mom's birthday [June 5]. It started around the time when two squirrels crawled up under the hood of the car and died in there."

Lee knew his parents had seen Caylee the weekend after that date, and questioned her timeline. "Well, either Mom or Dad would have smelled that."

"That's when it started," Casey insisted. "It started at that time and got progressively worse."

Lee asked her what she'd done to find Caylee, and Casey told him about her stake-out of Zenaida's apartment, when she sat there in her car watching the front door. It was, she said, the day she dropped Caylee off at the complex, but she began to mix up the date, saying it was June 9 and then June 15. When Lee called her on the contradiction, she said she'd watched the apartment on a number of occasions.

Finally, Officer Eberlin took Casey aside to get her statement. She claimed that the last time she had seen her daughter was on the 9th of June, when she'd left her with the baby-sitter, Zenaida Fernandez-Gonzalez, at 2863 South Conway Road and then went to her job at Universal Studios. In her statement, she wrote:

> I have spent every day, since Monday, June 9, 2008, looking for my daughter. I have lied and stolen from my friends and family to do whatever I could, by any means, to find my daughter. I avoided calling the police or even notifying my own family out of fear.
>
> I have been and still am afraid of what has, or may happen to Caylee. I have not had any contact with Zenaida since Thursday, June 12, 2008. I received a quick call from Zenaida. Not once have I been able to ask her for my daughter or gain any information on where I can find her. Every day, I have gone to malls, parks, anyplace I could remember Zenaida taking Caylee.
>
> . . . On Tuesday, July 15, 2008, around 12 pm, I received a phone call from my daughter Caylee. Today was the first day I have heard her voice in over four weeks. I'm afraid of what Caylee is going through. After thirty-one days, I know that the only thing that matters is getting my daughter back. With many and all attempts to contact Zenaida and within the one short conversation . . . I was never able to check on the status or well-being of my daughter. Zenaida never made an attempt to explain why Caylee is no longer in Orlando or if she is ever going to bring her home.

She described Caylee as three feet tall, weighing thirty-five pounds, with hazel eyes, light brown hair and a small birthmark on her left shoulder. When Casey had seen her last, she said, her daughter was wearing a pink shirt, blue jeans and white sneakers.

One officer went to South Conway Road, only to discover that the apartment number given by Casey was vacant and had not had a tenant for 142 days. Another policeman went to the apartment of Tony Lazzaro and his roommate, who consented to a search for Caylee and any evidence that might help find the little girl. He left with Casey's cell phone. A third officer was sent to North Glenwood Avenue in hopes of getting information about Caylee from residents there, but he came up empty handed.

Cindy was outside when the deputy returned with Casey's cell. She stood by his side providing relationship commentary as he scrolled through her list of contacts, calling every one of them.

A tearful, hysterical-sounding Cindy called Amy at 11 o'clock that night. She told her Casey's story about the kidnapping of Caylee. Amy said, "Casey emptied out my bank account."

After getting a few more details, Cindy excused herself from the call and then returned in a couple of minutes. "Casey is with the cops, but I asked her if she did this and she said she wrote all those checks."

Lee Anthony called Tony Lazzaro and explained the situation with Casey and Caylee. He then asked if he could come over to pick up the rest of Casey's things, including the laptop Casey used, which actually belonged to Cindy. Tony agreed.

Lee arrived around 2 in the morning. He got a leopard print duffle bag, a white backpack, a large purse filled with toiletries and cosmetics, and a slender black bag containing paperwork. He placed the computer in that bag. He was surprised at the neatness of his sister's possessions. She usually was very sloppy about her packing.

Tony pointed to a checkbook sitting on his dresser, telling Lee that it belonged to Amy. "I talked to Amy. She's going to come get this tomorrow. Do you want it?"

"No," Lee said. "If Amy's going to come get it tomorrow, you go ahead and keep it and just have her do that."

When he returned to his parents' home, Casey was outside in a circle of police officers. Lee carried all the items into the house. George Anthony complained that everything reeked of cigarette smoke. Cindy looked up at the officer. "I want to go through that stuff."

The officer said, "Dump it out on the ground." After the contents were spread out onto the floor, the officer left. Cindy rooted around through the contents and was surprised by what she didn't find. There were a couple of diapers and a few baby wipes, but usually the backpack was brimming with books, toys and clothing for her granddaughter. None of that was there. There were no little Baggies of pretzels or Cheerios. No tiny containers of juice.

Cindy pulled Casey's wallet out of the pile. She pulled out the cash—about $140—and stuck it in her pocket, saying, "It's probably mine or Amy's."

The officer returned. Cindy held up a credit card. "Look," Cindy said. "This is my JC Penny card that she took from me. Look," she said holding up another one from Sears, "this is another card that she took from me." Cindy then started to pull Casey's identification from the clear sleeve, but before she could see what was behind the driver's license, the officer reached down and plucked something out.

Cindy continued searching. She found a car key that did not look familiar. She made the assumption that it was Amy's, and set it aside. She pulled out multiple receipts, and Lee counted them—twenty-two in all, dated from June 20 to July 15. In going through them, Lee didn't find a single receipt containing purchases for Caylee—not for diapers or anything a small child would need.

Child abuse investigator Yuri Melich responded to the Anthony home and took over the investigation. He looked the part of a detective, with his stiff posture, close-cropped hair, sharp nose and pointed chin. He wore a serious, no-nonsense expression as he reviewed Casey's written statement and sat down with her apart from other family members. "Is this your version of what happened?"

"Yes," Casey said.

He explained that the incident was suspicious, and her version of events was questionable. He gave her the opportunity to correct, amend or walk away from the words she had written. When she demurred, Melich started the tape recorder.

CHAPTER 6

Again, Melich asked, "Are you telling me this is the story you want to stick with?"

"That's the truth," Casey insisted. "It's the story I'm gonna stick with, yes."

He asked where she'd dropped off her child, and Casey said, "At the Sawgrass Apartments on Conway and Michigan."

"Do you remember the address?"

"I don't remember the address, no."

"Do you remember the apartment number?" he asked.

"Two ten."

"Okay," Melich said as he jotted down the information on the location.

"It's on the second floor," Casey volunteered.

"If you were to pull into the Sawgrass Apartments, would the building be the one closest to the road, furtherest back, half way?"

"As soon as you go straight, you go over one speed bump and it's the first one on the right-hand side."

"Okay, is there a pool next to it? Or is there anything about the apartment that stands out?"

"There's a welcome sign, um, I guess there's a little shed close to the building, maybe about ten yards away."

"How long have you known Zenaida?"

"Almost four years," Casey said. "It'll be four years Christmas this year."

"Where did you meet her? And who did you meet her through?"

"A mutual friend named Jeffrey Michael Hopkins. I met him at Nickelodeon [an operating television studio and attraction] at Universal. I met her through him. She was . . . his son's nanny at the time."

"Does Jeffrey still work at Universal?" Melich asked.

"No he does not."

"How long has it been since he left?"

"About nine, ten months, give or take."

"Did he move back to Jacksonville?"

"He moved up to North Carolina for a short time and moved down to Jacksonville within the last three months."

"When was the last time you spoke with him?"

"About a week-and-a-half ago," Casey said.

When Melich asked for his phone number, Casey explained that she didn't have it because she'd lost the phone that contained his contact information. She said she still had her SIM card, but his number was saved on the phone itself. When she'd moved the card to another phone, his number was not transferred with it. She had no idea of where her phone could be. "I know I left it on my desk. And I haven't been to work for at least three or four days."

"And you said you made the report to Universal or . . ."

"Yes, with Security."

"When was that?"

"Nine days ago."

"Nine days ago?"

"Yes," Casey confirmed.

"Okay. So you met Zenaida through Jeffrey Hopkins?"

"I did."

"And his son Zack Hopkins, I guess, Zenaida used to watch over Zack?"

"Yes."

"And you say you've known Zenaida for about four years?"

"Almost four years, yes."

"So, you knew her before you had your child?" Melich asked.

"Well, I met her just before I was actually pregnant at the time, so . . ."

"And when did she start watching over your child?"

"Um, it's been within the last year-and-a-half, two years, that she started watching Caylee. I had another friend watch Caylee that I've known since middle school. When she went back to school, I was looking for a new nanny. Jeff offered to have Zenaida watch both kids. She agreed, and it kind of went from there."

"Before Zenaida started watching over your child, who was it— Who was the nanny?"

"Her name was Lauren Gibbs . . ."

"And when did Lauren stop watching . . . your child?" Melich pressed.

"Um," Casey said as she paused. "Maybe April of 2006."

". . . Would you drop the child off, or would she meet you somewhere?"

"I would usually drop her off. For a few months, we would go over to Jeff's house. He lived over in Avalon Park. That was a couple of years ago . . . It was in a nice centralized area. He had a decent-size house. It was good room for the two of them. Then I started bringing Caylee over to Zenaida's apartment," Casey explained.

After she described the two different places that Zenaida lived, Melich asked her to relate the events that had occurred on June 9.

"I got off of work, left Universal, driving back to pick up Caylee like a normal day. And I show up to the apartment, knock on the door. Nobody answers. So, I called Zenaida's cell phone and . . . the phone is no longer in service.

"So, I sit down on the steps and wait for a little bit to see if maybe it was just a fluke, if something happened. And time passed. I didn't hear from anyone. No one showed up to the house, so I went over to Jay Blanchard Park and checked a couple other places where maybe possibly they would've gone. A couple stores, just regular places that I know Zenaida shops at and she's taken Caylee before. And after about seven o clock, when I still hadn't heard anything, I was getting pretty upset, pretty frantic." The memory of the pain wasn't reflected in her voice. She spoke in a matter-of-fact tone, as if she were discussing a misplaced drink.

"And I went to a neutral place. I didn't really want to come home. I wasn't sure what I'd say about not knowing where Caylee was. Still hoping that I would get a call or, you know, find out that Caylee was coming back so that I could go get her. And I ended up going to my boyfriend Anthony's house, who lives in Sutton Place."

"Did you talk to Anthony about what happened to Caylee?" the detective asked.

"No, I did not," Casey admitted.

"Has Anthony ever seen Caylee before?"

"Yes, he has."

"Have you talked to anyone about Caylee, about your incident with Caylee? Or the fact that she's missing?"

". . . a couple of people, a couple of mutual friends."

"Who did you talk to about it?"

"Um, I talked to Jeff, Jeffrey Hopkins."

"Uh-huh," Melich said with a nod.

"I also attempted to contact Zenaida's mother, and never received a call back from her."

"Do you know Zenaida's mother's name?"

"Um, wow . . . and, um . . . I think it's *Gloria*."

"Do you know a telephone for Zenaida's mom?"

"I do not, no."

"Do you have any of these numbers programmed into your SIM card that you kept in your other phone?"

"No, I do not."

"How long did you have this old phone?"

"I've had the Nokia for almost a year."

Melich took care to keep the incredulity out of his voice. "So, after a full year of dealing with Zenaida and having her baby-sit, you don't remember . . ."

". . . Zenaida's number has changed a couple of times . . ." Casey answered.

"What about Jeffrey?"

". . . His number's changed a couple of times when he moved from Orlando to North Carolina and back down to Jacksonville."

"Okay . . . you talked to Jeffrey. Who else did you talk to?"

"I talked to Juliette Lewis. She's one of my co-workers at Universal."

"She works—you still work—at Universal?"

"Yes," Casey said.

"What do you do at Universal?"

"Event coordinator."

"Okay. What is Juliette? What position is she? Where does she work?"

"She's also an event coordinator. We work in the same department."

"You have a number for Juliette?" Yuri Melich asked.

"Oooh, off-hand, I can't think of one," Casey said with a rueful smile.

"She in your SIM card?"

"No, she's not. . . . Her number just changed because she just moved back up north. She . . ." Casey's words jerked as she realized that she had just contradicted herself. Quickly, she worked to recover. "Within the last two months, she has finished moving up to New York. She's sub-leasing her apartment."

"So, Juliette . . . doesn't work at Universal anymore?"

"No, she does not."

"When did she leave Universal?"

"About two months ago."

"Who else did you talk to about it?" the investigator continued to push.

"It's been within that small group. I've tried to find out information from people going out to different places. Like Fusian Ultra Lounge and a couple of bars that I know Zenaida had gone to downtown before to see if— just kind of random talk. If anybody heard about my nanny or talked to her lately."

"Did you tell anyone specifically that Zenaida took your child?"

"No. The only two people that I specifically told were Jeff and Juliette."

"And you don't have a number for Juliette?"

"Not off-hand, no, I do not."

"It's not on your phone? Might it be on line?"

"It's definitely on line—I know it's on one of our old work sheets. Um, her old number, which could still be active—I'm not sure if it is. But I know she does have a new number, which I just programmed into that new phone."

"When was the last time you talked to Juliette?"

"Hmm, about three weeks ago. Shortly after this happened."

"So, you talked to her after she left?"

"Uh-huh," Casey nodded.

"What's the reason— I asked you this before, and I'll ask you again for the record: What's the reason you didn't call the police before? Since right now, we're here because your . . . parents asked you about the child, and they were concerned, didn't get an answer as to where the child was, they called the sheriff's office."

"Uh-huh," Casey agreed.

"Why didn't you call prior to today?"

"I think part of me was naïve enough to think that I could handle this myself, which obviously I couldn't. And I was scared that something would happen to her if I did notify the authorities or got the media involved. Or my parents, which I know would have done the same thing. Just the fear of the unknown. Fear of the potential of Caylee getting hurt, of not seeing my daughter again."

". . . I asked you this at the onset before we went on tape, and I'll ask you again just to make sure we're clear. Is there anything about this story that you're telling me that is untrue?"

"No," Casey said with a shake of her head.

"Or is there anything that you want to change or divert from what you've already told me?"

"No, sir."

"Did you cause any injury to your child Caylee?"

"No, sir."

"Did you hurt Caylee or leave her somewhere and you're . . ."

"No."

". . . worried that if we find that out, that people are going to look at you in a wrong way?"

"No, sir," Casey insisted.

"You're telling me that Zenaida took your child without your permission . . ."

"She's . . ."

". . . and hasn't returned her?"

". . . the last person that I seen with my daughter, yes."

After a few more questions about Zenaida, Detective Melich turned the questions back to the missing little girl. "Does Caylee take any medications?"

"No."

"She doesn't suffer from any conditions—any medical conditions—that we need to know?"

"No, not at all."

Melich then moved the conversation to the stolen money and possible implications of that theft. "As brought up before about taking some money from some people, I want to make sure I get it on tape. Do you have any problems with drugs or narcotics, either prescription narcotics . . ."

"No," Casey interrupted.

Melich continued, ". . . or drugs like cocaine, ecstasy, meth—anything like that?"

"Nothing like that."

"Have you ever been committed for thoughts of suicide . . . ?"

"No."

"Is there any underlying cause to why Zenaida would've taken your child?"

"No, nothing, that . . ."

"She ever make any statements to you about . . ."

"Only how much she loves Caylee and how great of a kid she is."

"And have you talked— When you talk to Jeffrey afterwards, I'm assuming Jeffrey's child is still with him?"

"His child is still with him," Casey said and then spun a tale about Zenaida's family in New York and Florida, her attendance at the University of Florida, her Dominican and Puerto Rican ethnic heritage.

"When we finish this, would you be willing to drive with me to show me where her mom lives and the apartment that you used to drop her off at?"

"Yes," Casey agreed, and then raised her right hand and swore and affirmed that all her words were the gospel truth.

CHAPTER 7

Casey left the Anthony home in Detective Melich's unmarked car. They rendezvoused with a deputy and drove
to the corner of Glenwood and Robinson. Casey pointed to
a second-floor window in a building off of the northwest
corner of the intersection at 301 Hillside Avenue. She
claimed that Zenaida had lived there during the first half
of 2006 in a three-story apartment. The second story window had been Zenaida's bedroom—the one above it was
where her roommate had lived. The place she indicated,
however, was a seniors-only facility.

On the other side of the street, Melich spotted 232
Glenwood Avenue—an address found on a slip of paper
in Casey's car. He asked why she'd written it down.

"Because it's across the street," Casey said.

The answer didn't make a lot of sense to the detective,
but, for now, he let the remark go unchallenged. They
drove next to 2863 South Conway Road, where Casey
verified the apartment number she'd provided earlier. The
unit appeared empty to the detective. "Have you ever been
inside the apartment?"

"Yes."

"Is there any furniture?"

"Yes, there's furniture and children's toys."

"What type of vehicle does Zenaida drive?"

"A silver Ford Focus."

The third location they visited was in the Crossings at
Conway, a townhome community, near East Michigan

and South Conway Roads, where Casey said Zenaida's mother, Gloria, owned a condo. Casey also claimed that Zenaida had lived there from the latter part of 2006 and through early 2007, and that was where she'd left her daughter with the baby-sitter during that time. However, when they got to the complex, Casey could not identify the correct address.

The investigator drove up and down every street, but Casey still could not recognize the condo. "I stopped paying attention to it, since I came here so many times," she said.

Detective Melich parked the car and explained to Casey that he was going to knock on a few doors to see if he could find anyone who knew Zenaida or Gloria. "Let me know if anyone I talk to looks familiar to you."

Yuri Melich knocked on three different doors and spoke to residents. Casey recognized no one. And none of the residents knew Zenaida, nor recognized the photo of Caylee. They returned to the Anthony home. "I'll call you if I need anything," he said as Casey walked inside.

Before the detective left, George Anthony approached him. "I am concerned that my daughter is holding back information. My wife and I are afraid that something might have happened to Caylee."

In the midst of an intense investigation, how could anyone in law enforcement respond to that—particularly when the detective shared that fear? He changed the subject, asking about Caylee's father.

"Casey would only tell me his name was Eric and that he died in a motor vehicle accident in mid- to late 2007," he said, adding that Casey claimed to have saved an obituary, but she couldn't remember where she'd put it.

After briefing his supervisor, Sergeant John Allen, Melich headed back to the Sawgrass Apartments on South Conway Road. He met with maintenance man Dave Turner and apartment manager Amanda Macklin. The detective pulled out a photo of Caylee—no one recognized the child. Nor did Zenaida's name sound familiar.

They confirmed that the apartment in question had been vacant for 142 days since the eviction of the former tenant in February and in that time, had been undergoing renovation and repair. Dave took the investigator up to the apartment, where Melich personally verified the vacancy.

Back in the manager's office, Amanda an a search for Zenaida Gonzalez and found her. She'd never been a resident, but she had stopped by on June 17 and filled out a guest card. She'd been interested in renting a two-bedroom–two-bath unit for herself and two children.

Amanda called employee Harry Garcia to the office. Harry acknowledged that it was his handwriting on the card, adding that he remembered talking to the woman in Spanish.

Melich handed Harry a sheet with twelve photographs, asking if he recognized anyone there. Harry pointed to one of the shots, saying, "She looks familiar to me. I believe she may have been the person who visited the community as a prospect."

Amanda duplicated the guest card as well as the lease for the previous tenants in the apartment and turned the copies over to Melich.

Next stop for the detective was Universal Studios. There he met with Investigator Leonard Turtora. Once Melich explained the situation, Turtora went into the company's database and mined for information. Yes, Casey had worked for Universal, but she was fired on April 24, 2006, more than two years ago.

Of Casey's two outcry witnesses—the people to whom she claimed to have informed about the situation with her missing daughter—Turtora uncovered still more disturbing information. Jeffrey Hopkins had been an employee, but was fired on May 13, 2002. Juliette Lewis had never worked there. There was no record that Zenaida Gonzalez, whom Casey claimed was a seasonal worker, had ever been employed at Universal.

Yuri Melich pulled out his cell, punched in Casey's

number and turned on the speakerphone, allowing Turtora to hear the call. Casey confirmed that she currently
worked for Universal as an event planner. She gave the
main phone number, then said, "My office extension is
104." She added that Tom Manley was her supervisor.
Melich asked for the location of her office, but Casey
could not recall the building number or its whereabouts.
He asked if she had her current work identification card.
"I don't know where it is."

After disconnecting, Turtora said that the extension
Casey named was not valid. He called to prove the point.
He also told Melich that no one named Tom Manley
worked for Universal. Tom Mattson was the head of the
events department.

Melich called Sergeant Allen. "Could you go by the
Hopespring address [the Anthony home] and see if Casey
will agree to come to Universal Studios?"

Allen and Detective Appie Wells picked up Casey at
12:30 that afternoon. While they were en route, Turtora
was busy trying to ascertain if it was possible that Casey
did work for Universal, but for some reason was not in
the computer system.

Turtora and Melich met Casey, Allen and Wells at the
employee entrance. Casey spoke to the security officer. "I
am a current employee and I've lost my I.D."

"Who is your supervisor?" he asked.

"Tom Manley."

The security officer tapped on his keyboard, then
looked up. "No Tom Manley works here."

Casey had no response. Turtora offered to escort her
to the location of her office.

Casey strode with a purposeful air. She walked down
one block, making a left turn, crossing the street at the
next intersection. There, she entered a building with
Turtora and the Orange County law enforcement members following in her wake. She strode to the interior
hallway.

Halfway down the length of it, Casey stopped and

turned to face them. "I didn't tell you the truth. I am not a current employee."

No one was surprised.

Turtora secured a small conference room where Allen, Melich and Wells could sit down with Casey and get a second recorded interview. Before turning on the recorder, Melich told Casey that the door was unlocked and that it was closed for privacy only. She had not been arrested and was free to go.

Casey agreed to talk with them and have the conversation recorded. Still, there was no emotion in her face. Melich wondered if she would ever demonstrate any genuine concern for her missing child.

CHAPTER 8

Detective Yuri Melich had talked to a lot of people that morning before walking into the conference room with Casey. Amy Huizenga called to tell him that Casey had borrowed her car while she was out of town and picked her up at the airport the previous afternoon at 2:30. She said Casey had stolen her checkbook and wiped out her bank account. Amy told the detective that she lived with Rico Morales at 232 Glenwood Avenue—a room with the view of the senior citizens' residence pointed out to Melich by Casey earlier that day.

The detective also fielded a call from Tony Lazzaro, who openly discussed his history with Casey and said that he had not seen Caylee since about June 2, when she'd played in the swimming pool at his apartment complex. Since June 9, Tony said, Casey had told him Caylee was at Disney, Universal Studios or the beach with the nanny, but never indicated that her daughter was endangered or missing.

The investigator wanted to bring Casey's lies to an end. Casey and Melich sat around a long table with Sergeant Jones and Detective Wells. Melich began the interview. "Remember how I opened the whole thing this morning?"

"Yeah," Casey said.

"About saying that you know we need to get complete truth, and the snowball effect, and . . ."

"Absolutely," Casey agreed.

". . . how it goes? Okay. We're about halfway down that hill, three-quarters down that hill, and it's a pretty big snowball. Which means that there's a lot of stuff going on right now."

"Uh huh," Casey nodded.

"And I can tell you just for certainty, everything you've told me has been a lie. I can tell you with certainty, and let me explain why. Since I left you this morning . . . I've gone to every address that you've told me. I looked up every name, I've talked to every person you wanted me to talk to, or tried to."

"Uh huh."

"And found out all these names you're giving me are people that either never worked here or been fired a long time ago. Okay? So, where we are right now is in a position that doesn't look very good for you."

"Uh huh."

"I'm just being straight with you," Melich explained.

"Yeah."

" 'Cause obviously I know and you know that everything you've told me is a lie, correct?"

"Not everything that I told you," Casey contradicted.

"Okay. Ah, pretty much everything that you've told me. Including where Caylee is right now."

"That I still— I don't know where she is."

"Sure you do. And here's . . ."

Casey interrupted. "I absolutely do not . . . know where she is."

"Let me explain something," Melich continued. "Together, with combined experience in this room, we all have about thirty years of doing this."

"Uh huh."

"Okay. Both myself and John Allen worked for Homicide Division for several years. We've dealt with several people; we've conducted thousands of interviews between the three of us . . . And I can tell you for certainty that right now, looking at you, everything that you've told me is a lie. Including the fact that you know your child was last seen about a month ago. And that you don't know where she is. Yeah, I'm very confident, just by having talked to you the short period of time, that you know where she is."

"I don't," Casey objected.

"You do. And here's the thing, we need to get past that, because we could sit here and go back and forth all day long about 'I don't,' 'You do,' 'I don't,' 'You do.' It's pretty obvious that with everything that you've told us, nothing has been true. You know where she is. Now my question to you is this: We need to find Caylee. I understand that right now, Caylee may not be in very good shape. You understand what I am saying?"

Casey's silence was, in itself, an acknowledgment.

"She may not be the way . . . your family remembers her. We need to find out from you where Caylee is . . . This has gone so far downhill and this has become such a mess."

"Uh huh."

"We need to end it. It's very simple. We just need to end it," Melich urged.

"I agree with you," Casey said calmly. "I have no clue where she is."

"Sure you do."

"If I knew, in any sense, where she was, this wouldn't have happened at all."

"This stuff about Zenaida, the caretaker, or the nanny, taking care of . . ."

Casey interrupted again. "It's the truth."

"It's not the truth. Because we went to the apartment complex. There's no person that ever lived there by that name. The apartment's been vacant since March. That same apartment. Now the apartment that you pointed out to me—the two-story apartment? That's an old folks' home. It's right across the street from your ex-boyfriend's house, who you never mentioned. And you said you wrote the address down because it was across the street.

That's a lie, because I've already talked to him and we've already been by the house and we've already, you know, looked at everything we need to look at over there."

"Uh huh."

"Everything you told us is a lie. Well, now, there's a couple of ways that this goes . . . I've never met you before, so I can look at you in a couple of ways . . . I can look at you as a person, who's scared—who's concerned and who's kind of afraid what's gonna happen, because of something bad that happened before. Or we can look at you as cold, callous and a monster, who doesn't care—who's just trying to get away with something . . . bad that happened, and trying to cover it up."

"Uh huh," Casey said with chilling nonchalance.

"It's going to be one of those two options . . . Now what we would have to do is, we have to determine which way this is gonna go. Are you . . . a person who's scared about the consequences of what happened? Or are you scared about something that happened? Or are you . . . really this cold, callous person, who doesn't care about what happened? It's one of these two options."

"I'm scared that I don't know where my daughter is . . . I would not have put my entire family . . ."

Sergeant John Allen stepped into the conversation. "Hold on. I want to ask you something."

"Yes, sir?" Casey said.

". . . You're here willingly, right?"

"Uh huh."

"You're here 'cause . . . you're trying to help, right?"

"Oh, absolutely."

"Nobody's forced you to talk to us, right?"

"No," Casey shook her head.

". . . Now, let me ask you," John Allen continued. "I want you to put yourself in . . . my shoes for a minute, okay? . . . In an attempt to try and help find your daughter, you've given him bad addresses, okay?" he said pointing at Yuri Melich.

"Uh huh," Casey acknowledged.

"You drove me all the way out here. We walked from the gate back here all the way to your office, right?"

"Uh huh."

"Okay. To . . . an office that you don't have. We got all the way to the building into the hallway out here before you finally say, 'Well, I really don't have an office here.' But . . . we were walking to your office, right?"

"Uh huh."

"Okay, so, I mean, does any of this make sense to you?"

"I understand how all that sounds. I . . ."

"No. No. No. No. No . . . Here's the problem with that, okay? You can carry the weight of this room for a long time, it's not gonna get any easier, okay? . . . I've learned this: People make mistakes. Everybody makes mistakes. All— The three of us have all made some . . . mistakes in our lives—we've done some things we're not proud of, okay? But then there comes a point in time you either own up to it, you say you're sorry, you try to get past it—or you lie about it, you bury it . . . and it just never, ever, ever, ever, ever goes away."

"Uh huh."

"Okay. That's it, okay? Now you know I want you to stop and think about what's going on here, okay?"

John Allen waited for a response, but Casey did not oblige.

"At this point, we can explain that you're afraid," Allen continued. "You know that you were ashamed of maybe something bad that happened . . . We're giving you this opportunity, yet you continue to lie and you continue to lie. Then what happens, at some point, it becomes there's no excuse—there's no reason . . . A reasonable person can look at this and go, 'Wow, this is a person who really just doesn't care,' okay? . . . You called because you want our help. You want us to find your daughter, okay? 'I am calling you and I'm asking for you to help. I'm asking you to help me find my child.'"

"Uh huh."

"'That's been going on for a month, okay? 'And to help you help me find the child, what I've done to this point is, I've given you a bunch of bad addresses to go look at—addresses and people that don't exist.' Okay? 'Then, I take you to a place where I tell you that I work.' Okay? 'And I walk past the security gate.' Okay? 'All the way to an office that I don't have.'"

"Uh huh."

"Okay. You sort of get the picture?"

Again, Casey did not respond.

". . . Do you understand where we're headed here?"

"I understand," Casey said.

". . . By burying this . . . you are not going to get yourself to a better place, okay? What you are going to do, you're going to cause everybody else around you to suffer, okay? And at some point, this is going to come out. It always does."

"Uh huh."

"It always comes out, okay? Now your best bet is to try to put this behind you as quickly as you can. Go to your parents and tell 'em, you know, some horrible accident—whatever happened—happened. Get it out in the open now, okay? Instead of letting them worry and worry and worry and worry, okay? How old are you?"

"Twenty-two."

"At some point . . . you're going to want to mend things with your family . . . You let this drag out . . . You make us solve this some other way. We'll solve it, we always do . . . There's no point in coming forward to say, 'Oh my God, this is what really happened,' once we figured it out, okay?"

"Uh huh."

"You ever had anybody do anything wrong to you? Did anybody hurt . . ."

"Of course," Casey snapped.

". . . When somebody's hurt you in the past, and they've come to you and said, 'I'm sorry,' okay? 'I really am, from the bottom of my heart, sorry for what happened.' Do you forgive 'em?"

"Yes."

"What about somebody that does something to you and lies, lies, lies, lies, lies. You forgive them?"

"It's a lot harder to sometimes."

"A lot harder to," John Allen nodded in agreement. "Tell me the last time somebody hurt you over and over and then let you suffer for a period of time. And then lied about it when you caught 'em . . . When you caught 'em, that apology didn't mean a hell of a lot, did it?"

"No."

". . . Right now, your best bet is to just get it out in the open, whatever happened, and tell us now, okay? So . . . we can kind of start getting past this . . . There's nothing you're gonna tell any of the three of us that's gonna surprise us, okay?"

"Uh huh."

"I've had to sit down with . . . mothers who rolled over their babies accidentally. I've had to sit down with mothers whose kids drowned in swimming pools. I've had to sit down with mothers who had boyfriends who beat their kids to death—who felt horrible about what happened. And then . . . I had to . . . help them explain to their families, okay? And, then, I've also had to deal with people who have done horrible, unspeakable things to children. And then lied about it and lied about it and lied about it, okay? And I'll bet you somewhere near, I probably dealt with somebody who, maybe, made a mistake, but continued to lie about it. Maybe they weren't such a bad person. But maybe the whole world didn't see it that way. Maybe their family didn't see it that way 'cause they kept lying, lying, lying and lying about it. . . . Look at this from an outsider's perspective . . . What would you do? How would you see that person? How would you see that person different? You might see somebody, maybe a young mother who made a mistake and, you know, maybe, initially, was afraid to tell the truth. But at some point, she came forward and said, 'A horrible thing happened. I'm sorry, I feel terrible about it, but I have to tell you.'"

After all that talk, Casey still did not give an inch. "The horrible thing that happened is—this is the honest to God's truth—of everything that I've said, I do not know where she is. The last person that I saw her with is Zenaida. She's the last person that I seen my daughter with."

CHAPTER 9

Yuri Melich grasped the reins of the interview again. "We know that's not the truth."

"Absolutely is," Casey insisted.

"Listen. We know that's not true—that can't be the truth. Because if it were the truth, everything you told us would've been on the money. Everything else would have matched. If you had told us the truth, we wouldn't be here at Universal Studios at a place that you've been fired since 2006. With you trying to explain to us, you know, you got an office and all that stuff."

"Uh huh."

"We wouldn't be here. So, we know—and this is the part we need to get past—we already know that you're not telling us the truth. That you know what happened to Caylee and you know where Caylee is."

"No."

Melich kept at her for a while longer, and then Allen stepped back into the fray. "I want to go through this, and I want you to stop me at the part that isn't the truth, okay?"

"Uh huh."

"You take your daughter and you drop her off on June the ninth . . ."

"Uh huh."

"Okay. At . . . the baby-sitter's . . . apartment, okay? That's been vacant . . ."

Casey interrupted. "I dropped her off at that apartment."

"Okay."

"At those stairs."

"Oh, you just walked her— You dropped her off . . ."

"Walked her to the stairs. That's where I've dropped her off a bunch of other times . . ."

"Okay. And when you dropped her off, who took her at that point?"

"Zanny did. She took her at that point."

"You left her in Zanny's care?"

"Yes."

"On June the ninth? Okay? So far that's right?"

"Yes."

"Okay. You first called the police about this when your mother and father— Ah, you actually, you don't call the police to report your daughter missing. What happens is your parents find their car has been towed . . . from Amscot, and your parents ask you where your daughter is. And you tell . . . your parents that you haven't seen your daughter for over a month, right?"

Allen waited, but Casey made no comment. Then he continued, "So far, I haven't said anything that's not true, okay?"

"That's all true."

"Okay. . . . When your parents involve the police in an attempt to locate your child because they're worried . . . the first thing you do . . . is . . . lie to the detective whose job it is to try to find your daughter and get her back into safe hands, okay? You give him all kinds of bad addresses to look at, right?"

Again, Casey sits mute.

"So far, I'm on track, right?"

"Uh huh," Casey conceded.

"Okay. Then you bring us out to Universal, where you say you work in an office . . . to try to help find stuff that will help us find your daughter. I'm on track so far, okay?"

"Uh huh."

"And we get here. We walk all the way down the hall to . . . where you tell us you don't really work here. You don't have an office here . . . So far, everything I've said is true, correct?"

"Uh huh."

". . . I'm telling you this story. I'm saying to you: 'Listen. I drop my child off five weeks ago at the baby-sitter's house. And she's just disappeared . . . Now I didn't call the police and tell them. Matter of fact, I made some attempts to locate her on my own. But I didn't really get the police involved or anything like that.' Okay? 'And, oh by the way, I got my mom and dad's car towed, and when my parents asked me what happened to my daughter, I told 'em I hadn't seen her in five weeks. So, they call the police.' Okay? 'Now, what I did is, I lied to the police when they got there . . . I told them a whole bunch of crap that isn't true . . . I did all this to try and help find my daughter.' Makes sense to you, right?"

"Uh huh."

Incredulous, Allen asked again, "That makes sense to you?"

Casey said nothing.

Allen continued to push. "It makes sense to you, that 'I'm trying to help the police find my daughter by giving 'em a bunch of bad addresses'? That makes sense to you?"

"That's what I said, yes."

"No, I'm asking you, that makes sense to you?"

"That part of it, no, not at all," Casey finally admitted.

". . . We're here 'cause you brought us here. Right?"

"Uh huh."

"Now, I want you to tell me how that's helping us find your daughter."

"It's not."

"But everything we're doing is to find your daughter. That's the most important thing in the world to you right now, right?"

"Caylee's been up here. Maybe we could talk to Security, see if she's come through the front. I know she's come to the park. She's gone to Disney. She's been at SeaWorld."

"Whoa! Ho— Hold on . . ."

"She's been to other places," Casey continued.

"Let's go back to— Let's . . ."

"It's . . . a backwards way of . . . looking."

"Why do you think it's backwards? It's backwards 'cause you haven't been truthful with us, okay?"

"'Cause I've been reaching."

"You've been reaching, huh?" Allen said with a shake of his head.

"I've been reaching to try to figure out a place where she actually is."

"So—once again, okay? 'Cause you never did answer my question. You're reaching and helping find her by bringing us here to this office that you don't have. It's helping us find her how?"

"It's . . ." Casey began.

Allen cut her off. "Because what you're doing right now, is, you're doing everything you can to find your daughter. You have three experienced detectives right now, whose sole focus is here to help you find your daughter, okay? And we're here 'cause you brought us here, correct?"

"Absolutely."

"You directed us here because we're going to your office to find evidence . . . that will help us find her, okay? Now that we're here, I want you to tell me how that's helping. What is it we're doing here? What's helping us right now?"

Again, Casey had no answer.

"Well, coming to an office that doesn't exist . . ."

"It's not helping," Casey agreed.

Melich picked up the thread of the questioning. "So why'd you do it?"

"Honestly, I wanted to come up and try to talk to Security. Maybe pass around a picture of Caylee. I legitimately have not seen my daughter in five weeks. I don't want anything to happen to her. Except I trusted her with somebody—somebody that had been taking care of her—that had been taking good care of her. Someone that she was comfortable with—that I was comfortable with."

"What about Jeff?" Melich pressed. "You said Jeff worked here about two months ago?"

"No. He hasn't worked here for quite a while."

"Ten months? How long?"

"It's been at least ten months," Casey stalled.

"Okay, he got fired in . . . 2002. He hasn't been employed here since 2002. What about the girl?"

"Juliette?"

"Yeah. What about her?" Melich asked.

"She left two months ago. That's exactly what she told me," Casey said.

"Juliette Lewis never worked at Universal Studios."

Detective Appie Wells spoke for the first time in the interview. "Yuri. I'm sorry. Is the baby's daddy actually dead?"

"I still have a copy of the obituary at home," Casey said.

"Alright. Well, you've told us so many untruths right now, I'm confused . . . Would your parents be upset if you had given the baby back to the daddy to take back for . . . his parents to take care of?"

"He passed away last year. We hadn't even talked much before that," Casey said.

John Allen asked, "Let me ask you this: Is the obituary in your office?"

"No, I think I have a copy of the obituary at home. There's no office, so there's no anything, anywhere. We've made that clear already," she snapped.

"Right," Allen said.

"So if I have a copy of it still, it would be on my computer at home. I'm pretty sure I kept that. I don't think that's something I would've gotten rid of."

Melich jumped back in, changing the subject. "Zanny's never worked here. How do you explain that?"

"She has an I.D. She has an I.D. with her name on it."

"Just like you have?"

"I've seen it," Casey stated, daring him to contradict her.

"Just like you have an I.D.?" Skepticism etched a roughness into the tone of Melich's voice.

"I do have an I.D.—somewhere at my house. Both of my parents have seen it. Both of my parents know . . ."

Melich interrupted. "Just like you have an office."

". . . that I worked here. I used to have an office."

"Now, just like you have an office?"

"No. I don't have an office now."

Allen spoke up again. "We're here because, why?"

"To try and put things together," Casey said.

". . . Our purpose of coming here was to do what? Go where?"

In a surprising moment of honesty, Casey said, "I guess there wasn't a purpose. There wasn't a purpose whatsoever to come up here."

CHAPTER 10

Casey rambled on again, insisting that her prevarication was all a desperate attempt to reach for alternate solutions. Melich cut her off with a blunt demand: "I want you to tell me how lying to us is going to help us find your daughter."

"It's not going to," Casey said.

"Well, then . . . if the main thing you want to do is find your daughter, and you don't think lying to us is gonna help us find her, why would you do that?"

"Because I'm scared, and I know I'm running out of options. It's been a month."

"What are you scared of?"

"I'm scared of not seeing my daughter ever again."

John Allen began, "Okay, and if you're scared . . ."

"And I'm honestly petrified . . ." Casey insisted.

". . . if you're scared of not . . ."

". . . of not seeing her again," Casey said, completing Allen's sentence.

"Seeing your daughter again, okay?" Allen echoed. "I want you to tell me how lying is going to solve that problem and help find your daughter quicker."

"It's not," Casey said.

"Then why would you do that?"

"See, I don't know," Casey answered. "I'm telling you that I just dropped her off and that was the last time that I seen her. Even starting with that, everybody else is like, 'Well, and what happened after that?'"

Frustration and bafflement grew with each word out of

Casey's mouth. Appie Wells asked, "You remember the phone call you were telling us about?" alluding to her alleged brief phone call with Caylee.

"Uh huh."

"Is that true?"

"Yes."

". . . What day was it you talked to her?" Appie asked.

"Yesterday."

"You remember what time of day?"

"Around noon. It was from a private number."

"Okay, what did she tell you? What's your daughter say to you?"

"She said, 'Hi, Mommy.' "

"And that's it?" Appie asked.

"And she started to tell me a story, talking to me about her shoes and books and . . ."

"It's important that you tell me," Appie pushed. "I mean, maybe there's something in what she said that can help us figure out where she is. What did she say?"

"I tried to ask her where she was."

"Okay."

"And she just kept talking about the book that she's . . . reading. We have videos of her reading the story, and she's telling me the story."

Allen spoke up again. "So she seemed happy and . . ."

". . . fine," Casey said with a jolting nonchalance.

"She's fine, she's happy?"

"She seemed perfectly fine . . . There was nothing in the background."

". . . No sign of any type of stress at all?"

"Not at all," Casey said.

"Great, that's wonderful," John Allen continued. "Let me ask you a question: Your daughter hasn't seen you in over a month, and she's not, she . . ."

Casey interrupted, "She was excited . . . to talk to me. But at the same time, it's crazy that she didn't get upset when she talked to me. Which . . . had it been my mom . . . I know it would have been totally different."

"That makes sense to you?" Allen asked.

"She never gets upset when she talks to me—whether I haven't seen her for an entire day or if I had to work late at night and didn't see her almost an entire day until the next one."

"That last time . . . somebody took her and you didn't see her for five weeks was, when?"

"Never."

"Okay. She's been with . . . somebody for five weeks. Hasn't been in her own home, hasn't seen her mother in five weeks . . . That didn't upset her?"

"She was fine."

Allen repeated the line of questioning. "She went on about, you know, 'I miss you, Mommy,' none of that? She just talked like you said? She talked about that book and all that stuff, right? That's it?"

"And when I asked her to give the phone to another adult, to somebody else, she was fine, she was willing to do it. But the phone hung up. She doesn't hang up phones."

Yuri Melich interrupted. "And that's the phone she called you on? On your cell phone?"

"Yes."

"Can I see that real quick?" Melich asked as he picked up the cell and walked out of the room. When he checked Casey's phone, he found no record of that phone call—he hadn't thought he would.

He called Zenaida Gonzales, tracking her down with the information on the guest card he'd picked up at Sawgrass apartments. She denied knowing Casey or Caylee. She also said that she didn't baby-sit for anyone. She agreed to provide a sworn statement.

Then Melich's own phone rang. It was from the detective who was interviewing Rico Morales at the station. Rico was bothered by a text message he'd gotten from Casey earlier that day that read: "If they never find her guess who spends eternity in jail?" He also told the detective that Casey and Caylee had spent the night at his house on June 9, and left on the morning of June 10.

While Melich was out of the room, Sergeant Allen continued the interview. "Okay. You have this conversation with her after not seeing her or hearing from her for five weeks. The phone call's terminated. You don't get a chance to talk to an adult . . . The very next thing you do after that is what? Call the police—because now something really strange has happened, so you must've called the police right after that. Did you call the city police or do you remember who you called? Which police agency did you call yesterday?"

"I didn't call anybody at noon after I got that phone call. I sat down . . ."

"You— Whoa! You didn't think that was odd . . . ?"

"I thought it was extremely odd," Casey said.

"But not odd enough to call the police and try to get help?"

Casey did not respond. In the moment of silence, Yuri Melich stepped back into the room. "Let me throw something in, if you don't mind," he said to the other detectives, then turned to Casey. "You know Ricardo, right? Obviously, your ex-boyfriend?"

"Uh huh."

"We brought him down to the office and he's been busy talking to a couple of detectives down there. And he was able to help us because he's telling us something obviously, completely different than what you're telling us." He told her that the video from the surveillance camera across the street would corroborate Ricardo's story of the events of June 9–10."

"I was not at his place the ninth of that month."

"So, you stayed at your ex-boyfriend's the ninth of this month when you are staying at your other boyfriend's house—Tony—the rest of the month?"

"He'd been out of town, so . . . I wasn't staying in his apartment. I was staying with Amy and Ricardo and J.P. J.P. and Ricardo own the house."

"So why didn't . . . you tell us you were staying there? We drove right by that house this morning, didn't we?"

Casey didn't answer the question, so Melich continued. "Okay, why were you pointing at this old folks' home and saying Zanny lived there at one point, when she didn't?"

"Because she had gone there before. I seen her there."

"She went to the old folks' home?"

"Yes."

"But you never dropped your kid off to her at an old folks' home. You never went into the old folks' home . . . Yet across the street from this old folks' home, right there on Glenwood, is where Ricardo lives."

"Uh huh."

"With Amy and J.P."

"Uh huh."

"All of whom are at our station talking to our detectives right now. So, obviously, you know, we're not stupid. Okay? And what you're doing right now is treating us like we're stupid, which— I take that, you know, to be a personal insult . . . And unless we start getting the truth, we're going to announce two possibilities with Caylee. Either you gave Caylee to someone that you don't want anyone to find out because you think you're a bad mom. Or something happened to Caylee, and Caylee's buried somewhere, or in a trash can somewhere, and you had something to do with it. Either way, right now, it's not a very pretty picture to be painting . . . Everything you told us is a lie . . . Every single thing."

"No, it isn't," Casey stubbornly insisted.

". . . This needs to end," Melich demanded.

"The truthful thing . . ." Casey began.

"This needs to end."

Casey continued, ". . . is, I have not seen my daughter. The last time that I saw her was on the ninth of June."

"And what happened to Caylee?"

"I don't know."

". . . Listen, something happened to Caylee. We're not gonna discuss where the last time you saw her. I'm guessing something bad happened to her some time ago and you haven't seen her. So, that part is true if you say you haven't seen her, because she's somewhere else right now."

"She's with someone else," Casey said again.

". . . No. She's either in a Dumpster right now or she's buried somewhere. She's out there somewhere and her rotting body is starting to decompose, because what you're telling us . . ." Melich said, stunned that those words did not provoke an emotional reaction from Casey. "And here's the problem, the longer this goes on, the worse it's gonna be for everyone. . . . Right now, it's gonna be one of two things. Either we find Caylee alive, which is gonna help you out extremely by telling us the truth. Or we find Caylee not alive, which, if you start telling us the truth, might still paint you in a better picture. But here is where it needs to end. Here's where the truth needs to come out. No more lies. No more bull coming out of your mouth. We've been very respectful. We're taking our time and talking to you. But we're tired of all the lies. No more lies. What happened to Caylee?"

"I don't know."

"You don't know?"

"I don't know . . ."

"What happened to Caylee?"

". . . where she is. That's the God's honest truth."

"Okay, where was she the last time that you put her somewhere? Where was she?"

"The last time I saw her was on those steps at that apartment that I took you to this morning . . ."

"But you didn't give her to anyone while you were there."

"I did."

". . . Listen to me," Melich pleaded. "We even pulled a surveillance video from an apartment complex . . . and we're not seeing you over there . . . all that day. You think that we're stupid, and we're not gonna . . ."

"I know you're not stupid."

"Remember we had those two people that we were talking about: the person who had an accident or . . . made a bad decision, and a person who's just a cold-blooded monster? That's telling me that you're the second person. This cold-blooded monster . . ."

"I'm not."

". . . who doesn't care and doesn't want to help because she's afraid that something so heinous happened, that everyone's gonna look at her and say, 'She's a monster—she deserves to go away—she deserves to never see the light of day—this bad thing should happen to her.' I don't want to believe that right now, but you're not giving me a choice . . . We know that everything you told us is a lie. Tell us what happened to Caylee. Tell us what happened to Caylee."

"I dropped off Caylee. And that's the last time that I've seen her. I dropped her off . . ."

"Where did you drop her off?"

"I dropped her off at that apartment."

"No, you didn't."

"That's exactly where I dropped her off."

"No, you didn't. And who'd you drop her to?"

"With Zenaida."

"No, you didn't."

John Allen asked, "Zenaida give you any money that day?"

"No. I would not have sold my daughter. If I wanted to really just get rid of her, I would've left her with my parents and I would've left. I would've moved out. I would've given my mom custody."

Appie Wells had another question: "What about the baby's dad's parents? Would you have left her with them, too?"

"I haven't talked to them since we were probably six or seven years old—since we were little kids. That was probably the last time I saw . . ."

"You don't have a phone . . . for 'em?"

"No I do not. I would not have let anything happen to my daughter—except I made the mistake of trusting another person with her. That's it."

Melich told her about her mother's constant calls to his cell phone and that her parents and all her friends know that she's lied "completely and absolutely from the get-go."

Again, she insisted she was telling the truth.

"You could have called your mom five weeks ago," Melich said.

"I was scared."

"What does that mean?"

"I saw my mom's reaction right off the bat, and it would've been the same from the get-go."

". . . So, wait a minute. So you're more afraid of your mom's reaction than you are if you'll ever see your daughter?"

"No. I'm absolutely petrified. Absolutely petrified. I know my mom will never forgive me. I'm never gonna forgive myself, because there's that chance that I might not see Caylee again, and I don't want to think about that."

Melich jumped on her again about bringing them to Universal Studios on a wild goose chase. "You brought us here 'cause she might be here?"

"She could be anywhere."

"Boy. That's true, but why here? . . . Why would a person who has hid your daughter from you for five weeks . . . bring her to the building that you used to work at?"

Melich waited for Casey's response, but got nothing.

"I mean, did you think we'd walk in here and she'd be sitting in the lobby or . . ."

"No," Casey snapped.

The three detectives reminded her of the evidence that proved that she was not telling the truth. In rebuttal, Casey said, "I will lie. I will steal. Or do whatever I can to find my daughter . . . I put that in my statement, and I mean that with all my heart."

"But . . . we work off of the truth," Appie Wells said.

"I know that."

"And we want to find your daughter as much as you do. And I don't think you're a monster or anything like that. I think you might have some pressures in your life. Who . . . exerts the most pressure on you . . . ?"

"My mom does, absolutely."

". . . You'll never live up to your mother's expectations, right?"

"At least not right now," Casey admitted. She went on to talk about taking advantage of her mother, leaving the car in the Amscot lot when it ran out of gas and sending emails to Zenaida that bounced back, undelivered.

Appie proposed a scenario involving the safe return of Caylee, and then asked what Casey would do if her daughter ever disappeared again.

"I wouldn't hesitate to talk to my parents this time if something happened . . . I learned the biggest lesson from all this. I made the greatest mistake that I ever could've made as a parent."

In defiance of logic, Casey, once again, raised her right hand and swore that everything she said was true.

CHAPTER 11

After more than an hour of interrogation and still no answers, the investigators filed out of the conference room with Casey. Back out in the parking lot, Sergeant John Allen pulled up photos of all the women in the appropriate age bracket named Zenaida Gonzalez from Florida's Driver and Vehicle Information Database (DAVID) system. Casey could not identify any of those drivers as her nanny.

When Allen focused her attention on the Zenaida Gonzalez whom Yuri Melich had called that morning, Casey said, "She's too old."

John Allen and Appie Wells drove Casey back to the central operations building of the sheriff's department. Detective Yuri Melich drove back to the office alone, frustrated at his inability to crack Casey. Her friends were right—Casey was well practiced in the art of deception. They all told him she was a habitual liar.

Jesse Grund said that he'd received a call from Casey on June 25. She wanted to get together, saying she was alone because Caylee had gone to the beach with the nanny for the weekend. He called Melich, he said, because it was contrary to what Casey had been telling police.

Another friend, Kristina Chester, had another contradiction to offer. She said that Casey and Caylee had come to her house sometime between June 12 and June 14. She insisted that she was certain of the date range. The three of them had taken a walk together. Kristine was concerned when she heard that the toddler had been reported missing since June 9.

Melich arrived at the operations center and prepared a charging affidavit. While working on that, he called George Anthony and got his approval to pick up the Pontiac, laptop computer and a few other items. He sent Detective Charity Beasley to the home on Hopespring Drive.

The arrest document contained three charges: neglecting a child, providing false official statements and obstructing a criminal investigation. With the affidavit in hand, he sat down with Casey one more time.

He gave her yet another opportunity to change her statement—one last chance to provide the information they needed to find her child. Casey persisted in repeating her story, again as if the repetition would somehow outweigh all the contradictory evidence.

Melich must have been weary of her games. Perhaps he regretted being unable to charge her with murder, right now. But the evidence was not there. Not yet. By her own admission, Casey had neglected her daughter. By the testimony of others, he knew she'd lied and blocked law enforcement's efforts to find Caylee. Those charges would have to do for now.

He placed Casey under arrest at 4:33 that afternoon and escorted her to the jail. He vowed never to give up until he found the proof to charge Casey Anthony with murder—and to never stop until little Caylee was found. He hoped he was wrong about Casey. He wanted to see that precious toddler brought home safe and sound.

It was not impossible, but he knew that it was as unlikely as a rose blooming in the snow.

THE PAST

"The past is never dead. It's not even past."

—William Faulkner

CHAPTER 12

Alexander "Alex" Cuza was a first generation Romanian-American. During World War II, he served with the United States Navy as a radio operator on a ship stationed in the Pacific Ocean. After the end of hostilities, he married Shirley and they set up housekeeping in Warren, Ohio, the county seat of Trumbull County.

Located near the Pennsylvania state line, just fourteen miles north west of Youngstown, Warren was situated in the area that has now come to be known as the Rust Belt. In its heyday, it was a highly productive center for manufacturing and industry, with a strong emphasis on steel. When Alex and Shirley started their family, the population of the city was just under 50,000. In a dozen years, the city's population grew by more than 20 percent—with the Cuzas contributing four new citizens to that number.

Alex continued on with the Navy for a few more years, experiencing another wartime assignment in the Korean conflict. While in the service, his first two sons were born: Daniel on May 18, 1947, and Gary on October 16, 1948.

Money was tight for the young family eking out an existence on a serviceman's salary. They lived in project housing in a run-down neighborhood.

When Alex left the Navy, he worked for the Mullins Cabinet Company for fifteen years. Their third son, Rick, was born on June 4, 1953. Then on June 5, 1958, they had a daughter, Cynthia. Alex and Shirley were thrilled to have a girl, at last. All three boys were given middle names starting with an "A," in honor of their father. Little Cynthia "Cindy" Cuza inherited her mother's middle name, Marie.

The Cuzas' economic situation improved, allowing them to move to a nicer neighborhood in 1962. It was a close-knit, family-oriented community, packed with kids on every block. Then, Alex lost his job at Mullins. He worked maintenance jobs to keep food on the table and a roof over their heads until he was employed by Thomas Steel.

With a family of six, the budget was still tight. When Daniel graduated from high school, he went right to work at Packard Electric, where younger brother Rick joined him five years later. Gary finished high school in the top ten of his class. He received scholarship money, but it wasn't enough. His parents could not afford to contribute to his schooling, and Gary had to work full-time while attending classes. After a year, it was just too much. He dropped out and joined the Navy, where he became a medical corpsman.

Thomas Steel was absorbed into a European conglomerate and the plant closed. Alex was out of work again. He soon secured another factory job at a welding company and life got a little more comfortable for the Cuza clan.

Being the first girl after a string of boys gave Cindy exalted status in the family. She often took advantage of her position, causing her brothers to nickname her "The Princess." She steamed whenever her parents said "No." It wasn't unusual for one of her older brothers to say, "Look, you're the girl and the last child, but the world does not revolve around you."

As the youngest, Cindy benefited the most from the gradual improvement in the family's finances. Her parents gave her a car when she graduated from high school, and paid for her education at Trumbull Memorial Hospital, where she earned her degree as a registered nurse.

While still a student, doing on-the-floor rotations at the

hospital, Cindy tended to a young woman named Kathy Anthony. Her brother George came in for a visit—and he and Cindy hit it off right away.

George and Cindy married and set up a home in neighboring Niles, Ohio. George was in law enforcement—first with the Niles Police Department, then as a deputy in the Trumbull County Sheriff's Office.

Initially, Cindy did not work. Her choice to stay at home created tension between her and her brother Gary. He'd had to drop out of college because his parents couldn't provide monetary support. Now his baby sister, with her education paid in full by Alex and Shirley, wasn't even using her R.N. degree.

George and Cindy's first child, Lee, was born on November 19, 1982. Less than four years later, he got a baby sister when Casey arrived on March 19, 1986. Cindy continued the tradition established by her mother, christening her daughter with the middle name Marie.

Cindy thought George should be earning more. She talked to Chuck Eddy, husband of George's sister Kathy. He told her how well he was doing working at his dad's automobile business in Austintown. Cindy thought that was an excellent idea for George. His father, after all, had owned Anthony's Auto Sales in Niles for decades.

George was reluctant to leave the sheriff's department after putting in ten years there. But Cindy kept the pressure on him until he agreed. He turned in his resignation and went to work for his dad. At first, it looked like a brilliant idea. Cindy used some of the extra income to fix up their home—she even installed new tile by herself.

Cindy, however, didn't factor in the less-than-satisfactory relationship between father and son. George's father had gotten him out of a lot of scrapes when he was a younger man, and still held that against him. Complicating things further, both men were known for their hair-trigger tempers. Fights began erupting on a regular basis. Usually they were wars of words, but one day, after George had been working there for about three years, things got out of hand. The elder Anthony shoved his son, and George shoved back—a little too hard. His father went through a large plate-glass window and into the front parking lot.

His father was cut up a bit, but not seriously injured. Their relationship, however, was permanently wounded. "You shouldn't be working here," he told his son.

Cindy worked part-time, bridging the gap until George bought a used car lot with the help of a second mortgage. Cindy continued working half days, thinking all was well with her husband's business until the day George dropped the bombshell. His business was done. He'd made some bad investments, and as a result, he was losing the lot—and the house went with it. There was no choice but to declare bankruptcy.

"Why didn't you tell me we were in trouble? I could have gotten a full-time job," Cindy shrieked. She loved her house and had put a lot of work into making it a nice home. Now, it was gone.

CHAPTER 13

Alex and Shirley Cuza grew increasingly uncomfortable living in their once-nice but now deteriorating neighborhood. Making matters worse, Alex injured his back and had to undergo surgery for removing some discs in his spine and fusing the others together. The cold winters in northeast Ohio brought on excruciating back pain. The couple wanted to move to the warmer weather of Florida, but they needed help to do so.

Rick, one of the two brothers still living in Warren and working at Packard Electric, was the only one of the Cuza children with money to spare at that time. He and his first wife loaned his parents $10,000 to move south and purchase a home there. Alex and Shirley settled down in Mount Dora, in the interior of Florida, just northwest of Orlando.

Life as Cindy had known it was now in shambles. She thought about her parents' recent relocation and thought that Florida might be a way for her family to start over. She visited her mom and dad, hoping to find a job and a new home in the Sunshine State. She discovered both in Orlando.

She was hired by Dr. David Osteen, an orthopedic surgeon whose clients included the players on the Orlando Magic basketball team. Buying a home while under the shadow of bankruptcy was a more difficult task. But Cindy accomplished that one, too, by assuming the mortgage of the current resident at the Hopespring Drive house.

The new home came with the previous occupant's 11 percent mortgage rate. It was high, but for the Anthony family, with their bleak credit standing, it was a blessing. They closed on their new home on October 4, 1989, buying it for $90,000.

The strain between Cindy and George followed them to Florida. Cindy bore a lot of animosity toward her husband for losing the house and life that she'd loved. Her brother said it took her a long time to get past her resentment.

Casey was 3-and-a-half years old when they moved. At the age of 5, Casey formed a life-long friendship with a little neighborhood boy her age, Ryan Pasley. They were constantly in each other's company until his family relocated to Seminole County as he entered eighth grade.

The *Orlando Sentinel* hired George as a route manager, supervising the drivers who made home deliveries of the newspaper. With both parents working, Lee and Casey spent a lot of time together and formed a close bond.

Although Cindy and Casey went through a lot of the typical mother–daughter conflicts as Casey entered adolescence, overall, they had a strong and tight relationship. Casey was a good student and did not exhibit any behavior problems at school.

At Liberty Middle School, Jessica Kelly introduced Casey to someone who'd just moved to Hopespring Drive, Kiomarie Torres. Soon, the three girls were close friends. They had a favorite hiding spot in the woods behind Hidden Oaks Elementary School. They rode their bicycles down the hill beside the school, toting picnic basket and blankets. They hung out there for hours. Kiomarie liked the wooded hideaway so much that sometimes she came alone when Casey and Jessica were at track meets.

When basketball season rolled around, Jessica spent a lot of time practicing and playing with the school team. Casey and Kio made it a twosome in their special spot, talking for hours on end, while snacking on food until the street lights blinked on and they had to go home.

It was a great escape from parents for the three middle school students—and it added to their sex education. Often they spotted teenage couples doing "the mommy–daddy thing." It was also a refuge from parental bias. If George was the only parent at home in the Anthony house, Kiomarie was allowed into Casey's home and bedroom. However, if Cindy was there, Kiomarie was not welcome. According to Kiomarie, Casey said it was because her friend was Spanish, and Cindy didn't want Casey hanging out with Hispanics.

The secret meeting place lost its allure when the girls entered Colonial High School. After the graduation ceremony in the spring of 2004, the two girls lost contact. Kio doubted she'd ever see her school friend again, and never thought either one of them would ever return to their special hideaway in the woods.

Another friendship Casey formed in middle school was with Melina Calabrese. They met in seventh grade when they were in the same class for English and Math. They talked incessantly about boys, developing serial crushes on those in their orbit. Some weeks, it seemed as if they both were head-over-heels for a different guy in each class period.

Melina and Casey continued to hang out together through their high school years. Both were very social girls, interacting with their peers at school events, the mall and parties. But, Melina said, "We never did anything crazy." Unlike many high school students, Casey was "very adamantly against cigarettes and pot."

George injured his knee and lost his job at the *Orlando Sentinel*. After rehabbing from his accident, he landed a service position with a pest control company. One day, as George headed into a customer's house, he tripped over a curb and landed on his bad knee. He could barely walk. Once again he was out of work. This time, he underwent a more intensive round of physical therapy.

According to what he told his family, he got bored with the period of inactivity that kept him at home alone for days at a time. With the help of a credit card he obtained without Cindy's knowledge, he started gambling on line. Then, he got another and another, maxing out each line of credit as the amount he owed spiraled out of control.

While George was jeopardizing his finances, his son Lee was starting out on his own. Right after graduation, he got a job managing a group of storage units. When that business was sold to another company, he had to move on.

Lee got an even better job working with computers for a business that offered parking lot services for big events, including one of the largest of all, the Super Bowl. Not only did Lee earn good money for a young man without a college education, he also got an enviable perk—trips to the Super Bowl.

In the spring of 2004, Casey neared her graduation from high school—or at least, that's what everyone thought. About a week before the ceremony, Cindy asked, "Where is your cap and gown?"

Casey shrugged and said, "They haven't given it to me yet."

Three days before graduation, George and Cindy learned for the first time that Casey had a problem at school. Her counselor called and asked them to come in for a meeting. The Anthonys knew it was serious when they entered the counselor's office and saw that the principal was there, too. Casey was not going to graduate with her class. When Cindy asked why not, she was told, "We offered Casey many options to get the required credits, but she didn't take advantage of any of them."

George demanded to see Casey's school records. The administrators refused; Casey was 18 years old—their hands were tied.

George and Casey's relationship had deteriorated badly in the previous two years. They didn't want to add that volatility to the confrontation with Casey, so Cindy handled it on her own. Casey insisted it was not her fault. "I took an on-line computer class and they didn't give me credit for it," she said. "I'm just one half-credit short," she whined.

Cindy believed her, but Casey was not telling the truth. There were no on-line class options, and Casey needed more than a half-credit—she was a few short of the minimum. Her classmates said that she'd just stopped going to class in her senior year.

Although Cindy had invited her parents to the graduation, she didn't bother to call them and let them in on the new developments. George, Cindy and Casey went to the ceremony and met Shirley and Alex there. Shirley was puzzled when she saw her granddaughter. "Where are your cap and gown?" she asked.

Casey burst into tears, repeating her pitiful half-credit story. She told them she was sorry, but she wouldn't be walking across the stage with her class.

Back at the Anthony home, Cindy forbade her parents from telling any of her brothers that Casey did not graduate. Shirley and Alex promised they would not—and they kept their word. None of the siblings knew until more than four years later, when they were questioned by law enforcement.

CHAPTER 14

Cindy and George hadn't given up on their daughter, despite the graduation debacle. They offered to provide the money for any educational expense Casey needed to get her high school diploma, but Casey never pursued it. Knowing of her desire to have a career in photography, they found a number of scholarship opportunities for her, but Casey did nothing about them, either.

Instead, Casey got a job with Kodak, a company with a Universal Studios theme park contract. She snapped photos of people enjoying rides there and peddled those shots to the customers when they disembarked.

Her manager, Mike Kozak, thought highly of her and her performance at work. She went into the manager trainee program where Mike "taught her the ropes." He said that she had a pleasant personality and got along with the crew. She did have limitations because of her youth, immaturity and experience: Mike had to explain to her more than once that she couldn't manage people during the day and then go out and party with them at night.

To Kiomarie's surprise, she and Casey were reunited. Kiomarie was employed by Universal Studios in attractions and entertainment, and their work brought them together on Halloween Horror Nights at the park in October 2004.

Something about her high school friend had changed—and not for the better, in Kiomarie's opinion. Casey seemed a bit off, as if the pieces of her life's puzzle no longer fit together. Kiomarie suggested that she needed to get professional help.

Old friend Melina Calabrese also got a job at Universal after high school. But no red flags about Casey popped up in her mind. After Melina left her job, she and Casey maintained a casual connection through telephone calls and text messages.

Soon after New Year's Day in 2005, Casey met 19-year-old Jesse Grund at Universal. Jesse worked in loss prevention. Casey and Jesse began dating by the end of the month. He appreciated her sarcastic sense of humor and her energy. She was a lot of fun to be around, but, to his dismay, Casey got serious right away.

Two weeks into the relationship, Casey said, "I'm in love with you." That level of commitment, that soon, was intimidating to the young man. Even though Jesse felt the stirrings of love in his heart for Casey, he stopped dating her.

But Casey didn't step out of his life. She helped Jesse's brother get a job at Kodak and kept coming by the Grund house to see Jesse. In June 2005, Jesse's father, the Reverend Richard Grund, an ordained Pentecostal Holiness Church minister, now a practicing non-denominationalist, caught sight of Casey for the first time. When Richard noticed her in his home, he asked Jesse, "Who is that girl?"

"That's Casey, the girl I dated for a while earlier this year."

"Well, son, she's pregnant."

"Oh, no. No. She's only got female problems. I asked her about that," Jess explained. "That's what she's told everybody, including her family."

Richard shook his head. "No, I know a woman who's pregnant, and she's pregnant."

Jesse blew off his father's observation and maintained his friendship with Casey. But about a month later, when he was sitting in a training seminar, he received a phone call from Casey. "I need to talk to you," she said.

"I can't talk right now, send me a text message."

Soon the words came over the screen: "I'm pregnant and you're the father. That's it."

With dread and embarrassment, Jesse called his dad. He knew his father would not approve of his premarital sexual relationship, but he had to let him know. "I'm going to take responsibility for my actions," he promised.

Then, he met with Casey. After going over the facts with her, Jesse realized that there was a major flaw in the timeline. He patiently explained how the math didn't add up, but dropped his protestations in the face of Casey's insistence. He adopted another tactic: "Look, both of us are too young to be parents. Let's put this baby up for adoption to somebody who wants a baby, but can't have one."

"That's not an option. That's not going to happen."

Between that time and the day of Caylee's birth on August 9, Jesse's doubts about his responsibility for Caylee grew stronger. His family urged him not to have his name placed on the birth certificate unless he took a DNA test first.

Richard Grund was not the only person to take note of Casey's pregnancy that June. When she stopped by Gentiva Health, where her mother had been employed as the supervisor of visiting nurses since 2001, Casey was wearing a long black coat that covered her mid-section—but not quite enough. She rushed past the front desk without stopping to chat with Charles Crittenden as she usually did. To Charles, she looked as if she was pregnant—but that was odd, because Cindy had never mentioned that she was expecting a grandchild. He shared his suspicions with a co-worker, who went into the back to check out Casey. She, too, thought Casey was pregnant. Cindy, it seemed, didn't have a clue, even though it was there for all to see.

Other observers were Casey's brother Lee and Cindy's youngest brother Rick. Both Rick and his brother Daniel had remained in Ohio working for Packard Electric, making wiring for General Motors cars. The company had become Delphi when it spun off from GM in 1999. Both brothers retired Daniel moved to Florida and Rick to coastal South Carolina.

Rick planned his second marriage for June 4, 2005, the day of his 51st birthday. Rick and his fiancée Robin wanted a small, quiet ceremony on the beach, with just their parents and children and a few close friends in attendance. Rick didn't plan on inviting any of his siblings.

His mother, though, wanted her daughter to come with her husband. Rick relented and extended an invitation to Cindy and George. The Anthony couple drove up to South Carolina with Alex and Shirley. Unbeknownst to Rick, Casey had planned to fly up for the wedding. When Lee dropped her off at the airport in Orlando, he said, "Listen, if you are pregnant, or something's going on, tell me. Be honest with me."

"No, Lee," she said. "I'm just bloated."

When Lee later learned the truth, he felt betrayed by his little sister.

The other travelers met Casey at the airport in South Carolina before driving to Rick's house. When Rick answered the door the day before his wedding, he welcomed Cindy and George, but was surprised when he saw his niece standing behind them. "Oh, Casey, I didn't know you were coming."

He took a closer look at the 19-year-old. She was wearing a tight-fitting, stretchy, powder blue top that left her lower stomach exposed and protruding. Her belly button poked out about a half-inch. After inviting their guests inside and getting them comfortable, Robin whispered, "You told me you thought Casey was too skinny when you saw her last year."

"She was," Rick said. "I think she's pregnant."

As soon as he could, he pulled his sister and brother-in-law off to the side. "Cindy, George, what's up with Casey? You got something to tell me? What's going on here?"

The couple looked at him with puzzled expressions. "What?" they both asked.

"She's expecting?"

They looked at him like he was crazy. Rick turned to Robin, who shrugged her shoulders and rolled her eyes.

"Cindy, she looks like she's pregnant. Come on."

"Oh, no. She's not," Cindy said. "She's just putting on weight."

"Cindy, I've seen a lot of pregnant girls. I'm not an expert, but, man, she looks pregnant," Rick said.

"Rick, my daughter has female problems. She has a tumor on her ovaries," she hissed.

Rick didn't believe her, but he said, "That tumor is as big as a baby. You'd better get her to a doctor right now, 'cause she's going to die," and then he just walked away.

All day, though, the other guests kept asking, "Who's the pregnant girl?"

Rick believed his mom might know what was happening, so he said, "Mom, I think Casey's pregnant."

"That's what Dad and I thought. Cindy swears she's not pregnant," Shirley said.

"Mom, she's a nurse, for crying out loud. She can't see it?"

Shirley shrugged and shook her head. Rick went back to his sister. "Cindy, come on. You're kidding me, right? Now tell me: Is Casey pregnant?"

"Casey told me that she'd have to have sex first in order to have a baby, and she did not have sex with anyone," Cindy said.

Rick knew Casey was either lying or dying, and he suspected she was not being honest with her parents. He dropped the subject and focused his mind on his wedding vows the next day.

Only Cindy and Casey showed up for the ceremony. When Rick asked about George, Cindy blamed the new puppy they'd brought along with them on the trip. "He barks whenever we leave him in the room, and we've gotten complaints. George is staying with him, but he'll be over later."

Rick said, "I told you bringing that puppy was a bad

idea." He wondered if there was another reason for George's absence. He had noticed tension between his sister and her husband. Maybe that was the real cause of his absence.

George did eventually show up at the house, with puppy in tow, and enjoyed the barbecue in the backyard with the rest of the celebrants.

After they arrived home from the wedding, Cindy confronted Casey about the pregnancy and finally, Casey admitted it. They went together to tell George. Cindy first made him sit down on the sofa. Then, she said, "George, you're going to be a grandfather."

George cried at the bittersweet news. He recovered and asked a series of questions: "How far along are you? How are you? Who is the father?"

To the last question, Casey answered, "I think it's Jesse." She didn't offer a last name.

Her parents wanted to meet him. Casey said she'd make that happen, but never followed through on her promise. Her parents accompanied her to all her doctors' visits and were excited about being present at the birth.

Cindy told her daughter, "When I was carrying you, I played classical music to my belly every day." Casey wanted to do the same for her unborn child. Cindy helped her find the same selections that she had played to Casey in the womb.

Casey's middle school friend, Kiomarie, learned the news of Casey's pregnancy in July. Kiomarie asked, "What are you gonna do about it?"

"I really want to give it up for adoption," Casey said.

To Kiomarie, this was good news. She'd recently learned from her doctor that she could never have children of her own. Casey was a cute girl and bound to make a cute baby, and Kiomarie was married and in a position where she could afford a child. "If you are going to give your baby up for adoption, I would strongly consider adopting the baby from you."

"That's a good idea," Casey said. "I really don't want to have a baby right now."

A couple of days later, a disappointed Casey called Kiomarie. "I talked to my mom, and she told me no. I need to keep the baby, and I'm not putting it up for adoption."

Casey walked into Mike Kozak's office at Kodak and said, "Well, you know, I'm pregnant."

"You gotta bring in a doctor's note," Mike told her.

When she did, Mike treated her as he did all his expecting employees: He moved her into the Kodak office so that she wouldn't spend all day standing on her feet. Casey did light duty work there, filing, application processing and other miscellaneous clerical chores.

Cindy and George were with Casey when she went into the delivery room at Florida Hospital in Winter Park. After cleaning up the baby's airway, the nurse placed little Caylee into Cindy's arms, because the doctor had not yet finished caring for Casey after the difficult birth. Casey objected loudly, "Oh my gosh. You get a chance to hold her before I do."

That small act was in some ways a foundation for the bond between grandmother and granddaughter. It also planted a seed of resentment that thrived in the dark side of Casey's mind.

The moment Casey was out of the delivery room, she called Jesse. He rushed to her side and held the newborn in his arms. He told them that he would do everything he could for the baby, and acknowledged that he was the father.

It was the first time Casey's parents had met him. George was cold to him. He disliked the young man and it showed. On first sight, George disapproved of the sloppiness of Jesse's attire in the hospital. Any father might find it difficult to embrace the man responsible for his out-of-wedlock grandchild, and George was no exception.

When Jesse and Casey were alone, she said, "I want to put your name on the birth certificate."

"No, let's wait and do a paternity test first," Jesse said.

Casey recoiled in anger and refused to allow the test to be conducted. Jesse petitioned the courts and was granted legal authorization. He paid $550 and waited for the results. It would take eight weeks for them to return, but Jesse still spent as much time as he could with the little girl. Just in case he was wrong and Caylee was his baby, he didn't want to miss any part of her life.

The results confirmed Jesse's doubts—there was a zero percent probability that he was the child's father. Yet, by that time, his connection to the little girl was as solid as kiln-dried timber. He was emotionally devastated by the results, and remained ready and willing to raise Caylee as his own. When he gave a copy of the test results to George and Cindy, his disappointment was clear. Jesse proposed and Casey accepted.

George asked them, "What are you guys planning for the future?"

"We're getting married," they said.

"Just 'cause you're engaged, that doesn't mean you don't need a plan."

"I'm going to take care of her," Jesse said.

"Yes, but what are you going to do with her? What are you going to do with my granddaughter? That's a very relevant question. Just saying you're going to take care of them doesn't tell me what you're going to *do* to take care of them."

George did not get a satisfactory response, but since Jesse came by the house every day, he had to give the young man some credit. "He loved that little girl—I know it. You could see the compassion when he was holding her. I think he loved that little girl more than he loved my daughter."

Maybe that's why Casey tried so hard with the Grunds. She began participating in the religious Friday night family fellowship at the home. She was there for Bible readings and for the nightly family prayer before bedtime—anything to fit in with them.

She didn't stop there in her attempt to mold herself in their image. When she and Jesse had dated the first time around, he'd learned that she hated the Yankees—the team Jesse loved. Now, she professed to be an ardent Yankee fan.

In early September, Melina Calabrese, Casey's close friend from seventh grade through her high school years, stopped by to meet Caylee for the first time. Casey told her that Jesse Grund was the father. Melina and her fiancé Josh hung out with Casey and Jesse throughout the fall—Jesse and Josh even started rooming together.

Once the DNA tests were back denying the possibility of Jesse's paternity, Casey told a few people that the father was guy named Jesús.

Casey never mentioned Jesús to her parents. When they asked about the father, Casey refused to give her parents a name.

CHAPTER 15

A new baby in the house wasn't the only upheaval in the Anthony household in 2005. George finally received a check for $60,000 in his workman's compensation settlement. Cindy thought they had a cash windfall—maybe they should use it to refinance their home at a more reasonable percentage rate.

She talked to George about how to spend the money. George confessed that it was already gone—he told her that he'd used it to pay some of his debts from on-line gambling. The worst part was that he still owed a substantial amount.

The pain of past wounds surfaced. To Cindy, it was yet another betrayal. She threw George out of the house. He moved in with his parents in Fort Myers.

She got an equity loan on the house, making the budget even tighter, while she made two large house payments. She wiped out her 401K to catch up on car insurance and other past due bills she'd thought George had been paying. She had to pay a penalty to the IRS because George had cashed out his retirement account and not reported the income. Then, she was unable to add any funds to her retirement account—a difficult position for a woman in her fifties.

Cindy consulted a divorce attorney, who told her that even though she'd made all the house payments, George would still get half of the house, and she'd probably have to pay alimony to him because she had been the main financial support for the family since they'd moved to Florida. She told her mother, Shirley Cuza, "Ain't no way he's getting the house I paid for. Even if I sold the house and got an apartment, half the money would go to George. I can't afford a divorce—between George and Casey, I'm living paycheck to paycheck."

In the fall, after Caylee's birth, Casey stopped into the Kodak office once to show off her new baby. Then, suddenly, she disappeared. Mike had expected her to come back to work, but it never happened. Corporate filed paperwork terminating her for "job abandonment." Her lack of employment added to a fragile economic situation in the Anthony home.

Casey spent a lot of time in the Grund household, where she put pressure on Jesse. Casey wanted out of her parents' home. She told her prospective father-in-law, "I don't want to turn out like my mother. I don't want to be around my mother. I want out of that house." She added that she hated her father for the financial problems he'd created with his gambling.

Casey wanted Jesse to move into a place of their own immediately. Richard Grund frowned on that scenario. He told his son, "If you want me to perform your [wedding] ceremony, you can't live together beforehand."

But Jesse wanted to move in with Casey, driven in part by what he perceived as Cindy's negative attitude toward her. One day when Jesse and Casey were lying together on the couch in the Anthony living room, Casey and Cindy began arguing. Jesse interrupted, telling Cindy, "Please don't do this while I'm here. Don't talk to her like that. You know I love your daughter."

"Why do you want to be with somebody who's got no future?" Cindy snapped back. "She didn't even go back to get her high school education. You know she's got a job at a place where she really doesn't even make enough money to support Caylee. I'm doing that—I'm the one supporting Caylee."

Jesse hated to hear these words in front of Casey. He knew they made Casey feel as if she must be a failure in his eyes.

In the spring of 2006, reconciliation was in the air. George and Cindy made a few tentative dates to test getting back together. One night, after a pleasant evening of dinner and conversation, Jesse's pick-up truck was in the driveway when they arrived back on Hopespring Drive at 11:30.

They were surprised by the quietness of the home when they stepped inside. They found Jesse, fully clothed, lying on one side of the bed in Casey's room. Casey was asleep on the other side. Caylee nestled between them.

George erupted. He wanted to yank Jesse out of the bed and drag him out of the house. Cindy's cooler head prevailed. "Listen, George, we're going through enough right now—you and I. I'll handle the situation. I'll handle Jesse," she said to him in the hallway.

Back in the room, Cindy turned her attention to Jesse. "I don't want you in my daughter's bed. There's no reason for you to be in my daughter's bed."

"Don't tell me what to do. I'm not doing anything. I have a right to be here," Jesse snapped back.

"This is my house. These are my rules. You have no right to be in here. You guys are not married—sure, you're engaged, but you guys aren't married. Until you're away from here," she said referring to when they lived together in marriage, "this stuff doesn't happen in my house."

Initially, Casey seemed captivated by her newborn and wanted to spend every moment with her. Before Caylee was capable of moving about, she installed child-proof latches on all the cabinet doors and put protective covers on all the open electrical outlets. Within a couple of months, though, she grew restless and yearned for the carefree life of a typical 19-year-old, with fewer responsibilities.

That was when she turned to another high school friend, Lauren Gibbs. Casey often called and asked, "I've got to work today and I don't have anyone to watch Caylee. Can you watch her?"

If she could, Lauren headed over to Hopespring Drive and took care of the baby until Cindy or Casey returned home. She never charged Casey for watching Caylee. Lauren knew life wasn't easy for a single mother, and she was glad to help her friend out.

Initially, Casey had told Lauren that she worked at Universal. Then, her early childhood friend Ryan Pasley started working at Sports Authority on Alafaya by Waterford Lakes. Casey told Lauren, Cindy and others that she was working there, too. When Casey went out late at night, leaving the baby with her mother, she told her mom that she had to do inventory. Cindy was comfortable with the late hours because she knew Ryan would be there, too, and she trusted Ryan.

Lauren didn't harbor any suspicions until one day in April when she was watching Caylee and needed to call Casey at work. The person who answered the phone said, "She doesn't work here. I don't even know who she is."

Lauren called mutual friend Melina Calabrese and told her about her call to Sports Authority. "You need to tell her straight up you've already called the job," Melina said and advised Lauren to confront Casey to see what she had to say for herself.

Lauren took her advice, but even in the face of the stark truth, Casey would not confess. "I have an I.D. tag," she insisted.

"Why did they say you didn't work there?"

Casey didn't have a real answer. She blamed it all on a communication problem at work. Lauren didn't buy it. Casey was using her in order to be free to go hang out with other friends. Lauren's days of providing free baby-sitting were over.

Despite her protestations to the contrary, Casey did not have gainful employment, and therefore, she had no money. She asked her friend Ryan to loan her $400, claiming that she had to pay rent to her mom and dad. Ryan didn't believe the reason she gave when asking for the money, but he figured the need was real. He gave her $400 with no expectation that he'd ever see it again.

At the end of May 2006, Casey talked to her father about her relationship with Jesse. "He's too controlling, Dad. I can't do anything unless he knows about it. I can't make my own decisions."

"You can't be in a marriage where you're supposed to care about each other and have one controlling person. Your mom and I have had tough times, but we still meet in the middle somewhere and compromise."

Casey broke off her engagement with Jesse early in June 2006. She told Melina that she'd stopped seeing Jesse because he was not the father. The biological dad, she said, was Josh, she now claimed, a one-night-stand she'd met at Universal Studios.

"Is Josh going to be part of Caylee's life?" Melina asked.

"No. Josh has a girlfriend he's going to marry. They already have kids together. I'm not even going to tell Caylee about Josh until she starts asking questions on her own."

That summer, to satisfy her parents' curiosity about Caylee's paternity, Casey clipped an obituary of a young man named Eric who'd died in an automobile accident. She told her parents that he was the biological father of her daughter. Later she would write a memorial to Jesús, whom she told friends was the father.

She didn't contact Eric's bereaved parents to let them know they had a granddaughter. She never applied for the Social Security benefits that a child became eligible for when a parent died. She never had any DNA tests done to match Caylee and Eric. She simply said that Eric was the dad. That was her story and she was sticking to it.

* * *

Despite Jesse's disappointment in his relationship with Casey, he missed Caylee and wanted to be part of her life. That desire made him vulnerable to Casey's next request. She explained that she'd lost her sitter and needed to find someone to take care of Caylee so that she could go to work.

Jesse only had one day a week off from his job at Progressive Insurance. He gave up that Monday to take care of Caylee. It was supposed to be a temporary arrangement, but Casey seemed to be doing nothing to change the situation. Soon, she'd cajoled Deborah Grund, Jesse's mother, to assume responsibility for Caylee two additional days of the week.

Richard Grund liked the little girl, but having her around the house three days a week was a serious distraction for a man who worked from his home. Every time he talked to Casey, he asked, "Have you found anybody yet?" The answer was always "No"—until one day that summer, Casey surprised him.

"Yeah. I got that worked out. Oh yeah, I found Zenaida Gonzalez, and she watches my friend Jeffrey Hopkins' son Zachary. And Zachary and Caylee play together. They love to be together. So this'll work out great."

Richard expected a simple "yes" or "no" in response to his question. *Wow!* He thought. *That's a lot more information than I really needed.*

He didn't know the half of it. Although he'd already realized that Casey was not always honest, he had no clue that Jeffrey did not have a child, nor did he know anyone named Zenaida Gonzalez.

Halloween 2006, Casey attended a masquerade party dressed as a casino waitress in a form-fitting, skimpy black lace and red-ribboned costume. She shocked and titillated the other partiers when she stopped in the middle of the room to engage in an intense make-out session with a woman wearing an umpire's uniform. A little later the two women were joined by another, lip-locking, fondling and writhing. Casey didn't limit her escapades that night to the same sex. She was also seen rubbing provocatively against a man's crotch.

In October, one of Casey's high school friends, Annie Downing, moved into Sawgrass Apartments at 2867 South Conway Road, unit number 218. By the end of the year, Casey dropped by her place nearly every day. It was an address Casey would remember well.

CHAPTER 16

Casey exchanged messages in an on-line chat with Jesse Grund in January 2007. "I can hit my friend Annie for some Xanax. We'd be a good time." Annie later admitted to having these pills from an old prescription, but insisted that she'd never given any of them to Casey.

"Yeah, well that's an understatement . . . then again, we never needed medication to be a good time," Jesse responded.

"Again, very true. How's the fam?"

"Alive and well. My mom actually recommended me seeing you."

"Really? Whoa. What brought this on?" Casey asked.

"Yeah, well . . . I hadn't heard you talk, except in my dreams, for months. So . . . I called mom and we talked, and she said I should see you."

"Odd that we've been in the same place, as far as dreams and such goes. I passed the Progressive office on University last week, and at random, noticed your car, parked by the street," Casey confessed.

"Yeah, I have been in your neighborhood for calls and driven by your house," Jesse said, still smitten—a state Casey was more than willing to foster.

Rick Cuza had been concerned about his father's health since he'd visited his parents in the summer of 2006. At the time, Alex seemed out of it—as if he were sleepwalking through life. A subsequent ultrasound examination found no blockage in his carotid arteries—indication that he might have suffered from a stroke, for instance. Still, Rick worried.

In January of 2007, Rick and his new wife Robin set sail from Port Canaveral on a four-day cruise. At the end of the excursion, they planned to pay a surprise visit to Rick's parents.

Rick's cell phone rang on the last day of the cruise. He was amazed and delighted to get a signal that far from shore. His mood quickly turned dark when he answered and realized his sister Cindy was the bearer of bad news. Their dad had had a stroke and his condition was serious. After disembarking from the ship the next day, Robin and Rick headed straight to the hospital and met Cindy there. Since Cindy was a registered nurse, Rick questioned her about the ultrasound results and learned that they weren't always reliable. The dye tests conducted after his stroke showed considerable blockage, Cindy explained.

They placed Alex in a nursing home just a short walk from his house. At first, he couldn't talk at all. Gradually, his speech returned, but he remained difficult to understand. At times, he chose to write out what he wanted to say, rather than struggle with oral communication.

Shirley visited her husband twice a day—for breakfast and dinner. Initially, she walked between her house and the nursing home, but she soon abandoned that habit. Although it was Alex's stroke, the traumatic experience and its aftermath had aged Shirley, too. She lost weight and became frail. Robbed of her vitality, she had to make the short trip in her car.

Cindy, Casey and Caylee visited the nursing home often, at first. After a few months, Casey didn't bother, allowing months to pass between visits to her grandparents.

January was a tough month for Cindy. Casey dropped another load of stress on her mother's back, with her claim that she was pregnant again, this time with Brandon Snow's child. Casey shared the news with her brother Lee, who told their mother. Cindy hit the roof, probably imagining that much of the care of this second child would fall on her shoulders, as it did with Caylee.

Casey solved that problem by claiming that she'd had a miscarriage on Valentine's Day. Annie, among other friends, doubted that she'd ever been pregnant. Annie noticed that whenever Casey was able to go out without her daughter, Cindy called frequently, wanting to know when she would come home to take care of Caylee. Most of the time, Cindy was angry, yelling at Casey. Annie suspected the pregnancy scare was somehow part of it, but thought there was a lot more to the conflict than she knew.

In March, Casey dated Christopher Stutz, a young man she'd met a few months after Caylee's birth. They'd been friends for a little more than a year, since meeting on the football field, where Casey sat on the sidelines watching the men play. Casey decided to take their relationship "up a notch." They often went to the movies, and at midnight, Casey would get a text from her mother: "You need to come home." Casey would leave Christopher and head to Hopespring Drive.

Their romantic entanglement didn't work well because of distance, though. Christopher was in college at Florida State in Tallahassee. So they went back to being friends.

After their dating ended, she told him that a manager from Universal had come by Sports Authority and said they wanted her to come back to work at the theme park again. She claimed she'd gotten a job in event planning, but said that it was only temporary, that what she really wanted to do was become a personal trainer, and she was working out a lot to further that goal.

She and Christopher continued to hang out together when he was home from college—Putt-Putt golf was a favorite activity. When Christopher suggested going to a bar, Casey insisted that she did not want to go out drinking because she didn't want to leave her kid with her mom and dad that long.

* * *

The first quarter of the year, Casey seemed troubled. She showed up at Annie's job for lunch, saying she needed to talk. "I need to get away. I feel like I'm having a breakdown."

Casey would not tell Annie why she felt this way, but she added, "I want to go to an institution. Caylee can stay with my mom. I need help."

Later that day, a concerned Annie called Casey, who reassured her that all was well. "I talked to my mom and everything is okay."

Annie was perplexed. Casey's problems sounded too deep and too serious to be alleviated by a simple conversation.

Michelle Murphy, a long-time Anthony family friend, got the next crisis call from Casey in March. "I'm feeling crazy and need someone to talk to," Casey said.

Again, Casey did not explain why she felt that way, but she did talk about her miscarriage, and her disappointment in losing the baby she was supposed to have borne in October and the loss of her imagined life with Brandon. She also expressed fears about her inadequacy as a parent. "I don't feel like a very good mother to Caylee."

When Michelle called back later that day to check up on her friend, Casey blew her off and said everything was fine. It made Michelle suspect that Casey had fabricated the story of her distress simply to get sympathy.

Were these genuine cries for help? Or a way for Casey to garner attention?

Michelle moved in with Casey's brother Lee in May 2007. She saw a lot more of both Casey and Caylee in the six months she roomed with him. She listened when Casey talked about being an event planner with Universal, but thought it was odd, since Casey didn't have the required education. Lee's girlfriend, Mallory Parker, on the other hand, was currently going to school in order to get that kind of job.

Michelle, however, never confronted Casey about this discrepancy.

Michelle worried a bit that Caylee suffered from extreme separation anxiety: The little girl's distress was over-the-top when Casey put her down or stepped out of her sight.

In June 2007, Rico Morales met Casey at a birthday party Amy threw for her roommate Lauren Gibbs. At the time, Casey was seeing Steve Jones, though she told her mother that she was dating Jeff Hopkins.

Cindy wanted to meet Casey's boyfriend and his son Zack. She invited Casey to bring them to the house for a cookout. Cindy bought the food and made preparations for the occasion. At the last minute, Casey said that Jeff couldn't come, because Zack was sick.

A couple of weeks later, Jeff and Zack were supposed to stop by for dessert. Once again, no Jeff—Casey said he'd had to go to work. After a couple more repeat no-show performances, Casey announced that Jeff had moved to the Carolinas to live near his mother.

If Jeff had known about the stories Casey told her mother, he would have been quite surprised. Jeff didn't have any children. And he certainly had no recollection of ever dating Casey. Their relationship as he knew it was wafer-thin.

When Jeff was in sixth grade, he'd played volleyball with eighth-grader Lee Anthony. The next year, when Casey started at Liberty Middle School, they'd exchanged "hellos" when their paths crossed, but nothing more.

In high school, they'd traveled with different circles of friends. He did remember the big smile she always donned when they passed in the hallway—but that was it. After high school, they'd had a few accidental encounters, but not one of them was memorable.

Caylee turned two years old on August 9, 2007, and that was cause for celebration on Hopespring Drive. Casey's grandmother, Shirley Cuza, came down to spend the weekend and attend her great-granddaughter's birthday party. Casey slipped into the guest bedroom a couple of hours before the festivities began and reached into her grandmother's purse, removing a check from the back of the book. She went to Publix, and picked up a birthday cake and decorations for the Mexican-themed event, writing a $54 check on her grandmother's account.

A number of Casey's friends had been invited to the party. Among those in attendance was Brandon, who was still dating Casey and had not yet been apprised that she was telling friends that she'd miscarried his baby in February. Both Michelle and Annie were there, too.

Casey told Annie that her mother was "a horrible person," who was trying to control her life and take Caylee away from her. "She wants Caylee to call her 'Mom' instead of 'Grandmom,'" she claimed.

As Cindy sat behind Caylee, helping her open presents, Casey pulled Annie aside and said, "Oh my God, this is supposed to be Caylee's day. I'm her mom. She's not her mom. She's trying to play mom, or be mom." To Annie, it was obvious that Casey was jealous of the relationship Cindy had with Caylee.

Michelle noticed that tension, too. To her, it seemed as if Cindy and Casey were competing over the girl. Michelle thought Cindy was "overbearing" and "trying to run the show."

Casey told Michelle that she was afraid of disappointing her mother, and was worried that Cindy would find out about the "bad things" she'd done.

"What bad things?" Michelle asked.

"I was pregnant with Brandon's baby and had a miscarriage. And I planned to throw a party here in the house that my mom doesn't know about." She didn't mention that day's theft from her own grandmother.

And Shirley didn't notice a check was missing until days later, when she balanced her statement. She'd paid the utilities bill in Mount Dora right before traveling down to Orlando, and thought she might have accidentally pulled two checks out and sent in both the actual one and a blank one. She went to the utility office, but they didn't have the missing check.

Shirley stopped next at the police station. She showed her statement to an officer, who found the cancelled check in question. It had a license number on its back. He ran it on the computer. "Do you know anybody in Orlando?"

"Yes," Shirley said.

"Do you know a Casey Anthony?"

"That's my granddaughter," she gasped. She expressed confusion over the theft. "I would have gladly given her some money if she asked." It was difficult for Shirley to accept that her granddaughter had stolen money from her. Her thoughts drifted back a few years to the time she'd wondered if a missing bottle of nail polish had slipped into Casey's pocket. She wondered no longer—she was sure of it.

Shirley confronted her daughter and granddaughter with the ugly news. Casey said she was sorry. Shirley accepted her apology, but added, "Don't let it happen again."

Later that month, on the day that Annie graduated from the University of Central Florida, Casey dropped by her place for a visit. Cindy called and demanded that Casey come home immediately. Casey said that her mother was upset because she hadn't registered at Valencia Community College. Annie learned the real reason later: Cindy had found a credit card statement with exorbitant charges run up on her bill by Casey.

It may have been Cindy's bill, but it was the last straw for Annie—she was tired of all of Casey's lies.

It was still Caylee's birthday month when Casey told Melina that her daughter's father Josh had died in an automobile accident. She had told her parents about the car crash the year before, but in that version, Caylee's deceased father was named Eric.

Melina thought they didn't need a man in their lives; Casey and Caylee were simply adorable together. Sometimes they called her and sang duets on the phone. She occasionally joined them on outings to Target and Chick-fil-A, their favorite. Melina never heard Casey raise her voice to Caylee, even when the little girl got fussy, and she never saw her hit her daughter or mistreat her in any way. Melina didn't have children of her own yet, but she hoped that when she did, she would have a mother–daughter bond just like the one Casey had with Caylee.

Caylee had her own bedroom, filled with stuffed animals, in her grandparents' house on Hopespring Drive, where she lived with her mother. Scattered around the room were lots of caps, hats and sunglasses—Caylee loved to wear her headgear and specs. She also was crazy about music. She had two little keyboards, but what really got her excited were drums. She loved to pound on them, and was surprisingly good at keeping a steady beat. Her grandparents were trying to decide if they should get her a drum set for her 3rd birthday or if they should wait until she turned 4.

Caylee developed a cute habit that tickled her grandparents: Every night before she went to bed, even if it was rainy or cold, Caylee always wanted to step outside and see the moon and the stars before she went to sleep.

She'd formed affectionate relationships with many people in her orbit. She adored her "Unca E" and "Mau-Wee"—her mother's brother Lee and his girlfriend Mallory Parker. In the backyard, she loved to swim in the above-ground pool. The adults made sure the ladder was never left beside the pool—they didn't want her climbing up unsupervised and falling into the water.

Another big attraction behind the house was a white plastic playhouse with her own little phone and kitchen set. Jesse Grund said that whenever he'd played in the backyard with Caylee, in October and November 2007, she'd run straight to the playhouse. Her grandparents and Casey played with her a lot there, too.

Jesse and Casey resumed dating in November. It didn't last long.

CHAPTER 17

On November 8, after a night of hard drinking, Casey had a medical crisis. Jesse grabbed the phone and punched in 9-1-1. "My girlfriend just had a seizure . . ."

"What address are you at?" the operator asked.

"Uh, my girlfriend . . ."

"What address are you at?" the operator repeated. Jesse gave the street address and apartment number. "Hold on for Medical."

A couple of rings later, the connection went through. "Fire Rescue."

Jesse repeated his address when asked. Then the operator asked, "What's wrong?"

"She just had a seizure. Her pupils are dilated. Her pulse is racing right now."

"Okay, listen," the operator said. "I have some help on the way, okay?"

"Okay."

"Alright, I need you to do a few things for me before we hang up, please."

"Okay."

"What is your name, please?"

"My name is Jesse Grund."

"Jesse, I need you to check and see if she's still breathing for me."

A minute-and-a-half after the initial call, the dispatcher informed the medics in the ambulance that the patient was still shaking and unresponsive. Thirty seconds later, an important piece of information came to the emergency vehicle en route to the scene. "She's been nauseous all day and was drinking heavily last night."

She had classic symptoms of alcohol poisoning—a condition that, if ignored, can lead to irreversible brain damage or death. But help arrived less than eight minutes after Jesse had picked up the phone.

Jesse was attending the Orlando police academy that fall. In November, after spending time at the firing range, he, Anthony Rusciano and a few of his fellow trainees went to Subway. Casey and Caylee joined them there.

Anthony, meeting them for the first time, asked, "Is that your little sister?"

To his surprise, Casey said, "No, it's my kid."

The next time he saw Casey was when he was working as a bouncer at Latitudes, a bar on Church Street in Orlando. She and Jesse came in and were all over each other. Jesse seemed to be showing off, flaunting his newly reconstituted relationship. At the end of the evening, Casey was so sloppy drunk, Jesse had to carry her out to the car.

Although still dating a girl in Tampa, Anthony was intrigued by Casey. He became "friends" with her on MySpace and Facebook shortly before Christmas. By New Year's Day, his relationship with his Tampa girlfriend was history and his pursuit of Casey had begun in earnest.

A few days into 2008, he had Casey in his apartment for a sexual encounter. Five minutes after it was over, Casey was out the door. Anthony said, "That's when, you know, you kind of feel like the girl. You're, like, *Damn, man, I just got used.*"

It was the same way each time they hooked up. As soon as the act was complete, Casey was pulling on her clothes and saying goodbye.

While Casey was casually entwined with Anthony, her renewed relationship with Jesse was in free fall. For months, Casey told Jesse, with great emotion, that she didn't want to be anything like her mother. "I want to be a different person," she said.

In January, Jesse noted a contradictory entry on her MySpace page: "I can't wait to be like my mother when I grow up. I want to be just like her. I love her so much."

He asked Casey about it and she had nothing but positive comments to make about her mom. Cindy, she said, was her confidante.

Casey's feelings for Jesse had also changed—but in the opposite direction. Casey broke it off, leaving Jesse perplexed.

Rico Morales ran into Casey again at a barbeque at mutual friend Troy Brown's house. They started seeing each other, and at Rico's birthday party, on January 23, things got intense and intimate between the two of them.

She sent Rico a note through Yahoo! Messenger a couple of weeks later: "My life sucks—I can't do anything because of the kid." She went on, griping about not being able to participate fully with her friends because she was a mother.

Rico wrote: "You do have more responsibilities than everyone else 'cause you're a mother. But we do get to hang out with you a lot and see you pretty often. So it's not that bad."

Beginning the second week of that month, Casey spent four or five nights a week at Rico's. Caylee was almost always with her, and slept in bed with him and Casey. Early in the relationship, Caylee hit her head on a table and bruised her eye in his apartment. Caylee's photograph, showing that injury, later raised questions about child abuse.

Rico worked till 8 most nights, so when he got back home, Caylee was usually in bed or getting ready for bed. Caylee had about four teddy bears and a favorite little doll named Momma; one of them was always with her when she slept.

Rico thought Casey was a good mother, very attentive

to Caylee—feeding her, giving her juice, changing her diaper, making sure she had her teddy bears when she went to bed.

Most nights, Casey and Rico didn't go out. They just relaxed on the couch watching movies and talking. He said he thought Casey was a nice person—sweet, agreeable.

However, Casey seemed rather volatile to her friend Amy. "When something ticks her off, it definitely ticks her off—not violently, but she definitely gets worked up about it. I've never seen her strike out at anyone or anything, but she definitely gets a little riled up."

Her relationship with Rico bore the imprint of Casey's "emotional, headstrong" personality. "They would either be super-duper-duper happy, or she would just be pissed off at him," Amy said. "She was really mad that he smoked . . . or she'd get pissed if he drank too much beer . . . Never physically violent angry, but just, like, so pissed off, she'd have to go into another room."

Rico played and interacted with Caylee, but he was a bit awkward with kids, since he hadn't spent much time around them. But Caylee was always willing to give him a hug. Rico thought she was an average kid, with occasional tantrums like any 2-year-old, but not a problem child.

Casey's friend Amy thought Caylee was better behaved than the average 2-year-old. "She can get a little into stuff, but she's two . . . every two-year-old does. She's normal, happy and way less bratty . . ." than most children that age.

Amy thought Casey and Cindy were consistent with the little girl, making Caylee very good at recognizing that "no" meant "no." Amy wasn't always comfortable with Casey's parenting, though. "I didn't like that she'd bring her over when we'd be drinking or having a party or having a poker night . . . but she'd put her to bed on the couch and the kid slept through anything . . . it was amazing."

One weekend, Rico went to Tampa for a Sunday wedding. Casey met him up there on Saturday, hung out all day and came back that night.

Throughout the spring, Casey frequently dropped Caylee off at Gentiva Health, where her mother worked, at 5, with the excuse that she needed to go to work. She wore an employee I.D. on a string of Mardi Gras beads when she did this.

Rico believed she had worked at Universal for the past four years. She talked about it a lot, about her boss Tom and her friend Julia. She had a great schedule. She could work from home whenever she wanted. Sometimes with events, she had to work early in the morning, sometimes late at night. She tried to set up friends to attend concerts for free, but it always fell through because the concerts sold out, making it impossible for her to get passes.

In February, Casey told her friend Melina about her event-planning job. She said that she worked downtown and had her own office. Melina was envious. She was currently going to school to get her certificate in event planning—and there was Casey with the job Melina wanted, without going to school at all.

After learning about Melina's education efforts, Casey told Rico that she was taking classes at Valencia to get her certification. Her classes were on Thursday, she said, but explained her presence at home on that weekday by saying that she frequently had the day off from class.

On St. Patrick's Day, just two days before her birthday, police believe she accessed the Internet and made several searches: "chloroform," "alcohol," "acetone," "peroxide," "inhalation," and "death." Four days later, they believe she did the same. This time the computer searched blogspot .com, druglibrary.org and instructables.com for "shovel," "making weapons out of household products" and "how to make chloroform."

At her birthday party, Casey took Melina aside to complain about her mother. Cindy, she said, was "overbearing," and they had frequent "extreme" arguments, usually about Caylee.

One night in early April, Caylee was there when Rico

went to sleep, but not there when he woke up. Casey told him that her mother had called during the night and wanted her to bring Caylee home. Rico didn't quite know what to think of that.

Casey and Rico split up on April 14. According to him, it was his idea. Although it was a fun relationship, it wasn't getting serious. His feelings for her weren't growing, and he believed they should be. He said that Casey felt the same way. Casey told her friends that Rico was scared of commitment and because of that, the relationship was going nowhere. They didn't fight over the break-up, though. And later, when Rico was sick, Casey came over and cooked chicken soup for him.

But their relationship did not become purely platonic. Their sexual intimacy continued into early June. She came by often and hung out with Rico after their break-up—sometimes with Caylee, sometimes not. She once said that Caylee was with Zanny, her nanny. "Zanny?" Rico asked, "What does that stand for?"

"Zenita," Caylee said.

Rico accepted the existence of the babysitter, but never once met her, and never talked to anyone who had seen or spoken to the mystery caregiver.

CHAPTER 18

According to her family, Casey had by then made a habit of stealing. She slipped cash out of her mother's purse, stole her father's coin collection, pillaged Caylee's piggybank, ran up charges on her mother's credit cards and even wiped out her daughter's emergency bank account. George thought the account was growing, as $30 came out of each of his paychecks for deposit in Caylee's name. When he checked the balance in 2008, only $5 remained.

George had long suspected that Casey wasn't working, because every time he turned around she was asking for $5, $10 or $20 to pick up diapers or gas. George was convinced when he found a résumé with Casey's employment information. Beginning in 2006, Casey wrote, she'd been a nanny. He asked Casey, "What's this?"

"Well, that's something I was thinking about doing."

"Why would you put it down on a résumé? That makes no sense. If you're going to be taking an occupation doing that, you don't put it down unless you're already doing it."

George couldn't win that battle, though. Whenever he said anything to his wife or daughter, they both insisted that Casey was working. Casey often claimed her check was locked up in her boss's desk. On one occasion, she even forged three deposit slips for her mother's account—a total of $4,400—and ceremoniously turned them over to her mother, saying that she'd finally gotten her back checks, and believed in paying back money she owed.

Cindy thought the money was in the bank, and spent accordingly. It wasn't until her $700 house payment check bounced that she learned the ugly truth.

That spring, Cindy discovered another way her daughter was stealing money from her. Casey had hacked into her mother's checking account on line to send payments of $300 to $450 per month to AT&T for her cell phone. Cindy demanded that she stop, and Casey did. Next time she needed money to pay her cell phone bill, she extracted $354 from the account set up for her grandfather's care after he went into the nursing home. The two small checks he got each month were directly deposited into an account without check-writing privileges. Shirley transferred it to her checking account when she needed to pay bills or the balance got too high.

Shirley was surprised when she saw the transaction on her statement. She went into the bank, where a manager tracked down the expenditure to Casey. "I don't know what you want to do about it," he said.

Her patience this time had expired. "You can do whatever you want to. If you want to arrest her, arrest her. Press charges."

The bank, however, did not take any action. Shirley emailed Casey because she didn't want to talk to her. Casey wrote back: "Dear Grandma, I'm so sorry. I apologize. I'll come down and do some cleaning for you."

Shirley responded: "Casey, I don't want you down here."

Shirley called her daughter and told her about everything. Cindy said, "Mom, I'll pay you back."

"No, the bank paid me back," Shirley said. "But if the bank wants to arrest her, they're going to, because I told them they could." Shirley didn't want to file a complaint herself—Casey deserved it, but she couldn't do that to Caylee and Cindy.

Cindy demanded an answer from Casey. Casey explained that she'd been transferred into a brand new department at Universal, and the budget had not yet gone through. She and all the employees were asked to buy their own telephones. They would be reimbursed for the expense when the financials were all in order. Then, Casey claimed, she was going to pay her grandmother back.

Shirley didn't buy this explanation when Cindy relayed it, but she didn't get on her daughter's case about it. Casey was in the wrong, not Cindy. Shirley later figured out that she'd gotten off easy. By her estimate, Casey had taken her own parents for as much as $45,000.

Cindy went to see a counselor through a service provided at her place of employment. She later related the conversation to her mother. The counselor said she should not be supporting her adult daughter. "You should kick them out on the street."

"What about Caylee?" Cindy asked. "I can't kick my granddaughter out on the street."

"Then just kick out Casey."

"Casey would try to take her."

"Well, you need to file for custody."

Cindy told her mother she was going to look into the possibility. She said that she wanted Casey to still be part of Caylee's life, but she thought that she—not Casey—should be making the decisions about what was best for Caylee's welfare. She planned to pursue custody, she told her mother.

She also shared her concerns about the problems on George's side of the family. His sister, Sonie, she claimed, was bi-polar, and the symptoms included compulsive behavior and overspending. She saw those same traits in Casey, she said, and it worried her.

She explained that all the drama and upheavals George and Casey brought to her life had had a negative impact on her own mental health. "I've even thought of doing away with myself, and probably would if it weren't for Caylee, you and Dad. The only thing that keeps me sane is my work—I love my job."

* * *

Casey sent a text to Amy on the afternoon of May 3, 2008: "Any more details on that party?" Two hours later, she wrote, "Cross your fingers that my parents get back soon. God, I need this tonight." After 8 that night, she sent another message to Amy: "I'm trying to get a hold of my mom to see when they're coming home. Sitting around sucks." After 11 P.M., Casey begged off of the party and asked, "Downtown tomorrow? My mom owes me."

She also madly exchanged instant messages with Anthony, Jesse's colleague who was a deputy with the Orange County Sheriff's Office. He started the conversation with a simple message: "??"

Casey wrote back: "I'm going to have to call you in a bit. If I don't finish this shit for work, I'm screwed. I've been up since 5."

"Ok, well what are the chances of chillin' today at all?"

"Very good as long as I can get this stuff done, and sent to my boss."

Anthony pressed for a time and added, "Get over here woman." He then continued urging her to come to his place, no matter how late it was when she finished her work. Casey didn't show up. Anthony tried to get Casey's attention on May 4 and 5, but although she responded, her messages were short and desultory.

On May 5, Casey's excitement was apparent the moment Jesse answered the phone. "Guess where I'm going? Puerto Rico! Rico has family there that we're going to stay with. All we have to do is pay for the flight and some food and expenses while we're down there." Later when she shared her good news with her mother, Cindy refused to take care of Caylee while Casey cavorted in the Caribbean—another drop in the boiling pot of anger that Casey had for her mother.

After talking to Rico that Monday, Casey went over to Christopher Stutz's home. Christopher was out with friends when Casey arrived, and she chatted with his parents for a couple of hours. When Christopher returned, he and Casey went out.

The next day, she was more responsive to Anthony's messages. "Bring your fine ass over here sometime today."

Casey wrote, "When I can, I will," and then complained about having to rely on other people; at the moment, she said, she was waiting on her nanny to get back from her sister's wedding in Tampa.

"Is she willing to get the offspring?"

"As of right now," Casey affirmed.

Anthony griped about the indefinite nature of that response and then wrote, "I could def. see you moving into a g.f. role, but not if I don't see you. I know it's like beating a dead horse, but it's how I feel. My point in all of this . . . if it's going to work, whether I 'have to make this all up to you,' or whatever, you're going to have to suck it up, and come see me every once in a while, you're a lot more mobile than I am a lot of the time . . .

"As for the sex thing, let's clear this up right now. When it's as good as it has been, I need it, I told you me and my routine, but it's not my main concern for seeing but once in three weeks is a tease, plus again, your pretty damn good in bed."

Casey complained about Caylee wanting more lunch, and when she said she didn't know what to eat, Anthony offered to cook for her if she came over. Casey wrote, "Ha, want me to bring this little snot head? Didn't think so." She said, "Spending the day with Caylee is ten times more exhausting than working a twelve-hour event."

The afternoon wore on, while Anthony and Casey exchanged more messages. Throughout the hours, Casey provided running commentary on the nanny's current location—there always seemed to be one problem or another. Then Casey got serious. "I'm sad, I've been sad all day, shit, I've been sad for days . . . Too bad I can't move out tomorrow, would make some of this a lot easier."

Casey told friends she'd meet up with them on the night of May 10, but didn't make it. The next morning, she got a text message: "I thought you were coming out last night."

"Yeah, so did I," Casey complained. "Mommy duties." Once again, Caylee was her excuse.

The next day—Mother's Day—Casey did not spend the day with her mother. Instead she took Caylee and went over to one-time boyfriend Christopher Stutz's home.

On Monday, Casey told Anthony that her vacation—from the job she didn't have—started on Thursday. She put off seeing him that day, but dangled the promise that she would be free for twelve of the fifteen days she was off work.

On Wednesday evening, Casey went downtown to Voyage Nightclub with Rico and Troy. Afterwards they all went back to Rico's place, but Casey stayed there only ten minutes. On her way home, she hit a construction barrier on Route 408, running over something in the dark and popping two tires.

At first she kept driving, getting off of the highway and into a residential area. She traveled a half-mile before tire chunks and sparks from the rim forced her to stop. She called Troy and Rico for help. They came to her rescue.

Casey tried and failed to put on her one spare tire while she waited for their arrival. The two guys finished that job and then tried to put Rico's spare on the Sunfire. When it wouldn't fit on the rim, Casey insisted they drive her home, since she needed to be there for Caylee in the morning.

The next day, she told her father about her abandoned, crippled car and asked what she should do. His first concern was making sure that she hadn't been hurt. She assured him she was okay. George then wanted to know why she'd been on that particular highway if she was working at Universal as she'd said she had been that night.

Casey avoided answering the question by asking, "Dad, what should I do?"

"Just have it towed home," he said. "Let me take a look at it."

Amy loaned Casey the $80 she needed for the tow. After looking the car over, George bought two new tires for the Pontiac.

It was mid-May and the house where Amy rented an apartment was sold, and she had to vacate, moving in with Troy Brown on a temporary basis. She was counting on Casey, who told her that her parents were helping her buy a home. By the time she took up her new living arrangements, Casey told her that the deal had fallen through—someone else had made an offer on the house.

"But great news!" Casey added. "My mom is getting a condo in Winter Park. My grandparents are moving there from Mount Dora, since there's a better facility in Winter Park for my granddad. And, my mom is signing her house over to me.

"I'll take over the mortgage payments and we can just move in there. It's great news, 'cause I don't actually have to move and Caylee can stay in the place she's always been—that's awesome."

"Cool," Amy said. It sure beat her current nomadic existence. She made plans to move into the Hopespring Drive home in mid-June, when, Casey told her, the paperwork would be completed.

Ryan—who'd moved to Jacksonville in January to attend school—called Casey in May, to share his excitement about finishing his final exams. Instead of congratulating him, Casey attempted to top him. "Well, I'm working in event planning at Universal now. I even have my own office."

Ryan recognized her one-upmanship, but wondered when that competitive quality had slipped into their nearly life-long relationship. It seemed to have been happening for a while, but he couldn't remember when it had begun.

That Saturday night, Casey and Caylee spent the night

at Christopher Stutz's parents' house—his mom and dad were away for the weekend.

On Friday, May 23, Amy invited Casey out to a party, but Casey wrote, "I'm going to stay home," then suggested they go out together the next night. "I've already cleared it with my madre."

Amy didn't make it to the Friday night party, since Casey couldn't go—but Casey attended after all. In the wee hours, Casey sent another text to Amy: "The cops came around 1:15 and broke up the party."

Tony Lazzaro was new to town. He scouted around Facebook looking for interesting people in the area. He found "a good-looking girl" named Casey Marie Anthony, who claimed to be a student at Valencia Community College. He sent a friend request and she accepted. Soon, he had her phone number and called her on May 23 to tell her about a "no clothes" party the next night at the Villages on Science Drive near the University of Central Florida campus, an event where you had to dress in things that weren't normally worn. She said she'd like to go, and got directions. Over dinner at Waterford Lakes Buffalo Wild Wings, Casey invited Troy and Amy to go with her. They agreed. Later that night, she texted Amy about the party: "You will officially see the American flag in all its glory tonight."

Casey, wrapped toga-style in an American flag, was a bright flash of color next to Troy, whose chest was swathed in layers of plastic wrap, and some of the other attendees who simply wore large paper bags.

She met Tony Lazzaro and a girl named Jamie Realander at the party and hit it off with both of them. She and Jamie made plans to get together at Jamie's place in Ovieda in mid-June. When the time neared, though, Casey told her she'd just gotten a speeding ticket and didn't want to drive outside of Orlando. A convenient excuse—but unfortunately untrue. Casey had gotten her last ticket in 2004.

The meeting with Tony proved more fruitful. Casey was drawn to his stereotypical jaded New Yorker appearance with a natural expression reminiscent of Mickey Rourke's. Together, they played innumerable games of beer pong, a drinking game. The set-up consisted of a triangle of cups filled with beer, with contestants on the opposite end of the table. Each team attempted to throw a Ping-Pong ball into the cups. When a player succeeded, the other group had to drink the beer. The first team that emptied their cups, won.

She ran into Brandon Snow at the party, and informed him of the alleged miscarriage she'd had on Valentine's Day in 2007. It was an emotional, high-drama scene, with Casey crying loud, bitter tears. Brandon couldn't understand why she was dumping this on him now, more than a year later.

That week, Tony asked Casey to come over and hang out with him and another couple. She agreed, but then called that night to say she was staying with the nanny, as Caylee had woken up before she could leave.

Casey and Caylee spent the night at Rico's apartment on May 28 and 29. On May 31, Tony was the DJ for a pool party at Arden Villas apartment complex, where Jesse lived. Casey went up to Jesse's unit to encourage him to come down and meet Tony Lazzaro. Jesse felt as if Casey was asking for his blessing on the relationship. After five minutes, Jesse was bored. He left the complex to go birthday shopping for his brother.

Soon after he left, the weather turned nasty, bringing the party to an end. Tony and Casey went to the movies and then to the apartment of one of Tony's friends. When Casey dropped Tony off at his place late that night, he invited her inside, but she demurred, explaining that the special ring on her cell phone indicated her mother was calling. She heard that little riff many times that night and, though she hadn't answered any of them, she knew they meant she had to go home.

The next day, Casey picked up Tony and they went to

a barbecue by the pool at Pegasus Connection, an apartment complex off Alafaya and University, where one of Tony's friends lived. This time, when they returned to Sutton Place, Casey accepted Tony's invitation to come inside. They were intimate for the first time, but Casey did not spend the night.

CHAPTER 19

George and Cindy's relationship was working well at this time. They enjoyed evenings out and day trips to the beach, as well as working together on landscaping, pool maintenance and other needed chores around the house. But when Cindy took vacation week in early June, she planned to devote that time to bonding with her daughter and granddaughter. A visit to George's mother in Fort Myers and relaxation on the beach were on the agenda. Cindy had Caylee the whole week, but Casey was never around.

On Thursday, June 5, Caylee's presence brightened her grandmother's birthday—helping Cindy forget that her daughter hadn't bothered to call. Lee did show up with his girlfriend Mallory to wish Cindy a happy day. Lee did not know that it would be the last time he would ever see his niece.

When Cindy's mother called to wish her a happy day, Cindy sounded depressed. Shirley suspected her mood was due to her financial problems. Since she'd made her decision not to divorce and had taken George back, her husband had jumped around to three different jobs, causing Cindy to remain the only consistent breadwinner in the house.

Casey certainly wasn't any financial help. She constantly asked her mom for money, knowing if she said she needed it for Caylee, Cindy would not refuse. At the same time, Cindy was already footing the bill for Casey's car insurance and paying off high credit card bills created by charges her daughter had made.

Shirley tried to avoid those conversational landmines and instead asked, "Why didn't you go to Fort Myers?"

Rather than explaining that Casey had avoided her all week, Cindy claimed, "I didn't feel like going."

At work, Cindy complained to Debbie about always having Caylee. Debbie suggested that if she was the main caregiver, she ought to get custody of Caylee. Cindy became agitated and said that she couldn't afford the legal expense of doing that.

When Casey finally showed up on Saturday, June 7, to pick up her child, she told Cindy that the babysitter would be keeping Caylee from June 9 through 12 because Casey had to take an out-of-town business trip for Universal Studios. Cindy asked about the change of address for Amy Huizenga that had arrived in their mail.

"Oh, she just wanted a package sent here."

"That makes no sense, Casey. You don't change your address for that."

Casey just shrugged. She wasn't about to explain the fantastical scenario she'd cooked up for Amy.

Cindy wasn't the only person that week to feel the sting of Casey's indifference. On June 6, Rico made dinner for a group of friends. Casey told both Rico and Amy that she'd be there. When she was more than an hour late, everyone sat down to their meal without her. She finally called while they were eating; she said she had to work all day. Actually, she was too busy partying at Fusian with Tony Lazzaro to give much thought to her friends.

Early the next morning, Casey posted a comment on the MySpace page of Brittany Schreiber, a friend from kindergarten through high school: "Hey girl! Quick question. Do you know any girls that can sing? My boyfriend, Tony, and his business partners are looking for an up and coming female R&B vocalist. Let me know! I appreciate it."

That night, Casey, with Caylee still in tow, arrived at Rico's place after 11 P.M. She spent the night and left late in the morning of the 8th.

Rico saw pictures of Casey at the night club when he visited MySpace later that day. *Odd*, he thought. Casey told him that she'd never been to Fusian. He sent her a text message: "Did you go to Fusian Friday night?"

She responded. "Yeah, but my boss sent me there to spy on his daughter."

With Caylee in the car, Casey picked up Tony at school and drove him to the mechanic to pick up his Jeep on June 9. They took separate vehicles to Subway, where Casey bought three subs before heading back to Tony's apartment.

Casey and Caylee showed up at Rico's that night after 8 P.M. Casey claimed that she and her daughter had no place to stay. Rico invited them to spend another night at his place. He and Casey had their last sexual experience together that evening. Afterwards, they had a huge blow-up over Casey's involvement with Tony. Casey didn't own up to any sexual intimacy with Tony, but she did confess to kissing him. Rico thought that since the two of them were still involved, she shouldn't be messing around with another guy. Casey disagreed. That was the end for Rico.

The last time he saw Caylee was the morning of the 10th before he went to work. He came downstairs and Casey and Caylee were on the sofa. He said, "I'm going to work." Casey said, "Okay. I'm going to take a shower and then I'm going to leave."

That day, Tony said that he teased her about the possibility he'd move back to New York. Casey burst into tears and choked back sobs. "You're taking this way too seriously," he warned. "Things are going a little too fast here. Relax, you know I'm moving soon. I'm just here for school and then I'm out."

She and Tony had another discussion that added to Casey's distress. Tony told her that if he ever decided to have children, he wanted sons. He knew how difficult it was to raise little girls, because he had two sisters.

That evening Maria Kissh and her boyfriend Clint House planned to stop by Tony's place when Maria got off work. Clint said that in between classes, he'd met Casey's daughter. "She was really cute and talkative to all the guys."

"Tony doesn't mind having her around?" she asked.

"No. She's the cutest thing."

"Well that's really cool that Tony doesn't mind that Casey has a child, and that she brings the child around," Maria said, looking forward to meeting the little charmer that evening.

When Maria and Clint arrived, Caylee answered the door. The little girl sat down with the couple and the roommates, but for a while, Casey and Tony were back in the bedroom.

Caylee struggled to put on her socks and shoes, and Maria came to her rescue. Maria didn't mind helping Caylee, but it didn't seem right that her mother wasn't there for her.

Casey and Tony joined the group, and Casey talked to Maria about the job she had at Universal and the nanny she paid $400 a week to take care of Caylee. Casey told Marie that she and Caylee lived with her parents off Narcoossee Road. Her parents were moving out the first of July and leaving the house to them.

A little later, Caylee wandered out to the balcony overlooking the lake. Maria followed her. Casey didn't seem to be paying any attention to her daughter. Caylee pointed out the birds she saw.

Maria asked, "Have you seen any alligators out there?"

Caylee shook her head making her ponytail fly through the air.

Clint stuck his head out and told Maria it was time to leave. She knew she couldn't just leave Caylee in such a dangerous spot, but was amazed that Casey was oblivious and trusted the care of her little girl to strangers. Maria made sure Caylee was safely inside before she left.

On Wednesday, June 11, despite Casey's anxiety over her relationship with Tony—or maybe because of it—she changed her social networking pages to include Tony Lazzaro as her boyfriend. Then, she sent Christopher a text message: "Hey! What's up? Where have you been? Have you checked Facebook or MySpace? I've been dating somebody."

Tony, Casey and Caylee went to the Mall of the Millennia in Casey's car that day. Casey and Caylee went shopping while Tony promoted his hip hop showcase on Friday at Fusian. When he finished handing out all his fliers, they met up, and Tony treated them to a late lunch/early dinner at The Cheesecake Factory.

Casey dropped Tony off at his apartment and drove off with Caylee. Tony never saw the young girl again.

On Friday, June 13, Casey was supposed to drive Amy to Jacksonville to pick up a car to replace the one she'd totaled earlier that month. Amy texted Casey shortly after 6 A.M. to make sure her friend was awake.

Casey responded immediately, writing that she was on her way to the hospital with her dad. She added that she would let Amy know what was up as soon as possible. While Amy waited, she looked into alternative ways of getting to Jacksonville.

Amy's phone signaled that a text message had arrived. She read that Casey's dad had had a mini-stroke. She typed back, "Honey, don't worry about it. Take care of your family. I'll get myself up there. Don't worry about it."

Amy, driving up in a rental car, got a call from Casey while she was on the road. Amy said that Casey perpetuated the story of her father's health crisis and chatted about her increased use of marijuana since she'd started spending more time with Tony. Then Casey invited Amy to join her at Fusian Ultra Lounge in the Waterford Lakes area that night. Amy declined—the music wasn't to her taste, and it wasn't the kind of place where she thought she'd have any fun.

In the month of June, Casey was seen often at Fusian. That night, she met Tony at his place and rode with him to the hip hop party. She sent a mass text message out to all her male friends to promote Tony's showcase: "You guys should definitely come. $5 cover, super hot shot girls, a hot body contest." It was the first time Casey had slept until morning in Tony's bed.

Throughout that week, tempers flared between Casey and her mother. Neighbor Jean Couty was mowing her lawn when Cindy stepped out of her home with Casey on her heels. Casey screamed at her mom. Cindy responded, but never raised her voice. She got into her car and drove away.

Jean was outside washing her car when she witnessed another unpleasant event. Casey burst out of the house screaming again. "Just shut up, Mom! I don't want to hear it anymore!" Cindy said nothing, she just hung her head down as Casey heaped on the abuse. Casey turned away and headed out for a jog around the neighborhood.

On Father's Day, June 15, Cindy took Caylee to visit her great-grandfather at the nursing home. Caylee ran up to Alex and jumped into his arms. While Cindy and her father talked, Caylee played. Nursing home employee Karen Angel approached the little girl and said, "Hey, cutie. Tell me your name." Caylee blushed from shyness.

"Can I have a hug?"

Caylee reached up to Karen, who picked her up in her arms. Caylee laid her head on the woman's shoulder, content. When Karen set her back down, Caylee said, "Bye." To Karen she appeared to be a very happy little girl.

After their visit, Cindy and Caylee went up the street to visit Cindy's mother. Shirley made chili and cornbread for dinner. Thinking Caylee might not like it, she fixed a peanut butter and jelly sandwich for her great-granddaughter.

Caylee tasted the chili and liked it, but ate very little and barely touched her PB & J. An over-indulgence in popcorn at the nursing home had left her without much of an appetite. She spent much of her time during her visit playing with her great-grandmother's cat. Shirley could watch that child forever. Caylee's sunny disposition brought a lot of joy to her life. She could never remember seeing the little girl upset about anything.

Casey's early childhood friend, Ryan Pasley, was in town that weekend and Casey was supposed to meet him at his aunt's house on Sunday for a family cookout. Ryan was in contact with her all day by phone and text. He kept expecting her to arrive at any moment, but she never made it.

Cindy and Caylee took a swim in the pool after returning home. When they finished, Cindy removed the ladder and locked the gate. Cindy confronted Casey that evening, slapping down one photo after another that she'd printed off the Internet—shots of Casey at the no-clothes party. "You're at work? Huh? I watched Caylee that night so that you could go to work." She told Casey she was an unfit mother and threatened to obtain custody of Caylee.

According to the story Lee shared with a friend, the fight had escalated from screaming into physical confrontation. Cindy, he claimed, had wrapped her hands around Casey's throat and squeezed.

On June 16, at 12:50 in the afternoon, Casey sat down in a La-Z-Boy recliner next to her father. "Hey, I'm gonna be working a little late. Caylee's gonna be staying with the Nanny. I'll see you and Mom tomorrow afternoon. I've already talked to Mom. Mom knows I'm gonna be staying over."

"Okay, just be careful and . . ." George said.

Casey cut him off. "I'll see you tomorrow."

Wearing a pair of gray pin-striped slacks and an off-white top, she walked out of the house with her daughter. Caylee looked adorable that day, dressed in a blue jean skirt, a pink top and a pair of white sunglasses. Her hair was pulled back in a perky ponytail and she wore a white knapsack, decorated with monkeys, on her back.

It was a memorable impression of the little girl. Unfortunately, it was the last time George ever saw his granddaughter—the brightest light in his trouble-ridden life.

THE CRIME

"The truth does not change according
to our ability to stomach it."

—Flannery O'Connor

CHAPTER 20

A Note to the Reader

*Under United States law, a person is presumed innocent until proven guilty, and Casey Anthony has yet to be tried by a jury of her peers. What follows is merely the author's recreation of what **might** have happened, if the charges against Casey are true. This recreation is based on the author's analysis of the law enforcement forensic evidence, the medical examiner's autopsy report, and other available information. Casey Anthony's movements during the critical period were documented by the pings from her cell phone. Time frames are estimates, based on evidence and interview statements.*

After Casey left her parents' home with Caylee on Monday, June 16, 2008, she hovered around the neighborhood as she waited for her father to leave for work.

She returned to 4937 Hopespring Drive when the house was empty. Caylee raced to her bedroom and changed into a pair of striped shorts and a tee shirt proclaiming: "Big trouble comes in small packages."

The police found evidence that three months earlier, someone using Casey's computer had conducted internet searches for chloroform recipes. Police believed that person was Casey, and now was the time to put that knowledge to use. Assembling the materials needed would not have been difficult—pool chlorinator, a bottle of acetone, a glass container, and lots of ice. She would have also needed an abundance of caution to avoid inhaling any of the escaping vapors.

When the process was complete, it would have been easy to persuade Caylee to inhale the sweet-smelling fumes. It would not have taken many whiffs to render the small girl-child unconscious. When she was out and unable to defend herself, multiple layers of duct tape were wrapped around the little girl's mouth and nose and into her hair to ensure that she never awoke from her chemically induced sleep.

Law enforcement suspected Casey carried the limp body to the bedroom where the red heart sticker was placed on the tape over her daughter's mouth. Then, Caylee was wrapped in her Winnie the Pooh blanket, slid into a waterproofed canvas bag and stuffed into a black plastic garbage bag.

Then, in this scenario, she carried the delicate bundle out to her car and placed it in the trunk. Mission accomplished, she drove to Tony Lazzaro's apartment, where Tony would have been unaware of Casey's actions or of Caylee's whereabouts.

Ironically, records indicate that the couple went to Blockbuster that evening and rented two videos: *Jumper*, about a 5-year-old child abandoned by her mother, who masters teleportation; and *Untraceable*, about a kidnapper and killer. Casey remained at Tony's all night.

Casey drove back to her parents' empty house on Tuesday. Normally, Casey pulled straight into the driveway and parked outside of the garage. On this day, she backed in, raised the automatic door and parked with the rear-half of the Buick hidden from view inside the garage.

Neighbor Brian Burner was in his freshly mowed front yard, clearing clippings and other debris with a leaf blower. Casey approached him at about 1:30. "I can't find the key to the shed, and I need to dig up a bamboo root I've been tripping over. Do you have a shovel I could borrow?" she reportedly asked.

Brian handed her a round-bladed shovel with a rubber grip. She stepped into her parents' garage, disappearing from his view. At that point, it was suspected that she carried the garbage bag from the trunk into the backyard, looking for a place to bury her daughter, setting the bundle down in three different locations—next to the playhouse, near the screened patio porch and at a spot behind the swimming pool.

At the latter location, evidence indicated that someone started to dig a twelve-inch-wide hole, but quit after achieving a depth of five inches and covered up the effort. The backyard no longer seemed a viable option. The garbage bag went back into the trunk, and the lid slammed shut. Casey walked over to the Burners' home, knocked on the front door and returned the borrowed shovel. Brian noticed nothing amiss—no strangeness in Casey's behavior, no dirt on her shorts or sports bra.

Casey drove around looking for other disposal options. Cell phone pings tracked her meandering through a remote spot near the airport. And also showed her travelling to a sparsely populated area in the vicinity of the University of Central Florida.

Casey spent that night and the next day at Tony's apartment. On Thursday, June 19, according to the authorities, she went out on another scouting mission. She roamed around Blanchard Park and Little Econ Park. She was running out of time.

In the sweltering heat of a Central Florida summer, the smell in the car would have become unbearable. Documents indicated that no later than June 26, she settled on a location within her comfort zone. She stopped at the woods of scrub pine, red maple, saw palmetto, wax myrtle and heavy undergrowth less than a mile from her parents' house—the same overgrown area she'd frequented with her friends in middle school.

She must have held her breath as she lifted the foul-smelling bundle out of the trunk of her car. She carried it a little ways into the woods, dumping it into a patch of fern, ground cover and fallen leaves, where poison ivy and air potato vines snaked across the ground and embraced tree trunks in their effort to stretch out of the gloom and toward the sun.

If the pending charges are true, Casey then turned and walked away, leaving behind the remains of her child, her flesh and blood—the beloved granddaughter that George and Cindy Anthony would never again see.

CHAPTER 21

During that dark week, Casey showed few signs to her friends and family of being emotionally impacted by the fate of her daughter. On Tuesday, she posted a message on Amy's Facebook page! "Cheer me up lady. I love you and can't wait to finally get you moved in."

One night, she stopped by Christopher's house shortly after 7 P.M. She was driving a dark-colored Jeep Cherokee with New York plates. She told Christopher that her car had broken down and she was borrowing a friend's.

She greeted his mom, who was working out on her new treadmill for the first time. Casey and Christopher then watched television and chatted. She seemed happy, but said that she was a bit depressed about her parents splitting up. Her dad, she said, was cheating on her mom. Her mom, she said, explained about the divorce and told her, "We're going to be together and Dad's going to be out of our life."

Casey also said that she was buying a house at a subdivision near the dump on Curry Ford Road. It would be a home for her and Caylee, but her mom was helping her pick it out. She blew off $250,000 as a cheap price to pay for a home.

She also told Christopher that she had a strong relationship with her mom, but not so much with her dad. He wanted to get too involved in her life, she said, pushing his beliefs on her, telling her how she should act and insisting that she worked.

* * *

Casey made herself at home in Tony's place to the delight of his temporary roommate, Nate Lezniewicz. He and Tony were in school full-time, bopping in and out of the apartment between classes. Casey always seemed to be smiling and happy. But better than that, she kept the house in order, did the laundry and often cooked dinner. Nathan told Tony, "Don't screw this up. I'm eating better than I have in a few months."

Despite the fact that Casey seemed to be there every day, all day, Nathan, Tony and the other roommate, Cameron Campina, all thought she was employed by Universal as an event planner. Casey's answer to any questions was simple: her boss allowed her to work from home. They accepted that explanation. And besides, Casey brought home bags of groceries from time to time. She'd have to have a job to do that.

Caylee had been a frequent visitor at the apartment the first half of June. Nate thought Caylee was a "very sweet, very smart" girl who was fun to have around. He often sat with her watching her favorite shows, *The Pink Panther* and *Dora the Explorer*. Caylee amazed him with her ability to count to 45 in Spanish—something she'd learned from Dora.

At times, Nathan and Caylee played a little game with his laptop. He'd call out a letter and she'd hit the key, getting it right almost every time. Caylee's favorite phrase cracked him up: She'd say "What's up, dude?" every time someone entered the apartment.

One afternoon when he and Cameron took a nap in the living room, Caylee pulled out Tony's drum pad and a pair of drumsticks. She woke them up, pounding out a beat and chanting, "Wake up, Nate. Wake up, Cam."

But her presence disappeared in the middle of that month. Nathan teased Casey about Caylee's absence. "I'm beginning to think you don't have a child. Where is she? How come we haven't seen her around?"

Every time the subject came up, Casey greeted it with

a chuckle. "Oh, she's at Disney World with the nanny"—Or at Cocoa Beach or the Universal theme park. She explained that there were problems and constant fighting at her parents' home. She said she didn't want Caylee subjected to that environment. While she was here, she claimed, Caylee was with the nanny. Life at the apartment with three single guys often got a bit too rowdy for a 2-year-old girl.

Casey was right about that. There were lots of late nights with partying both in the apartment and out at clubs. Initially, according to Tony and his roommates, Casey had been reluctant to use marijuana. The guys teased and coaxed her with a chorus of "Come on, Casey," and "Hit this bowl."

Casey always gave in and took a toke. Soon, it was a nightly habit and Casey needed no persuasion. She wasn't a typical user, though. It took very little to get her high. Tony described her as "giggly and happy" when she smoked, though he was quick to add, "She's been happy the entire time she's been here."

On the morning of June 19, Casey called high school acquaintance Matthew Crisp to find out if he still leased apartments. Her boyfriend, she said, wanted to break his lease and find a new apartment. Matthew said that he was still in the business and asked her to come by.

She came by with Tony, upbeat and full of smiles. Matthew showed an apartment to Tony and he liked what he saw. As they were leaving, Casey gave Matthew a hug—a very tight hug, to Matthew's surprise.

John Azzilanna and Teddy Pieper, students and club photographers, worked at Fusian on Friday night, June 20, after midnight, shooting pictures until the club closed at 2 A.M. One of their subjects was Casey, who was wearing a blue dress. She seemed happy. She seemed all about having a good time. Just a typical clubber—without a care in the world.

The only thing that struck Cameron as odd were Casey's cell phone calls. Any time her phone rang, Casey stepped outside. He'd watch her pace around in the grass behind the apartment. Although he didn't know it, many of those calls were from Casey's mother asking about Caylee.

While Casey partied, her parents suffered. Cindy called constantly begging to see her granddaughter. Casey's excuses never ended—they were in Tampa, they were in Jacksonville. She promised to come home one Monday, but when that day arrived, she called and said the nanny had been in an accident and was now in Tampa General Hospital being treated for a concussion. Casey, her girlfriends and the kids were staying at the hotel in Tampa until Zanny's family arrived.

She was supposed to return to Orlando one Friday. But, she said, she'd gone to Jacksonville to see if she and Jeffrey Hopkins had a future, and while there, her car had issues. Jeffrey didn't want her to drive all the way to Orlando without taking care of the problems first. He put the car in the shop. Casey knew that excuse would please her dad. He'd gotten on her case for traveling out of town when the car needed an oil change, a tire rotation and other work.

Then, on the weekend she'd said she would come home, she begged off again. This time, she said, Jeff's mother was remarrying and she and Jeff needed to go to a brunch on Sunday.

When Cindy simply pleaded for a chance to speak to Caylee, her timing was never right, according to Casey. Caylee was with the nanny, taking a nap or getting ready for bed.

In her frustration with her daughter, Cindy called Casey's friend and former neighbor, Ryan Pasley. According to Ryan, Cindy said, "I don't think it's a good idea for you to talk to Casey anymore, 'cause she's a sociopath. I don't want you to get hurt. She's been lying about a lot of stuff. And she stole from me and her grandmother." Cindy elaborated on the details of her daughter's lies and theft.

Ryan was shocked. He knew Casey was "a little bit of a white liar," making dishonest statements about insignificant matters, but what Cindy was saying went far beyond that. He didn't know what to think or what to say. He ended the conversation with "Okay. I understand," but he wasn't sure that he did.

Cindy didn't understand a lot of things, either. Why, she wondered, was Casey keeping Caylee away from her? Until mid-June, Caylee had lived in George and Cindy's home all of her life. Now her grandparents missed her presence like crazy, and they were sure the little girl must miss them, too. Cindy's complaints about not seeing her granddaughter became an endless, painful litany.

CHAPTER 22

Monday, June 23, Cindy spoke to co-worker Debbie Bennett. "I think someone was swimming in my pool."

"That's what people do," Debbie said with a grin. "They swim in the pool."

"No. You don't understand. Someone's been in the pool when I haven't been home."

"What makes you think that?"

"I came home one day and let the dogs out. They headed for the gate and started to shove their way out—it wasn't locked. We always keep it locked. And the ladder was on the pool. We always take it off and put it away so Caylee can't climb in the pool."

Early that afternoon, Casey posted a message to Troy's Facebook page about her impatience with the progress of her move with Amy into her parents' house. "Hell, in the past nine days, I haven't even been living in the house. Drama. I'll fill you in on it later."

Casey left Tony's apartment to go to her parents' house. She wasn't gone long before she called Tony to tell him she'd run out of gas. "Just drive toward my house and you'll see me on Chickasaw."

In about twenty minutes, Tony spotted her walking southbound on the sidewalk by Saint Isaac Jogues Catholic Church. He picked her up and drove her to Hopespring Drive. They went through the garage and into the house, passing through the sunroom on the way to the backyard.

The padlock on the shed door didn't stop Casey from getting what she wanted. They broke it to get into the outbuilding and returned to Tony's Jeep with two full, five-gallon gas cans. Casey directed him to Anthony Lane, where her car was parked on the side of the road. Tony passed it, made a U-turn at Killian and pulled into a grassy spot in front of the Pontiac.

Opening the tailgate, they walked back to the car, where Casey opened the gas flap on the passenger's side. "I'll pour the gas for you," Tony offered.

"No," she snapped. "I'll do it."

Emptying the first can, she handed it to Tony, who screwed on the cap, setting it on the ground, and passed the second one to her. She emptied it into her tank and screwed the top on before stepping behind her car, opening the trunk and placing it inside. As she went for the second can, Tony walked to his Jeep, closed the tailgate and got inside. He never had a clear view of the trunk and its contents. Gas fumes overwhelmed any other smell that may have been coming from the car.

Casey followed Tony out of the subdivision. En route to his apartment, Tony's cell rang. After finishing the conversation, he called Casey. "What a crazy day. We've got to go drop off your car, and then we need to go pick up my friend who got in a car accident."

Before they arrived at Sutton Place, though, another friend had come to the stranded caller's rescue. Casey and Tony went inside and stayed there the rest of the day.

On June 24, Jesse Grund resigned from the Orlando Police Department. He'd gone to the academy because he wanted to be an investigator. Assessing the political reality of that goal, it appeared as if he'd spend a good part of his life on patrol. That idea did not appeal to him at all.

Still, it was distressing to let go of his dream. He needed a sympathetic ear, and called Casey. She did her best to cheer him up and offered to see him. "I'm free next weekend, if you want to get together and do something."

That morning at 10:30 A.M., George Anthony went outside to cut the grass. He went to the shed to get gas for his mower. He was surprised when he saw the shed door four to five inches ajar. Peering inside, he noticed the gas cans were gone and the broken padlock had been laid neatly on the floor inside the shed. *Odd*, he thought. *Why wasn't the lock just left where it fell?*

George called the Orange County Sheriff's Office, and a deputy arrived about twenty minutes later. After filing an incident report, he called Cindy. "Hey, guess what happened today?"

"What?"

"Someone broke into our shed and stole the gas cans."

"You're kidding me."

"I'm not joking," George said with a laugh. He then confirmed the plans to meet Cindy at Bank of America at 2 o'clock to endorse their stimulus check, allowing Cindy to deposit it in her account. After returning home, he went inside to get ready for work.

He began to wonder if Casey was responsible for the missing gas cans. She'd taken gas from them before. He told her he didn't mind, but he expected her to replace what she'd taken. He remembered another minor theft in the neighborhood recently, and dismissed his suspicions.

He heard the garage door open. He wasn't expecting anyone, and his car was in the garage. He moved toward the noise to check it out. Casey burst into the house. "Hey, Dad, how you doing? I don't have much time. Gotta go back to work for an event."

"Wait a second, Casey," George objected as she blew past him. "Where's Caylee? What's going on?"

"Oh, she's staying with Zanny."

"We haven't seen the girl in over a week, how's everything? We haven't talked to her—it sure would be nice to hear her little voice."

"Dad, I don't have time for this. I got ten minutes. I gotta get back to work," she said as she headed toward her room. She shouted down the hall, "Oh, by the way, I talked to Mom. I understand something happened here at the house."

"In reference to . . . ?" George queried.

"Oh, the gas cans," she said.

"Yeah. Isn't that something?"

"Oh, yeah, Dad, that's terrible."

Something in Casey's tone of voice did not sit right with George. His suspicions stirred again. He thought she was hiding something. Were his gas cans in her car? "Hey, Case, you know in the trunk of your car, we got these metal wedges you put underneath the wheel so if you jack up your car, it doesn't move? I wanna get one out of your car, 'cause I already have one in the garage and I need another 'cause I'm gonna go ahead and rotate your mom's tires over the weekend. In case you're not home, I'd like to be able to do it."

"Oh, Dad, I'll get it for you."

"I've got an extra set of keys. I'll go to the trunk and get it."

It seemed to George that Casey's focus of getting in and out of the house fast was now overwhelmed by an urgent need to keep her father out of her car. When George opened the door from the house to the garage, she brushed past him. "Dad, I'll get your thing."

Casey's walk was almost a run as she hurried to keep ahead of George as they crossed the garage floor. "Dad, I'll get it. I know where it's at."

"Casey, I'm capable of reaching inside your trunk and unbolting that thing."

"Dad, I'll get it," she insisted.

George kept following her. He was on the side of the car near the taillight when she pulled something out of the trunk. "Here are your effing cans," she sneered and slammed the lid shut. George did not get a glimpse inside.

"Thanks a lot," George said. "Now I look like a stupid ass. I made a quick report to the Orange County sheriff's department and now you got the cans. Why do you have them?"

"Well, I've been dragging, driving back and forth to Tampa to see Zanny."

"Wait a second, you're supposed to be working, but now you're in Tampa? This doesn't make sense to me," George said. Shaking his head, he continued. "Listen I'm not gonna deal with this right now, but where's Caylee? What's going on? I believe I need to know."

"I'll talk to you and Mom later," she said as she slid into her car. George stood dumbfounded, with a gas can in each hand, as his daughter peeled out of the driveway.

On June 25, Casey posted a comment on Brittany Schrieber's MySpace page. It was the third one she'd written to her friend enticing her to come out to Fusian Ultra Lounge. "You and the girls should try and come out to Fusian this week. There's a hot body contest, first prize is $50 and a bottle. It's the ALL WHITE PARTY [meaning everyone coming should be wearing that color]. Give me a shout, it's be great to see you!"

Casey called Amy that day to complain about a worsening problem in her Sunfire. "There's a horrible smell in my car. Maybe my dad ran over something when he borrowed it. It smells like something died in there. But maybe it's the engine."

CHAPTER 23

Tony awoke on June 27 to find Casey sitting up in bed looking at the video of Caylee's visit to her great-grandfather on Father's Day. At first, he thought she was crying, but there was no trace of tears on her cheeks—not even a glistening of moisture trapped in her lashes. She rubbed her eyes and brushed back her hair. It seemed to Tony that she was going through the motions, but there were no genuine emotions behind them.

Later that morning, Casey left the apartment. Once again, she ran out of gas. First she called Jesse. "My car ran out of gas. Can I borrow a gas can?" she asked, knowing that Jesse kept one in his pick-up truck.

"Where are you?"

"I'm at Fifty and Goldenrod."

Jesse was at his parents' house on the other side of town. "There's just no way I'm going to be able to get over there to help you out." He asked why she'd run out of gas, but couldn't get a satisfactory answer.

When Jesse wouldn't come to her rescue, Casey called Tony for help. "I'm on Goldenrod," she said. "Somebody helped me push the car into the Amscot lot."

Casey disconnected the call and texted Amy. "Ran out of gas. Two weeks in a row. How does that work?" Once again, Casey mentioned the nasty odor in her car. "There definitely was part of an animal plastered to the frame of my car," she said. "I got rid of it."

Amy called Casey to find out if she was all right, and

to see if there was anything she could do. Casey assured her that she was just waiting for Tony to pick her up.

She was still talking to Amy when Tony drove past Amscot on the opposite of the divider in the middle of the street and stopped at the red light before making a U-turn. He spotted Casey standing between her car and a Dumpster in a patch of shade, talking on her cell. The Pontiac Sunfire certainly looked like it had been pushed. It sat cockeyed, straddling two parking slots.

He pulled up and she clutched two bags as she hopped inside. One contained clothing, the other had the booty she'd plundered from her parents' freezer—a box of Tyson's fried chicken and another of freezer pops.

Casey abandoned her car in a lot that her mother drove past every day. With the clumsy way it was parked, Cindy couldn't overlook it for long.

"How?" Tony laughed. "I mean, who runs out of gas?"

She shrugged and blamed her fuel gauge.

"So what do we need to do with your car?" he asked.

"Don't worry about it. I'll take care of it. You worry about school and packing for your trip to New York. I'll take care of it while you're away."

That afternoon, Casey sent out a big batch of messages, inviting friends to join her at Fusian. She sent one of them to Jesse Grund. He was reluctant to go. He believed the environment there was very drug-friendly and he didn't care for the music they played. Casey pressed. She was worried about him, she said, insisting that a night partying at Fusian would cheer him up.

"Who's watching Caylee?" he asked, knowing of the rift between Casey and Cindy.

"She's at the beach with the nanny for the weekend," she said.

On Saturday, Casey texted Amy, asking if she could borrow Amy's gas can. Amy explained that all her stuff was in storage and it might take her some time to locate it.

* * *

On Monday, June 30, Casey, driving Tony's Jeep, dropped him off at the airport for his flight to visit family and friends in New York. At 9:45 A.M., Amy's phone rang, waking her up. "This is Casey. Come open the door."

"Are you outside of it?" Amy asked.

"Yes."

"I'm asleep."

"Open the door and go back to bed," Casey insisted.

She came into the apartment chattering away. Amy knew it was senseless to try to stop Casey when she was on a roll. She knew she couldn't sleep through Casey's non-stop monologue. She abandoned her plans to get more rest.

Casey asked again about Amy's gas can. Amy said, "Well, why don't we go to Target? I'll buy a can and you can use it and give it back to me. I can always use another one."

They hopped into Tony's Jeep and went shopping. Casey complained about not being able to see Caylee. "But it's better for her. She's just playing and having fun. They're going everywhere. They were at Busch Gardens for a while. At least, she's in a good place and not in volved in all this other stuff." She launched into a repeat performance of one of her stories about her parents' con stant fights.

The two hung out together until Amy had to go to work that evening, and Casey spent the night there. She woke up Jesse Grund the next morning at 10:15. "Please, I need a favor," she said.

"What is it?"

"Well, I need to take a shower before I go to work. I've been staying at Tony's, but I don't have a key to get back into his place, and he's out of town. I can't go to my parents' place."

"Okay, fine. You can come over."

Jesse was surprised when she arrived. She didn't look

like a woman in desperate need of a shower—she looked neat and clean already. And, to Jesse's disappointment, Caylee was not with her. After she cleaned up, they sat around watching television and talking for a couple of hours until Casey left for "work."

She got her nails done that day and arrived at Rico and Amy's place after 11 P.M. and spent the night. When Rico woke up, he thought that Casey had left—but then she emerged from the garage, where she had been doing laundry.

That night, she and Tony talked on the phone until they fell asleep. "Did you ever get that car taken care of?"

"Yes," she said. "My dad took it to a dealership." That was another lie. The car had been towed to an impound lot on the same day Tony flew to New York. Her father thought the car was with Casey in Jacksonville.

Another night, Tony teased her again about staying in New York. "I'm going to have to probably get a job. I have to work to get money, to save it up for school, before I come back down."

Once again, emotion flooded out of Casey. She was overwrought. Tony was surprised that her reaction was, again, so over the top. The intensity of her commitment made him nervous.

On July 2, Amy said that Casey ripped off her stash of vacation cash. Amy, in a panic, asked Casey if she knew what had happened to her money. Casey made up a story that Amy had been sleepwalking and hidden the money in a safe place somewhere in the apartment.

While Amy searched high and low, Casey visited Cast Iron Tattoos on South Orange Avenue, where she was a regular customer. Her usual artist, Bobby, put a new tat on her shoulder blade. The design proclaimed "Bella Vita," Italian for "A Beautiful Life"—not exactly the sentiment you'd expect from a woman whose child was nowhere to be found.

That night, Casey posted a poem on her MySpace page:

On the worst of days
Remember the words spoken.

Trust no one,
Only yourself.

With great power,
Comes great consequences.

What is given,
Can be taken away.

Everyone lies.

Everyone Dies.

Life will never be easy.

CHAPTER 24

On July 3, Cindy posted a sad message on MySpace titled "My Caylee is Missing."

> She came into my life unexpectedly, just as she has left me. This precious little angel from above gave me strength and unconditional love. Now, she is gone and I don't know why. All I am guilty of is loving her and providing her a safe home. Jealousy has taken her away. Jealousy from the one person that should be thankful for all of the love and support given to her. A mother's love is deep, however, there are limits when one is betrayed by the one she loved and trusted the most.
>
> A daughter comes to her mother for her support when she is pregnant; the mother says without hesitation, it will be okay. And it was. But then the lies and betrayal began.
>
> First it seemed harmless, ah, love is blind. A mother will look for the good in her child and give them a chance to change. This mother gave chance after chance for her daughter to change, but instead more lies, or betrayal.
>
> What does the mother get for giving her daughter all of these chances? A broken heart. The daughter stole money, lots of money, leaves without warning and does not let her mother now speak to the baby that her mother raised, fed, clothed, sheltered, paid

her medical bills, etc. Instead tells her friends that her mother is controlling her life and she needs her space. No money, no future. Where did she go? Who is now watching out for the little angel?

That day, Troy Brown dropped off his visiting out-of-town girlfriend, Melissa England, to spend time with Casey while he went to work. Melissa didn't know Casey, but Troy gave her some background, including the fact that Casey was a single mother. Melissa thought it was odd that Casey only made a single reference to her child and that was in an overheard cell phone conversation. They were in Target when Cindy called. Casey's tone of voice made her irritation toward her mother obvious. In response to a question, Casey snapped, "The kid is with the nanny."

That night, Troy, Melissa and Casey went to the Dragon Room off of Orange Avenue. Casey was there partying when she answered a cell phone call from her brother Lee. With panic and distress in her voice, Casey told her friends that she had to leave the club right away. "My brother is coming here to get me."

Troy agreed to leave, but thought that the whole week had been a strange roller coaster ride with Casey. Most of the time, she seemed more carefree and happier than he'd ever seen her; but as soon as she was contacted by a family member, she went into instant distress. He couldn't figure it out.

Jesse Grund received a text message from Casey that sounded like a reaction to Cindy's post. "There's something going on in my family right now. If my mom or dad try to call you, don't answer, but for right now, just stay out of it. I'll take care of it."

The next day Casey contacted him asking what he was doing for the Fourth of July. He said that he was spending the day with his family and asked for an explanation of her text message. Casey didn't offer one, she just said, "It's a long story, and I will probably call you when I get drunk to tell you."

Amy provided something for Casey to do on the holiday when she invited her to go to Will Waters' house for a party. They had to leave early because Amy had promised to put up the decorations. Casey didn't know Will, but volunteered to help anyway.

They finished dressing up the back deck and went with Will to pick up beer and food. They purchased a keg, made multiple stops in search of a place that still had ice in stock on this holiday weekend and then went to Target, where they picked up a kickball and a football.

While most of the partygoers celebrated outside, Casey was in the house, sweeping, cleaning, straightening up the place and taking care of any problems. Will came inside when he got a cut on his face and Casey was there with a cold towel and sympathy. Will was fascinated. Her energy amazed him. Her personality intrigued him. His friends noted her generosity on Will's behalf, and kidded him. A couple of them cocked their heads in her direction, and expressed their awareness of his good fortune for latching onto a good-looking woman who cleaned, bandaged and performed other domestic chores, with one word: "Dude!"

After taking care of Will's minor injury, the two of them stood on the back porch watching a game of kickball. Casey said, "You know I have a daughter?"

"Yeah," Will said. "Amy told me." It wasn't a big deal to Will. It seemed to him that every girl his age had a kid around.

The party packed up at 8:30 and headed over to Lake Eola to watch the fireworks. At 9:10, Tony called Casey. He said that his dad wanted him to stay in New York.

"Well, why would you bring this up now?" Casey asked.

He told her that his dad said that he could send for his car and stuff so that he wouldn't have to go back to Florida at all.

"Well, I don't want to talk about this now. It's not a good time to be talking about negative things while I'm watching fireworks," Casey retorted.

Casey told Will that she didn't know what was going to happen. Her boyfriend was supposed to return the next day, but right now that looked like a 50/50 proposition. The party returned to Will's place when the fireworks ended. Amy and Casey left that night at 1:30 A.M.

The next morning, Casey got up early and jumped right to her laptop. She was clicking away at the keys when Amy arose. Revved up and giddy with excitement because she now knew Tony was returning that day, she got on Amy's nerves.

Will wrote Casey a text—"Are we going to hang out again?"—and then went into the bathroom and took a shower. He checked his cell when he got out of the shower at 9:30, but there was no response. For a moment, he was deflated, but looking outside, he spotted Casey coming up his steps.

He greeted her with a grin. "So, what are we going to do?"

They decided to go to Ikea. Will had already planned a shopping trip there and Casey said she was getting a new place soon and she needed some things, too. They had lunch at Zaxby's chicken, where Casey told Will her daughter was with the nanny. She shared her plans to get an apartment with a friend who also had a child. They'd both hire the nanny as a live-in. They stopped at Target for some bubble gum and coffee before spending three hours in Ikea. Will picked up what he needed for his re-decoration, and Casey window-shopped for the new place she claimed she was getting near Valencia Community College.

After leaving Will's, Casey headed out to pick up Tony. She stopped at a car wash near the airport to clean off the road dirt on Tony's Jeep. She called Will from there and kept him on the phone as she drove away, parked in the lot and ascended on the escalator. Finally, Will said, "Alright, bye. I've got things to do. I got my motorcycle to work on."

Five minutes later, Casey called again. "Well, Tony's

not here yet." At the time, Will didn't mind talking to her. Some people got annoyed because she talked so much, but not Will. On reflection, he realized that her need for constant connection was probably not a good sign—an indication that Casey needed more attention than was healthy.

Tony noticed nothing amiss when Casey met him at the airport. She pointed out the car wash where she'd taken his Jeep as they drove past it. Then they stopped at Winn-Dixie to pick up groceries before going to Tony's apartment.

The two of them went to Buffalo Wild Wings at Waterford Lakes for a late dinner. They sat at a long table with a bunch of Casey's friends whom Tony met for the first time. Casey saw old beau Christopher Stutz, across the room with a woman she didn't know. She sent a text: "Hey, I hope you're enjoying your date."

He looked around, didn't see her and typed back, "What do you mean?"

By the time he hit "SEND," Casey was standing beside him. "Hello," she said. They chatted for a few minutes and then she excused herself to go back to her friends.

Even though Tony was back in town, Casey maintained contact with Will, accepting him as a MySpace friend and exchanging messages nearly every day. Will appreciated one in particular. It arrived on his cell on July 7. In it, she said he was the sweetest guy she'd ever met.

She called or texted him often, during the day while Tony was at school. She asked him a couple of times to meet her for lunch at Houlihan's, but he said that he was at work and couldn't get there. "Don't you ever go to work?" he asked.

"They email it to me and I work with the photography on the computer," she explained.

On July 7, Casey ran into Matthew Crisp, her high school acquaintance, at Subway. They sat together, ate lunch and chatted about what they did for the Fourth of July.

Matthew asked, "How's the little munchkin?"

"She's good. She's actually at a play date out in Sanford."

They talked through Matthew's lunch hour and ended only when he had to get back to work. Matthew thought she seemed a little bit needy or lonely. He attributed it to Tony being out of town, as Casey told him—though he'd actually been back in Orlando for two days.

At 6 A.M. on July 8, Amy's cell phone rang. It was Casey, but this time, she didn't wake her friend. Amy was across the street from Tony's Sutton Place apartment at a 7-Eleven pumping gas into her car. Casey was going to drive Amy to the airport for her flight to Puerto Rico. In exchange, Casey got the use of Amy's car while she was gone. Amy wanted to leave Casey with a full tank of gas.

That morning, Cindy's mother Shirley sent an email message to her sister Mary Lou expressing her concerns about Casey's extended visit to Jacksonville. Mary Lou wrote back:

> I am with you thinking something might be amiss with Caylee. I can't believe she would be that upset to speak to and hear her grandmother on the phone??? I just hope that little girl is OK. I wonder how much of Caylee's clothes and toys Casey took when she left??? How much of her own things did she take??? Seems to me, they would be running out of things to wear, etc. Of course, I guess Casey could be buying things as time goes along?

They exchanged other thoughts about Cindy's situation through the next day, both commenting on how good it was that Cindy and George were getting along, because Cindy needed his support during this trying period of time with Casey.

Mary Lou wrote:

I know Cindy is between "a rock and a hard place" with this "Casey affair." Even though Casey has been supported in everything she has done, by her folks, she is an "ingrate" and for some reason has turned her back on the people who care the most for her.

Rico was scheduled to return to Orlando from a trip to Boston on the same day that Amy flew to Puerto Rico, but at a later time. Casey sent him a text, asking for his arrival time and offering to pick him up. He told her that picking him up didn't make much sense, since he had a flight to Puerto Rico just five hours later. "But if you want to come and get me and we can chill at Chili's and then you can bring me back to the airport."

By the time Casey got his response, she had already made other plans. Casey told him to send her a text when he got in. He did. But she didn't acknowledge his message. Rico was not surprised.

Throughout the day, Shirley and Mary Lou continued emailing about the pros and cons of Casey having a new love interest in Jacksonville, including the possibility that the result would be a second child for Casey—one that Cindy would be forced to raise. Mary Lou added:

I smiled when you said Cindy says she doesn't think Casey is PG [*pregnant*]. I don't think she thought Casey was PG the last time around either??? Something is keeping Casey from facing her mother??? (I was so devastated last time when Casey was pregnant. It was almost like it was my own child.) I just felt terrible and I could imagine how letdown Cindy felt.

CHAPTER 25

Late on the night of July 8, Casey posted an image file on line. It was a picture of a sad little girl looking up at a noose wrapped around the neck of a teddy bear that has x's for eyes. Beside the little girl were the words: "Why do People Kill people, who kill people, to show people that To Kill People—is Bad?"

Casey woke up in a cold sweat three or four nights that week. Tony asked what was wrong. Casey said she'd had a nightmare and blamed it all on the uncertainty in their relationship.

Will got off work at 5 P.M. on July 10. Casey was supposed to meet him at 6:30 for a helicopter ride to Saw Island. When she was ten minutes late, Will called. No answer. He sent a text. She didn't respond right away, as she usually did. He texted again: "I need you to reply so I can cancel the helicopter trip."

Still nothing. He sent another message: "I need to know something. I've got reservations and people are on hold."

Twenty minutes later, she acknowledged his messages: "I can't make it. Sorry."

Cindy had taken more vacation days the week after the Fourth of July holiday, counting on Casey's promises that she'd have a chance to visit with Caylee. Every day, Casey opened up her bag of excuses and doled out another to her mother. On July 10th, Casey claimed she had come by the house. She said she'd seen her dad while Cindy was out running errands. Cindy questioned George, who denied seeing either Casey or Caylee.

Cindy sent a despairing email to her daughter:

I can't sleep, stupid hot flashes wake me up then I start thinking about you and Caylee. Dad said he went to work at 9 am and got home at 6:30 pm, he said he did not come home in between. I don't know who or what to believe anymore.

You've told me every day that you were going to call me and you haven't but you choose to call when you know I won't be home. What the hell is going on? I've tried not to bug you to death but I still haven't gotten to see pictures of Caylee or gotten to speak to her. It's been over a month now.

Am I ever going to see her again? Are you still with Jeff? Are you going back to work? . . . I'm not sure how much longer I can continue on this day to day course. I'm going freakin' nuts not knowing what's going on with you. I've had a breakdown at work, can't take much more stress.

Casey posted a poem by rap artist Tupac Shakur on her MySpace page on Friday, July 11. The words encouraged people to stop trying to make sense of a bad situation and instead, to walk away from your problems and move on with your life.

The postman walked up to the front door of the Anthony home on Friday and stuck a piece of mail in the crack of the door when no one answered. The family always went in and out of the house through the garage. No one noticed the letter.

Casey called Will and told him she was working with the "shot girls," the girls who serve shots, at Fusian and invited him to join her there that night. Will was flabbergasted. "No. Why would I want to hang out with you when Tony is supposed to be there. . . . Why would I want to hang out with you and Tony if you know I have a crush on you? Why would I put myself through that?"

It was not a good night for shot girls. One was grabbed and scratched on the stomach by a rowdy customer. They all went home early. On Saturday, Casey was supposed to hang out with Will. She begged off once again.

That Sunday and Monday, Casey exchanged instant messages with Iassen Donov, the Army buddy of a former boyfriend. Innocuous on the surface, the dialogue revealed a lot about Casey's state of mind and her willingness to go to great lengths to protect her lies. On Sunday, she told him that she was tired because she hadn't been sleeping well.

"You should exercise more," Iassen wrote.

"This is true. I can't wait to get my new place."

"When is that happening?" Iassen asked.

"Probably within the next week."

"Oh, true, you and Tony?"

"No sir. Just me and the kid."

"Where?"

"Possibly in the Winter Park Villas." She explained that she really didn't want to live in an apartment, but getting a house didn't seem to be a good idea at that time.

"So what do u do when u work? With the kid that is."

"I have a nanny. I love her," Casey wrote.

Iassen asked her why she wasn't moving in with Tony, and then wrote, "Where's the other guy? The Spanish guy?"

"Ricardo and I aren't really even friends anymore."

"Sucks, doesn't it?"

"We stopped dating in March right around my birthday."

"Still have feelings for him?"

"Ha, definitely not. The other way around actually."

"Oh. How did u get over him so quickly?"

"I didn't have the same feelings. He said I led him on.

I never really ever saw him as more than a friend. It sucks but I was honest."

"I thought u were the one who wanted a relationship," Iassen wrote.

"I did, for a little bit, but he wanted to wait."

"And it bit him in the ass. Are u happy now?"

"I am very happy now."

While Casey chatted away, her parents worked in their front yard. George planted plugs to restore a couple of dead patches in the lawn. Cindy weeded the flower beds near the house. She noticed something stuck in the front door and got up to retrieve it. "George, we got a certified letter from somebody by the name of Johnson's."

"Yeah?"

"Yeah. Can you pick this up?"

"Yeah, I'll do it Monday."

That day, though, George was called into work early and didn't get a chance to get to the post office until Tuesday, July 15.

On Monday, Casey took Iassen's advice and worked out at the fitness center at Tony's complex, and reconnected to let him know and continue their IM conversation. She asked him to go to the beach with her.

"Ok u wanna go on a date with me to the beach while u have a boyfriend, that looks grrrrrrrrrrrrrrrrreaaaaaat."

"Hahahaha. It wouldn't have to be a 'date.' But you need a friend. I miss my friend. It's a win, win."

"Lol. I wanna know, have I ever hurt you? Like emotionally."

"Most definitely not. You seriously are one of the nicest guys I have ever met. Hands down . . . I've had a consistent crush on ya for a long time."

"Nuts. We didn't even hang out that much."

"It's one of those things. You get a good vibe from someone, it sticks," Casey wrote.

"I'm sure u wouldn't want anything with me right now, I'm in the worst state of mind to commit to somebody."

"Even outside of a relationship, I'm probably not in the best spot either."

"Why?" Iassen asked.

"I'm pretty much hung up on Tony, and realistically, if he moves back to New York next year, my relationship will end. Sucks to know that inevitably, unless I were to drop everything, I'm going to lose someone close to me."

They bounced messages back and forth, talking about her feelings and the alternatives to Tony's expected departure, and then Casey wrote, "If you're going to take a risk on something, of all things, why not let it be love? It is the most damaging and rewarding thing in the entire world."

"Because it's the one risk that hurts the most."

"It is."

"People may not die of a broken heart but they wish they did."

"Absolutely," Casey agreed.

"The person that can make you the most happiest in this world, is the same person who can make you the most miserable."

"It's a powerful thing to hold someone else's heart in your hand," Casey wrote.

CHAPTER 26

Jamie and Casey exchanged text messages, on Tuesday, July 15, about the unpleasant incident at Fusian the previous Friday night. Because of what happened, Jamie told Casey that she wasn't going to work there as a shot girl again. Jamie asked what she was doing that day. Casey said that she was going to work at Universal.

Jamie mentioned the little girl in the photographs on Casey's MySpace page. "Is she yours?"

"Yes," Casey wrote. "She has a birthday next month. She'll be three."

Casey left the apartment and stopped by the Bank of America branch on South Conway Road. She went up to the teller with one of Amy's checks and walked away with $250 in cash.

Her next stop was Cast Iron Tattoos to make an appointment for herself and a friend for Saturday, July 19. Recognizing her as a regular customer, tattoo artist Danny Colomarino came out front to greet her. "Hey, how you been?" he asked, then inquired about her daughter.

"Caylee is with her nanny. I'll bring her with me on Saturday," Casey said. She pointed to the car in the parking lot and said it belonged to a friend. "I'm going to the airport to pick her up, and three other guys who are coming back from Puerto Rico." She explained that she was supposed to go on that trip, too, but she had to save her money to move out of her mother's house and into a place of her own.

Danny thought he heard a bitter edge in her voice, but he didn't blame her. He knew he'd be "a little bummed" if his friends all went on an island vacation and left him behind.

While Casey was chatting up Danny at the tattoo parlor, George and Cindy were running head-first into Casey's lies. Their daughter couldn't have driven to Jacksonville as she'd said. The car was right here in Orlando at a tow yard.

Cindy explained the situation to her supervisor, Debbie Polisano. "Go get the car, get Casey and go home," Debbie advised.

After retrieving the stench-filled Pontiac, George suggested that they call the police. Cindy refused. She had to find Casey first. Cindy returned to work around 2 that afternoon.

Co-worker Debbie Bennett was surprised to see Cindy entering the office. She turned away from the copy machine to ask her what happened.

At this point, Cindy didn't seem worried, but sounded very angry at her daughter's irresponsibility. "The car is a mess. Caylee's car seat, her backpack, her clothes and her favorite baby doll are in there. It smells like a dead body in that car."

"Cindy, there's something wrong. You need to call police," Bennett urged her. "It doesn't sound right."

"No. I'm going to give Casey a chance to explain herself. I'm going to try to get hold of her. I'll call her employer."

Concerned about Cindy's state of mind, Bennett went to their supervisor, Debbie Polisano. The supervisor went to Cindy's office to talk to her.

"There's a really, really bad smell in the car," Cindy told her.

"Did you open the trunk?" Polisano asked. When Cindy didn't respond, she asked another question. "Where is Casey?"

"I don't know."

"Cindy, you need to go home and call the police."

"I can't," Cindy said, shaking her head. "I have a lot of work to do."

Exasperated, Polisano went to the area director, Nilsa Ramos. Nilsa told Cindy she had to go home and deal with her family problems.

Finally, Cindy relented. She pulled into her driveway and went straight to the car in the garage. She pulled out the purse that Casey had left on the seat and found a phone number for Amy Huizenga.

Casey drove Amy's maroon four-door compact to the airport and met Amy and the other three returning revelers. It wasn't possible to fit everyone and their luggage into Amy's small car. Rico, Troy and J.P. waited at the airport while Amy drove Casey to Tony's apartment. On the way, Amy listened to Casey's excited chatter about a cell phone call she'd received that day from Caylee. Amy then returned to the airport to pick up the guys.

After they got back to their apartment, J.P. wanted to get an iPhone, and Amy went with him to The Florida Mall. Twenty minutes after they arrived, Amy received a harried phone call from Cindy Anthony.

At Sutton Place Apartments Tony and Nathan played MLB 2K8, a major league baseball video game while they waited for the All Star game to commence on the television. Casey sat beside them on the sofa tapping on her laptop.

When he heard a knock, Tony shouted, "Come in." The door opened and he looked up at Amy, who appeared totally miserable.

"I need to talk to you," she said to Casey.

Casey went outside and closed the door behind her. Nathan and Tony returned to their game. Drama intruded on their concentration just two minutes later as the door flew open and Casey came inside loudly arguing with her mother. As Casey rushed back to the bedroom, Cindy spoke to Tony. "I hope you're rich, 'cause Casey's going to take all your money and leave you high and dry."

Tony and Nathan exchanged looks of bewilderment. "What are you talking about?" Tony asked.

Casey zoomed back into the room and told her mother to shut up. The door slammed and they were gone. *What was that all about?* Tony wondered. He waited for Casey to contact him with an explanation. After two hours, when it hadn't come, he picked up his cell and wrote a text message. Just a moment after he hit SEND, he heard a tone across the room. Casey had forgotten her phone.

He picked it up, looked for Amy's number and gave her a call. She told him that Casey had taken her checkbook and used it to steal money from her. Cindy's last words before leaving now made sense. *But what else was going on?* He remained in the dark until he got a call from Casey's brother Lee.

CHAPTER 27

After dropping off Amy, Cindy said, "Casey, I'm going to take you to the police department. Maybe they can talk some sense into you and tell me where Caylee's at."

"Mom, go ahead, go ahead. I can't take you to see Caylee tonight."

Cindy pulled into the parking lot of the Orlando police substation on Pershing Avenue, but the office was closed for the day. Cindy turned to her daughter. "Casey, come on, tell me what's going on."

"Mom, I can't."

"Someone's going to help me," she said as she called 9-1-1. When the operator answered, Cindy didn't quite know what to say. *She won't take me to see my granddaughter?* she thought. *That isn't a crime. But I need to talk to a detective.* She blurted out, "My car was stolen."

Cindy and the operator went back and forth in a confusing dialogue about where she could meet the officers. Cindy called it quits, deciding she'd just call them back when she got home. She wanted to shake Casey and force the answer out of her, but she was afraid if she started, she wouldn't be able to stop. In her current state of rage, she worried that she could not trust herself to maintain her self-control.

Back on Hopespring Drive, Lee waited outside for his mother and sister. Once there, Cindy questioned Casey again, hoping Lee's presence would get her to talk. But it didn't. Frustrated at her inability to get satisfactory an-

A collage of images found on Casey Anthony's computer by the Orange County Sheriff's Department.

The Anthony home on Hopespring Drive.

—*Diane Fanning*

Caylee Anthony's bedroom.

— *Orange County Sheriff's Office*

Casey Anthony's bedroom.

— Orange County Sheriff's Office

A collage of photos of baby Caylee hanging on the wall of Casey Anthony's bedroom.

— Orange County Sheriff's Office

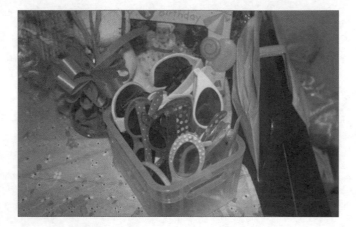

Caylee Anthony was a true child of the Sunshine State—she loved her sunglasses and had a pair to match every outfit.
— *Orange County Sheriff's Office*

An envelope addressed to Caylee with the backing of a heart-shaped sticker stuck to its surface.
— *Orange County Sheriff's Office*

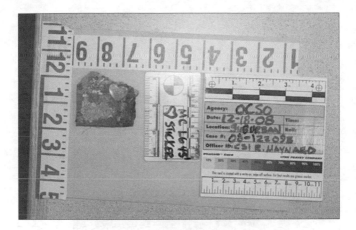

The heart sticker recovered from the location where Caylee's body was found. — *Orange County Sheriff's Office*

Unit 210 at Sawgrass Apartments. Casey claimed to have left Caylee with Zenaida Gonzalez at the bottom of these stairs. —*Diane Fanning*

Have You Seen Me?

REWARD

Caylee Marie Anthony

3 Year Old, White Female, Brown hair, Hazel eyes, Birthmark on left shoulder, Approximately 3 feet tall.

The Orange County Sheriff's Office is currently trying to determine the whereabouts and well being of this child. If you have seen Caylee Marie Anthony in the company of another since June 9, 2008 call 407-254-7000.

www.HelpFindCaylee.com

A flier created by the Kid Finders Network. The Anthony family had many printed and distributed throughout Orlando. It was also available on-line for the general public to print and to use and distribute as they wished.

Crime scene technicians dig for clues in the woods on Suburban Drive where Caylee's body was found.

— Orange County Sheriff's Office

An Orange County Forensic tech uses a magnifying glass to make sure he finds any small piece of evidence among the debris found on the forest floor.

— Orange County Sheriff's Office

An aerial view of the location where Caylee's body was found. The road running through the middle is Suburban Drive. Hopespring Drive is the street on the right closest to the wooded area. — *Orange County Sheriff's Office*

The memorial on Suburban Drive next to the woods where Caylee's body was found. — *Diane Fanning*

swers from her daughter, Cindy called the police again to report her car stolen.

While Cindy was on the phone, Casey spewed out her kidnapping scenario to Lee. She repeated the tale to her mom. Cindy punched 9-1-1 again—this time in an all-out panic. She informed the authorities that her granddaughter had been missing for thirty-one days—she'd been kidnapped by the baby-sitter. At the operator's request, she put Casey on the phone.

George pulled into the driveway and saw his wife pacing, crying and waiting for the police to arrive. "Someone's got Caylee. Caylee's gone! Someone took her," she wailed.

A police car pulled up just moments after George. The responding officer took statements from everyone. When Detective Yuri Melich got to the scene, he sat down with Casey and a tape recorder.

Lee called Tony and got the go-ahead to come over to Sutton Place and pick up the rest of Casey's things. He arrived at 2 in the morning. The laptop sat on the kitchen counter, plugged into an outlet. He started it up, but only got a blue screen. A message popped up warning that the computer had been shut down improperly. Lee rebooted. The plain screen came up again, followed by the error message. He assumed that a virus had deleted or corrupted some of the files needed to open Windows. He turned off the computer.

He couldn't ask Casey about the cause of the problem when he returned to the house because she was out with the detectives, pointing out the current and past addresses of Zenaida Gonzalez. On another computer, he logged into Casey's Yahoo! account and discovered a total absence of incoming and outgoing messages dated before July 15—even all the spam was gone. Lee knew someone had to have manually removed them from the account. He began to doubt that a virus caused the problem with the laptop. It appeared as if the damage might be intentional.

* * *

Before dawn on July 16, Cindy's mother, Shirley Cuza, sat down at her computer and sent an email to her sister. In the middle of her update about her cat's health and questions about her sibling's dog, she wrote:

> I guess you haven't heard from Cindy? I just can't imagine what's going on with Casey??? Unless she and Cindy had a "spat" before she left last time, there doesn't seem to be any reason for her to do this to her mom???

For now, Shirley simply believed that her granddaughter Casey was playing games with Cindy. She did not suspect that her great-granddaughter Caylee had come to any harm.

A little before 7 that morning, Casey began a text message exchange with Tony. "I'm so sorry for not telling you what happened. We obviously need to talk. I need you and I love you more than you know."

"Where is Caylee?" he asked.

"I honestly don't know."

"Don't know? R u serious? When did u find out?"

"I've been filing reports all night and driving around with multiple officers looking at old apartments I had taken her to. Everything. Too long. Let's just leave it at that."

"Y wouldn't u tell me of all people? I was ur boyfriend that cares about you and ur daughter. Doesn't make sense to me. Why would you lie to me?" Tony asked.

"I lied to everyone. What was I supposed to say? I trusted my daughter with some psycho? How does that look?"

"Idk [I don't know] what to say. I just hope your daughter is okay and I'm gonna do whatever I can do to help ur family and the cops."

"I was put in handcuffs for almost 10 minutes and sat in the back of a cop car. The best and most important person in my life is missing. I am the dumbest person and the worst mother. I honestly hate myself. The most important thing is getting Caylee back but I truly hope that you can forgive me. Granted, I will never be able to forgive myself."

"Who is this Zanny Nanny person?" he asked.

"Someone I had met through a mutual friend almost 4 years ago. She used to be my buddy Jeff's nanny before she became mine. I'm scared."

"R u home?"

"Yeah. Almost 12 hours of stuff. Finally getting a shower. I feel like shit."

"Where did u drop off Caylee last time u saw her?"

"At her apartment. At the bottom stairs."

"Where?!"

"Sawgrass Apartments. Have told and showed police the apartment. Told them and drove out there with two different officers. I just got back from the second drive. If they don't find her, guess who gets blamed and spends eternity in jail?"

"Yeah, no shit," Tony agreed. "Why wouldn't u say something sooner bout this? To anyone? Oh and why are u texting and not calling?"

"I talked to two people that have been directly connected to Zanny. How can I sit there and be so blind and stupid? It's my fault. I was scared to admit it. I was scared that something was going to happen to my baby."

Iassen Donov received a call from a friend telling him to check out Casey's MySpace page. He did. Everything had changed. "Caylee's missing," dominated the page. He called Lee's girlfriend, Mallory Parker. She explained what was going on with Casey and Caylee. Later, Lee called asking him to spread the word.

Matthew Crisp read the message on his cell phone. "Caylee is missing. She has been for thirty-two days now. Please if you have any information call me on cell or at home."

"Are you serious?" he typed.

"Yes," she responded.

"I believe we had lunch since then and it never came up."

"It's a long story," Casey typed. "Posting on MySpace and Face Book shortly. Please pass it on."

When Melina Calabrese heard the news of Caylee's disappearance, she was perplexed. *Oh my gosh, why didn't she call me? My gosh, why didn't you call anybody? Five weeks? I mean, I'm one of her best friends.* Melina could not understand why Casey had not reached out to her, her parents, her brother or the cops in all that time.

Lauren Gibbs received the message about Caylee and called Casey right away, breathless. "Omigod, Casey."

Casey was matter-of-fact in her response. "Yeah. Caylee's missing. I haven't seen her. I talked to her yesterday, so I know she's fine. It was from a private number."

"Do you have any idea who it could be?" Lauren asked.

"No," Casey said.

Childhood friend Brittany Schrieber woke up that morning to discover the same text message from Casey waiting on her cell phone.

Brittany typed, "Caylee missing?"

"Yes, she has been for a few weeks."

"What happened?"

"Her nanny. Someone I trusted took her. No calls until yesterday," Casey claimed.

"I'm sorry. If you need anything, let me know."

"Thank you."

"Is there anything I should keep my eye open to watch out for."

"A silver Ford Focus, four-door," Casey responded.

A lot of people received a similar text message that morning. Some received similar responses from Casey, some got no response at all and others received a phone call from Lee explaining the situation and asking for assistance to find Caylee.

Brittany seemed to get everyone's attention. After she'd

texted with Casey, she received two calls from Lee. The first was an explanation and a plea for help. The second was a wrong number—he thought he was calling someone else—and a complaint about Casey giving the family false phone numbers. Cindy made contact with her as well. She walked the short distance up the street to visit in person after Casey left on another excursion with the police just after noon. "Casey is hiding something," Cindy told Brittany. "She told me she was going to Jacksonville for a month for a job, and was going to drop the baby off with a sitter."

Cindy explained that she hadn't offered to take care of Caylee while Casey was out of town because of the jealousy issue over Cindy's relationship with her granddaughter. Cindy said they knew Casey wasn't in Jacksonville when they found out that her car had been towed from Amscot.

"The car seat, diapers and Caylee's baby doll were in the car—Caylee never leaves without her baby doll. It's been her baby since she was born."

Cindy moved on to Casey's behavior in the last month. "She made sure I wasn't there before she came to the house. She'd go and take the stuff she needed, and stole money every time. But she never took anything for Caylee. No shoes, no pajamas, no dolls, no anything."

CHAPTER 28

Detective Yuri Melich spent the day of July 16 chasing down leads and talking with Casey Anthony. It was clear to him that every detail provided by Casey turned into a dead end. The claim of the last place she'd seen Caylee, the tale of the kidnapping nanny, the story of a job at Universal—one falsehood piled upon another.

Melich gave Casey the opportunity to change her story—again and again. She stubbornly persisted, as if repetition could magically transform reality.

Although the investigator hoped for Caylee's safe return, he feared that the prospect of finding her alive was already passing through the improbable phase, and quickly approaching the impossible. He didn't have the evidence to charge Casey for her daughter's death, but he could arrest for her false statement and child neglect.

As he prepared the charging document, he called George Anthony and asked for permission to pick up everything that had been in the white Pontiac Sunfire at the time George retrieved it from Johnson's Wrecker Service.

With George's agreement, Melich sent Detective Charity Beasley to the Anthony home. George wrote a statement affidavit for the detective allowing the Orange County Sheriff's Office to "search and provide evidence to help bring back my granddaughter—Caylee."

Beasley pulled evidence tape across the doors and trunk of the Pontiac. From inside the home, she recovered Caylee's cloth-body, unclothed baby doll, a *Dora the Ex-*

plorer backpack, a child's toothbrush, a dinnerware knife and a leather bag containing papers, along with other miscellaneous items. The Anthonys volunteered a Compaq laptop used by Casey.

Cindy told the investigator that she'd already washed a vile-smelling pair of pants she'd found in the car, as well as all of Casey's smoke-filled clothing, which Lee had picked up at Tony's apartment. Because of the laundering, Detective Beasley did not confiscate them.

On the basis of the evidence he had thus far compiled, Yuri Melich arrested Casey and ordered her transported into the Orange County Jail. The 22-year-old moved into a single-occupancy cell at the county female detention center. She was in a foul mood when she phoned home that night.

After Cindy greeted her daughter, Casey dished out a snide comment: "Mom, I just saw your nice little cameo on TV."

"Which one?" Cindy asked.

"What do you mean, which one?" Casey snapped.

"Which one? I did four different ones, and I haven't seen them all. I've only seen one or two so far."

"You don't know what my involvement is in stuff?" Casey asked.

"Casey . . ." Cindy pleaded.

"Mom . . ." Casey said in a mocking tone.

"No, I don't know what your involvement is, sweetheart. You are not telling me where she's at."

"Because I don't fucking know where she's at!" Casey yelled. "Are you kidding me?"

"Casey, don't waste your call screaming and hollering at me."

"Waste my call sitting in the jail?" Casey sputtered.

"Whose fault is it you're sitting in jail? Are you blaming me you are sitting in the jail? Blame yourself for telling lies. What do you mean, it is not your fault? What do you mean it's not your fault, sweetheart? If you would have told them the truth and not lied about everything . . ."

"Do me a favor and just tell me what Tony's number is. I don't want to talk to you right now. Forget it."

"I don't have his number."

"Well, get it from Lee," Casey demanded. "I know Lee is at the house . . . It was just on the news. They were just live outside the house."

"I know they were."

"Well?" Casey snarled. "Can you get Tony's number for me so I can call him?"

Cindy handed the phone to Lee. "Hey?" he said.

"Hey. Can you get me Tony's number?"

"I can do that, but I don't know what good it's going to do you at this point."

"Well, I'd like to talk to him anyway because I called to talk to my mother and it is a fucking waste," Casey complained. "By the way, I don't want any of you coming up here when I have my first hearing for bond and everything. I mean don't even fucking waste your time coming up here."

"You know, you are having a real tough year, and making it real tough for anybody to want to try to, even if it is giving . . ."

"See, that is just it, every . . ." Casey interrupted.

"You are not even letting me finish," her brother said.

"Go ahead."

"First, you are asking me for Tony's phone number so you can call him and then you immediately want to start pressing toward me and saying 'don't even worry about coming up here for all this stuff' and trying to cut us out."

"I'm not trying to cut anybody out."

"I'm not going around and around with you," Lee warned. "You know, that is pretty pointless. I'm not going to put everyone else through the same stuff that you've been putting the police and everybody else [through] for the last twenty-four hours, and the stuff you've been putting Mom through for the last four or five weeks. I'm done with that. So, you can tell me what's going on. Kristina [another young mother whose children often played with

Caylee] would love to talk to you, because she thinks you will tell her what's going on. Frankly, we are going to find out—whatever is going on is going to be found out. So, why not do it now?"

"There is nothing to find out. There is absolutely nothing to find out. Not even what I told the detectives. I have no clue where Caylee is. If I knew where Caylee was, do you think that any of this would be happening? No."

"Anyway, you only have a couple of minutes with this, so I'm not going to let you completely waste it. Here is Kristina."

"No, no," Casey objected. "I want Tony's number. I'm not talking to anybody else."

"Hello," Kristina said.

"Hi." Casey's voice softened. "I'm glad everybody is at my house, but I'll have to call you later, or I'll have to call to get somebody to get your number. Do me a favor and get my brother back, because I need Tony's number."

"Okay. Is there anything I can do for you?"

"I'm sitting in jail. There is nothing anybody can do now."

"I'm just trying to be a . . ." Kristina said.

"I know you are, honey," Casey said. "I absolutely know you are, and I appreciate it and everything you are trying to do, but I'd like to call Tony. He's not at my house, is he?"

"No, it's just me and your parents and Lee."

"Well, can you do me a favor and get my brother back so I can get the number from him, please?"

"Does Tony have anything to do with Caylee?" Kristina asked.

"No. Nothing."

"Okay, so why do you want to talk with Tony? You probably don't want to tell me, do you?"

". . . Tony had nothing to do with Caylee," Casey insisted.

"Oh, then why do you want to talk with him?"

"Because he is my boyfriend and I want to actually try

and sit and talk to him because I didn't get a chance to talk to him earlier. Because I got arrested on a fucking whim today, and because they are blaming me for stuff that I would never do. That I didn't do."

"Well, I'm on your side, you know that?" Kristina said.

"I know that, I just want to talk with Tony and get a little bit of . . ."

"Casey, you have to tell me if you know anything about Caylee. If anything happened to Caylee, Casey, I'll die." Kristina's voice quavered with emotion. "You understand? I'll die if anything happened to that baby."

In a situation like this one, with a friend breaking down, a lot of mothers would have fallen apart. But not Casey Anthony. Instead of displaying tears, she gave rein to her impatience. "Oh my God! Calling you guys— A waste, a huge waste. Honey, I love you. You know I'd never let anything happen to my daughter. If I knew where she was, this would not be going on."

"Then how come everyone is saying that you are lying?" Kristina asked.

"Because nobody is fucking listening to anything that I'm saying. The media misconstrued everything that I said. The fucking detectives . . . got all of their information from me, but at the same time they are twisting stuff. They already said they are going to pin this on me if they don't find Caylee. They've already said that. They arrested me because they said . . ."

"Yeah, 'cause they said that the person you left Caylee with doesn't exist," Kristina pushed.

"Because, oh look, they can't find her in the Florida database," Casey Anthony said. "She is not just from Florida. If they would actually listen to anything that I would have said to them, they would have had their leads. They maybe could have tracked her down. They have not listened to a fucking thing that I've said."

"You know that whoever has Caylee, nobody is going to get away with it—nobody."

"I know, nobody is going to get away with it, but at the

same time, the only way they are going to find Caylee is if they actually listen to what I'm saying, and I'm trying to help them, and they are not letting me help them."

"So, how can I help them find her?" Kristina asked.

"The best thing you can do, baby, is to listen to me. They need to look up her information in the New York database and a North Carolina database," Casey said. "And other places that she's lived outside of Florida. That is what I told them, even again today. I told them that four times today. I sat up at the police station. The county police station . . ."

"Is she the one who has Caylee, or did she transfer Caylee to someone else?"

"Honey, I have not talked with her. I don't know. I have not talked to her."

"How come everyone is saying that you are not upset, and that you are not crying, and you show no caring of where Caylee is at all?"

"Because I'm not here fucking crying every two seconds because I have to stay composed to talk to detectives, to make other phone calls and do other things. I can't sit here and be crying every two seconds like I want to—I can't," Casey shrieked.

"Okay, Casey, don't yell at me, I'm on your side," Kristina said.

"I know you are on my side. I'm not trying to . . ."

"Nobody is saying anything bad about you," Kristina said. "Your family is with you one hundred percent."

"No they're not. That is bullshit, because I just watched the fucking news and heard everything that my mom said. Nobody in my own family is on my side."

"Yes they are. Nobody has said . . ."

"They just want Caylee back. That is all they are worried about right now, is getting Caylee back," Casey complained, and then added, "And you know what? That is all I care about right now."

"Casey, your daughter, your flesh-and-blood and baby girl . . ."

Casey cut her off. "Kristina, please! Put my brother back on the phone, I don't want to get into this with you right now. I love you, honey, and I'm glad that you are there. Thank you for your help. I will let you know if there is anything that you can do."

"You can't tell me anybody who can find Caylee?"

"No. No, because everyone that I've tried and every number that I've called is disconnected—nothing. I can't get ahold of anybody."

"But that girl was the last person to have her?"

"She was the last person to have her," Casey said. "That was the last time I saw Caylee."

"Lee said he doesn't have Tony's phone number."

"Yes, he does. He has Tony's phone number in his phone. He needs to stop fucking lying. He just told me a second ago that he'd give me the number."

"So, if I go and get you Tony's number, are you going to finish talking to me?" Kristina asked.

"I will call you tomorrow. I want to talk to him really quick. I wanted to actually try and call tonight. I haven't slept in four days. I have not slept in four days."

"Listen, if you are going to talk to anybody, you can talk to me," Kristina urged.

"I know I can talk to you, but at the same time, I know that I can talk to Tony and that is who I want to talk to now. I have not gotten the chance to talk to him since this morning. Since all of this stuff happened, with trying to set up the MySpace, and I made the MySpace—"

"Do you know the password for MySpace?"

"I made all of it."

"What's the password to MySpace so we can see if anybody has written any leads of where Caylee might be?" Kristina asked.

"You can go on line and see it. As far as messages, I don't know if anybody is going to be messaging," Casey Anthony said, then gave her the log-in information.

In the background, Lee said, "Hold on for a second," as he looked up Tony's number.

Kristina passed the phone number on to Casey and asked, "Can Tony tell me anything?"

"Baby, Tony doesn't know anything. And I have not even talked with him since this morning."

"Has Tony seen Caylee?" Kristina asked.

"Tony has not seen Caylee since the beginning of June. What's Tony's number, again?"

Kristina repeated the number.

"Thank you. I will find a way to call you later. Leave your number at my house with my mother and I can get it either later tonight—"

"How can I get ahold of you?"

"I'm at the jail, you can't."

"You don't have a way to write my phone number down?" Kristina asked.

"No, I have no way of writing it down. I have to remember Tony's number. I have to try to memorize his number right now. Just leave your number with my mom and I will try to call you in the morning if I don't get a chance to call you tonight."

"So, how can I find information about that girl?"

"Have them look up a New York license for Zenaida Fernandez-Gonzalez," Casey said. "They've just been looking up the last name 'Gonzalez' or the last name 'Fernandez.' If they look up her entire name, they might actually find her. They have not done that. They haven't listened to anything that I've said."

"How do you spell 'Zenaida'?"

"Z-e-n-a-i-d-a."

"Where does she live? Because they went and looked at her place and . . ."

"Baby, you are not telling me anything that I don't already know. Again, I've only been in jail since about eight thirty tonight. I was with them all day. I know that. I was with officers pretty much since nine P.M. last night up until this evening when I came up here."

"But you are telling the whole truth and nothing but the truth?"

"That I have no clue where my daughter is?" Casey asked. "Yes, that is the truth. That is the absolute truth."

"They'll find out, and whoever . . ."

"Okay, Kristina, I'm hanging up. I need to make this other call before I forget the number. So, I'll call you later."

When old friend Melina Calabrese heard the tape of this phone call on television, she was furious, and came close to punching her TV set in her frustration. "That's not the Casey I know . . . I just couldn't understand how she was so rude . . . It just didn't sit well with me, and it really upset me that that was her way of talking to her parents and her brother and [Kristina]. And then to ask for Tony's phone number, I just don't think that . . . should have been her number-one priority, especially during whatever may have been going on."

The driver that night for Johnson's Wrecker Service answered a towing request call from the Orange County Sheriff's Office. He called manager Simon Burch at home.

"Hey, that car that we released today that you were telling Nicole about, with the smell in it? Was that a white Pontiac?"

"Yeah," Simon said. "Why?"

"Well, I'm picking it up right now," the driver said.

"Why?"

"I'm picking it up and taking it to the Crime Lab."

"Oh, that's kind of weird." The pieces of the puzzle didn't fall into place for Simon until the next morning.

CHAPTER 29

At 7 P.M. on July 16, Detective Jerold White went to the only address that law enforcement had for Jeffrey Hopkins to interview him about Caylee's disappearance and Zenaida Fernandez-Gonzalez. He wasn't there. Jeff's parents, Jeffrey and Melissa, lived at that location, and said their son had not resided in the house for five years. They promised to tell Jeff that police wanted to talk to him. They asked the detective why they had received a call from Casey's phone at 5 A.M. that morning.

White visited Rico Morales at 9:30 that night. He answered all of the detective's questions without hesitation, until White asked, "If you were me, you were the police, and you'd been tasked with trying to figure out what's going on, where would you point me to look?"

Rico stammered, "If I was— From what I feel right now— I don't— I know just about as much about Casey as you probably do. Everything I thought I knew about this girl was not the truth."

"Um huh," White encouraged.

"So I feel like the person we're talking about now, and the person I knew before are two different people. I don't really feel like I know her. Apparently where she worked wasn't true. Her nanny? No one knew her. I really don't know what to think."

"Where did she tell you she worked?"

"At Universal Studios."

"She ever take you there?"

"As an event? No never took me there."

"Never got you a free pass?" White asked.

"No, we tried a few times to go to a concert or something, but it always fell through and—maybe because she didn't work there—but she talked about it a lot, to the point where I would never guess that it is not true. Like she had her boss, Tom, she had a best friend named Julia that she talked about—and it all added up. I don't know. I mean, I had no reason to question it or anything."

At 10 P.M., Amy Huizenga was at police headquarters filing a fraud report against Casey for the theft of her checkbook and the money in her account. Detective White found her there and interviewed her about the missing person case.

At his home, Christopher Stutz's cell phone rang. It was a call from the Orange County correctional facility asking if he'd accept a collect call from Casey Anthony. He hung up without answering and called his parents. They warned him not to take it. Three minutes later, the phone rang again. This time, he refused the call.

Simon Burch, manager at Johnson's Wrecker Service, woke around 6 the morning of July 17, and turned on the news. He saw George and Cindy sitting on a sofa answering a reporter's questions. It all came together in his mind. *Oh crap. Garbage bag. Dumpster. Smelly car. Oh shit.*

Simon was in his pajamas, but he didn't take time to dress. He just slipped into a pair of flip-flops and raced to the receptacle. He felt sure he could locate the bag. At work, they used black garbage bags with red drawstrings. The one from the Anthony car had been white with yellow pulls.

He looked down at the contents of the Dumpster. The last garbage pick-up had been on Monday, but there was already an amazing amount piled up in the big metal container. When he didn't see the white bag, he climbed inside. He picked through the trash expecting to spot a flash of white or buzzing flies without any trouble. But it wasn't there.

Still standing knee-deep in the filthy container, Simon called the sheriff's department and talked to someone he knew at Dispatch. Eventually, he and Detective Melich connected. He spilled out the whole story of the Anthonys picking up the car, the discovery of the bag and his early morning search. "But I can't find the garbage bag."

"Thanks, okay," the detective said. "I have it."

"What do you mean, you have it?"

"I have the garbage bag."

"How did you know about the garbage bag, and how did you get it back?"

"We came to your yard last night and your night driver let us in, and we took the garbage bag out of your Dumpster and took it away." Melich went on to explain how he got the information from George Anthony.

Another drama played out that morning in Mount Dora. Shirley Cuza was surprised when she had a 6 A.M. visitor. Cindy knocked on the door and then used a key to come inside. She called out to Shirley, who asked, "What the heck's wrong?"

"Lee's out here. Come on out. I've got something to tell you."

"Well, give me a minute," Shirley said. She left the bathroom and went into the living room, where she sat down. Cindy stood in front of her wearing a solemn expression on her face. "Who died?" Shirley asked.

"Nobody died," Cindy said. "Casey's in jail and Caylee's missing."

Goose bumps raced up Shirley's arms and across her scalp while Cindy explained how the abandoned car had led to Casey's arrest. Cindy's next stop was the nursing home. She needed to prepare her dad for the day's news, too.

Cindy called Ryan Pasley at 8:30 A.M. He hadn't watched the news yet, but he caught up with the coverage later that morning and listened to details Cindy hadn't shared—the Zenaida kidnapping story, the Jeffrey Hopkins connection and the suspicion swirling around Casey.

Cindy called Amy, too. "I'm so sorry for any hurt that happened, that Casey may have lied to you or betrayed you or anything like that. I'm very, very sorry."

"Don't worry about it," Amy reassured her. "I still believe in Casey."

Detective Pedro Rivera went to Cast Iron Tattoo, where he interviewed Sean and Jonathan Daly and Danny Colamarino. Danny told him about Casey's visit on July 15, and said, "It truly blows me away how normal she was."

In court that day, Casey, with her newly hired attorney José Baez, appeared before Orange County Judge John Jordan. He denied the motion for bail, chastising Casey: "You left your two-year-old child with a person who does not exist, in an apartment you cannot identify, and you lie to your parents about your child's whereabouts. It appears to the court you care so little for your child, you did not even report her missing until five weeks later."

The judge ordered a mental health evaluation. On the current charges, Casey faced a maximum sentence of 7 years.

At last, Casey had a place of her own—but not exactly the one she'd envisioned. Her residence was s 12.5-foot–by-7-foot cell, with a floor-to-ceiling door of Lexan, a clear glass substitute, located in Protective Custody Level One, in the high-security section of the Orange County correctional facility. It is the same area of the jail where love-crazed astronaut Lisa Nowak was once housed after she'd made headlines for assaulting a fellow astronaut's girlfriend in a parking lot in Orlando.

There was no illusion of privacy in Casey's new room. She was allowed to leave for one hour a day to take a shower, sit in the day room, make collect phone calls or select books from the library cart. She had another hour for exercise in the jail yard where the only equipment was a volleyball and a basketball. The remaining twenty-two hours a day was spent in her fishbowl cell, unless she had visitors.

Her attorney could visit her any day of the week, any time of the day or night. Family and friends had to adhere to the jail visitation schedule. When they did, they never were in the same room as Casey—they communicated via a remote video feed.

For a party girl who found the rules in her parents' house stifling, this total absence of freedom must have felt like cruel and unusual punishment.

CHAPTER 30

Detective Yuri Melich went to the Sutton Place apartment complex on July 17 and asked Tony Lazzaro and Cameron Campina if he and his detectives could look around and see if there was any evidence there to indicate that something had happened to Caylee. When Tony and Cameron agreed, Melich put three other investigators to work searching for clues while he talked with the two residents.

Cameron expressed surprise at the turn of events: "I would never expect anything like that to happen . . . it seemed like a happy and loving relationship . . . It feels like we had the rug pulled out from under us."

At 3 o'clock that afternoon, Detective Appie Wells met the Anthonys' neighbor Brian Burner at his place of work. He told the detective about the shovel Casey had borrowed from him in June. Wells followed Brian to his home on Hopespring Drive, where they met a crime-scene investigator who took the tool into custody.

After an hour-and-a-half-long interview with Brian, Wells went next door to the Anthony home and knocked on the front door. The Anthonys welcomed the detective inside. Three attorneys sat in the family room talking to Cindy—two of them represented Casey; the other was a friend who was looking out for Cindy and George's interests.

Wells explained the purpose of his visit to Cindy and the lawyers, and received her permission to examine the house and the yard. George walked out on the back porch with the detective. Wells told him about the borrowed shovel and said, "We want to examine the backyard for any evidence of freshly turned soil or any suspicious disturbed areas." George walked through the area, with Wells pointing out spots that he thought might look suspicious.

He unlocked the door to each of the three outbuildings in the yards to allow access. "My wife and I already searched through the sheds, but you're welcome to check behind us. Cindy even moved Caylee's playhouse and looked underneath it for anything suspicious."

After consulting with his supervisor, Wells called for a more thorough search, complete with cadaver dogs. K-9 Deputy Jason Forgey and his dog, Gerus, had already been put to work at the forensic bay of the Orange County Sheriff's Office on West Colonial Drive. On command, Gerus worked from the driver's-side front fender in a counter-clockwise direction, alerting Deputy Forgey at the rear passenger fender, indicating that the dog detected the odor of human decomposition in the trunk of the Pontiac.

The dog and his handler reported next to the Anthony home. They pulled up by the single-story home and walked to the wooden fence and through the gate to the backyard. After the crime-scene investigator had made thorough photographic documentation of the area, Gerus received the command and responded. Gerus zoned in on the plastic playhouse sitting on twenty-five pieces of square concrete that covered a 36-foot-square patch of ground. He did not alert at the 12-inch-wide and 5-inch-deep area of disturbed soil behind the swimming pool.

Osceola County Sheriff's deputy Kris Brewer arrived with her cadaver canine, Bones. That dog alerted in the same spot as Gerus, but also found two other areas of interest—a patch of ground near the screened patio porch and a spot to the east side of the playground area. All three areas were flagged.

The detectives moved the playhouse off of its platform

and, using hand shovels, they excavated the area of disturbed soil behind the pool, but found nothing of interest. Darkness descended on them as they worked. The investigators called off the search until the next morning. They wrapped the backyard in yellow evidence tape, planning to return the next morning at 8 A.M.

On Friday, Crime Scene Investigator Melissa Cardiello moved the 16-inch-square flat concrete blocks to examine the ground underneath. The weed barrier appeared to be undisturbed. She removed the weeds in one corner and saw that the roots had likewise not been disturbed.

At a spot marked the previous night, she found an area of wood chips. She scooped them up. The next layer was a black plastic weed barrier that had no breach in it. In three other areas, she found the same covering of mulch atop a similar barrier. Beneath one, she found three hair ties and a piece of plastic. A plant root grew through the center of the tie. None of the locations showed any signs of disturbance.

Cardiello also searched through the three sheds. In one, she found a teddy bear in a plastic bag. It was shown to Cindy Anthony, who didn't recall ever seeing it before. In addition to the outdoor search, detectives went into the home and seized electronic equipment belonging to Casey and her parents.

Investigation of the car continued in a bay at the Orange County Sheriff's Office forensic garage. They found a page of paper filled with different variations of the signatures Casey would sign if she married Tony Lazzaro and took his name. Crime Scene Investigator Gerardo Bloise collected dirt from both rear fender wells and secured it in marked petri dishes. Using an UltraLite-ALS (alternate light source), he examined the interior and exterior of the car, finding two suspected stains on the carpet in the cargo area. He recovered hairs from the trunk, as well, and removed the spare tire cover for analysis in a lab.

After photographing the stains, Crime Scene Investigator Michael Vincent used swabs and sterile water to take samples from the suspected areas. Presumptive blood tests came up negative.

CSI Bloise moved the Pontiac to the auto theft garage in order to put the vehicle on a lift. He collected dry vegetation and a leaf before returning the car to the forensics garage.

Shirley wrote an email and sent it to both her sister Mary Lou and her son Rick, giving a synopsis of the events that had led to her granddaughter's arrest:

> Even before the judge the next day, she wouldn't say truthfully where she was or is. Everything she told them and wrote in her statement proved to be a lie.

> She talked about Casey not working for two years and

> running up bills and also using Cindy's credit. She *[Cindy]* is wiped out. Now Cindy is talking bonding Casey out. So, she's as nuts as Casey is. Where does she think Casey would go, except to her house and finish stealing her blind . . . I'm really a mess over this.

One thing that often occurs in the case of a missing child, didn't happen here. Authorities did not issue an AMBER Alert, because of the length of time since Caylee had disappeared, and because the known information did not meet the requirements of the established criteria.

CHAPTER 31

The afternoon of July 18, George and Cindy roamed around their house and yard trying to think of any little thing that could have happened to their granddaughter. "You know, George," Cindy said, "I hope she didn't—something happened—she didn't panic. Caylee coulda got outside real quick." They both thought back to the day that Cindy had come home and found the pool ladder propped beside the pool.

That day, Attorney Baez attacked the sheriff's office, saying, "police really haven't been looking for Gonzalez, they've been digging in the grandparents' backyard."

Law enforcement was in fact looking for the missing little girl by running down leads—forty of them had already been received by the end of Friday, and they kept coming in by phone, fax and email in Orange County as well as on the hotline at the National Center for Missing & Exploited Children. Some were actual sightings, sending officers out to investigate and verify or eliminate. One person reported seeing Caylee at Chuck E. Cheese's on the day of her mother's arrest. On Thursday, someone else thought they'd seen her in the lobby of a Bank of America branch.

Throughout the investigation, a large number of tips came from people whose knowledge was indirect—psychics from around the world, people who'd had dreams of Caylee and those who claimed they'd received a special message from the Lord. The leads were all over the place.

Conflicting visions abounded. Caylee was covered with leaves, next to a stream, or in a barn, or buried in a field full of telephone poles, in the Anthony backyard, in a playground, or in a landfill. One believed that Caylee was in Lucedale, Mississippi, with the KKK, who'd paid for her because they use children in their cult rituals.

Another, claiming that she'd gotten all of her information from Caylee's great-great-great-grandmother, had a story about a person finding Caylee on a bus and turning her over to Child Protective Services—but Caylee was now dressed as a boy and going by the name "Robert." This caller explained the stench in the Anthony car by saying that Caylee had bought a cat and forgotten it in the trunk of the car. Someone else thought it was vital for the police to know that Caylee's Care Bears lunch pail was filled with "Dingos and M&M's" and stashed inside of a cupboard in a house on Centennial Drive.

Kid Finders Network, an organization in West Palm Beach that helped families in searches for missing kids, donated fliers and began building a mobile billboard detailing Caylee's disappearance, scheduled to hit the roads of Orlando the next week.

On Saturday, July 19, two dozen family members, friends and volunteers gathered at the Publix grocery store at Lake Underhill Road and Chickasaw Trail. They set up a tent, marked car windows with urgent messages and sallied forth to distribute fliers in the area.

Gentiva employees—Nilsa, Charles, Deborah and Debbie—stopped by the Anthony home to pick up fliers. Cindy no longer appeared angry. She seemed calm, focused and determined. Before they left, Jesse Grund arrived. Cindy threw her arms around his neck and said, "We've got to bring this little girl home. We've got to find her."

The team from Gentiva canvassed Tony's apartment complex, handing out fliers. Other groups distributed them at the University of Central Florida in the Conway area, in downtown Orlando, at large retailers such as Wal-Mart and Target, and at major intersections.

George made arrangements for more posters to be picked up at Staples downtown. A family member needed to run that errand, and Cindy volunteered. She stopped by the tent at Publix first. There, she spotted Annie Downing writing on car windows, and thought it would be a good opportunity to take her aside and ask her about what she knew. "Annie, you wanna go with me to Staples?"

During the ride to the office supply store, Cindy found comfort chatting with one of Casey's friends. She brought up her desire to gather up a bunch of Casey's friends and try together to create a timeline of Casey's movements in recent days. Annie thought that was a good idea.

After dropping Annie off at the Publix tent, Cindy returned home, where Jesse and Lee sat at opposite ends of the dining room table working on the logistics of the search for Caylee. "Annie and I just had a really great talk. I think it'd be helpful if we get all of Casey's friends together and kind of do a timeline over the last month and see where her head was at and what was going on."

"Mrs. Anthony, let me volunteer to be in charge of that timeline," Jesse offered.

"Well, Jesse, a lot of these friends I'm gonna be talking to, you don't know. And I'd kind of like to talk to her friends first. Certainly, you can interject your stuff in the timeline."

"I really want to participate," Jesse said.

"Fine," said Cindy, pulling out a pad of paper and a pen. She took notes as Jesse told her all he could remember. At this time, Jesse thought he recalled talking to Casey on the telephone the last week of June—more than a week after anyone had seen Caylee. He thought he'd heard Casey tell Caylee to get off the table during that conversation. He later told police that he believed he was confused about the date of the call.

On Sunday, July 20, Christopher Stutz, Amy Huizenga, Troy Brown, Rico Morales, Jesse Grund and other friends gathered at the Anthony home to provide information to Cindy and each other. They vented their frustrations and concerns about the current situation and plotted out events on calendars.

While they worked, George went next door to Brian Burner's house. When Brian answered the door, George handed him a flier and told him that they were having a vigil for Caylee on Sunday evening. "You're the one that turned in the shovel, right?"

"Yeah, I turned in the shovel," Brian said, wondering why he'd even asked, since it had already been all over the news.

"Well, we're trying to set up our own timeline, and want to know when you gave her the shovel."

"I think it was the week of the sixteenth, but I'm not sure," Brian said.

"I'm sorry we haven't been able to come over and speak to you about what's going on, but everything has been crazy."

Brian assured George that he understood and said, "I didn't turn in the shovel to make it like something bad had happened in your yard."

Kiomarie Cruz called Yuri Melich at 8:30 that night to tell him about the woods where she and Casey used to hang out in middle school. An hour later, the two met at Hidden Oaks Elementary School and walked back to the wooded area, just blocks from the Anthony home. Kiomarie was the first to point to this location—but she would not be the last. Those woods would haunt the investigation for months.

Sixty people showed up in the Anthonys' front yard for the first Caylee vigil on July 20. They prayed together and shared comforting thoughts with the family. José Baez stepped up to speak to the group in defense of his client. "I'd like to make it clear that my client, Casey Anthony, at no time refused to speak with law enforcement.

A lot has been reported about this matter and that I am in some way standing in her way. I'd like to . . . direct everybody's attention to the arrest report, which clearly states that the police were called out on the fifteenth of this month, and she spoke with them immediately on that day, and then on the following day, practically the entire day she spent with law enforcement. Only upon being arrested and might be detained that she invoked her right to counsel, as I think anyone would do in this country. We are focused on trying to find Caylee."

Cindy Anthony appeared on the *Today* show on the morning of July 21. She asked that police release her daughter so she could help investigators. Cindy also said that Casey had gotten a mysterious telephone call from Caylee last Tuesday, July 15.

Ann Curry asked, "Cindy, if you could speak to your daughter, what would you say to her?"

"My first words probably be: 'I forgive you.' I have not said that to her, although I told her that I love her and that I support her."

"Why would you say, 'I forgive you'? Forgive her for what?"

"For not telling me sooner, for not telling the police sooner. You can't, you can't understand, someone can't come to grips until they're forgiven. So she's probably not going to be able to tell me everything until I can forgive her," Cindy explained.

"Well, what could possibly explain why it took her five weeks to report her missing daughter, Cindy? You know her."

"I have no idea. I know her, and I know Casey knows. I know Casey doesn't know where they're at right at the moment, but I don't know anything else right now, because I can't speak to my daughter, and we're trying to get that changed very quickly. I'd like to make a plea to the prosecutor and the judge to let her out so we can all talk to her."

* * *

In the Orange County Sheriff's Office forensics garage, Dr. Michael Sigman collected two separate air samples from the Pontiac Sunfire. He used a large gas-tight syringe to extract them. He placed each one in a separate Tedlar polymer bag, a sealed clear package designed to capture and hold gas vapors and air samples. He prepared the bags for shipment—one to the Oak Ridge National Laboratory in Tennessee, the other to the National Center for Forensic Science.

On Tuesday, he collected an additional sample using an SPME filter—a piece of equipment widely used in research laboratories studying odor pollution from pig and poultry farms. The smell from the garbage bag recovered from the impound lot was studied, but no trace of decomposition odor was detected in the trash or the bag itself.

Cindy clung to the rotten pizza story as an explanation for the wretched stench emanating from the car.

CHAPTER 32

Casey, with José Baez by her side, appeared in Circuit Court Judge Stan Strickland's court for a bond hearing on July 22. Casey appeared calm, undisturbed by the drama swirling around her. Baez, with his slicked-back black hair and expensive suit, seemed confident and ready to do battle.

Assistant State Attorney Linda Drane-Burdick called Detective Yuri Melich to the stand. He testified that the forensic specialists "found hair samples in the trunk of the car that are a similar color to that of Caylee. They also set a stain inside the trunk of the car that came up under black light that's questionable, and we need to process. They also found some dirt inside the trunk of the car that needs to be processed. I actually went into the car to smell what the smell smelled like. Briefly, just before I came into the job, I was a homicide detective for two years with Lawrence County Sheriff's Office. And in my experience, the smell that I smelled inside the car was the smell of decomposition."

"Right now, what we are dealing with is that you have a child who is missing for a lengthy period of time . . ." Drane-Burdick began.

"Yes," the detective agreed.

"That wasn't reported by the mother for several weeks . . ."

"Correct."

"That there was an abandoned car that contained evidence of human decomposition."

"Correct."

"Is Casey Anthony a suspect, a possible— I don't wanna misstate this. The evidence of human decomposition would lead you to believe, would it not, that there is a possibility that this child is no longer alive?"

"Yes, that can be concluded," Melich nodded.

"All right. And is Ms. Anthony a suspect in that circumstance?"

"I wouldn't use the word 'suspect' I would use the word 'person of interest.'"

Jason Forgey, K9 Deputy with the Orange County Sheriff's Office, stepped up next to testify about his trained cadaver dog, a German Shepherd named Gerus, responding to the odor in the car. "He jumped up into the trunk with front claws, stuck his head in, backed up, did the eye contact and moved to the right rear passenger side, rear fender/trunk–taillight area and gave me a fine train of alert."

"What's that mean?" Drane-Burdick asked.

"He alerted to the odor of human decomposition."

"In the trunk of that car?"

"Yes, ma'am."

When cross-examined by the defense, all the witnesses with the Orange County Sheriff's Office insisted they were still looking for the girl alive, and urged anyone with information to step forward. As of this date, they had received more than one hundred tips and were investigating every credible lead. The detectives told Baez that they had not been able to find the baby-sitter or prove that she even existed.

Linda Drane-Burdick turned to the judge. "The risk of her flight if she is released on some low bond increases exponentially, especially now that she's heard this additional evidence, and knows that she is their person of interest."

Cindy Anthony testified for the defense, acknowledging that her daughter had lied before, but said that Casey was a caring mom. Cindy said she would sell her home to free her daughter, and that she believed Caylee was alive. "I know Casey as a person. I know what she is as a mother, and I know there's only one or two reasons why Casey would be withholding something about Caylee. I believe that it's something that someone is holding over her, and threatening her in some way."

Cindy said that despite her statement that she had not seen her granddaughter since June 9, she now remembers taking Caylee to the nursing home to visit her great-grandfather on Father's Day, June 15. She also remembered looking in on her when she was getting ready for bed that night.

She described her daughter as her best friend, second only to her husband. She couldn't verify whether Casey had had a steady job since Caylee's birth. She and George had provided everything for Casey and Caylee, including food, shelter and the car. "Casey's lied to me in the past," she admitted, but added that either she or her son Lee can get to the "bottom of the truth" if they could talk to her outside of the jail.

Baez asked Cindy questions about Casey's behavior as a mother. "She gets down on Caylee's level," Cindy said. "If Caylee's sitting down on the floor, she'll go down on the floor. Or if there's a table or countertop in the kitchen and we need to talk to Caylee, she sets her up there. This is something Casey's been adamant about, to pick Caylee up and put her on the counter, look her in the eye and say, 'Caylee, look at Mommy.' She's always done that, instead of intimidating and looking down and scolding her. Casey doesn't yell at Caylee, she talks to Caylee."

Baez asked, "Who taught her to discipline a child that way?"

"No one taught her. She probably learned by example."

"Whose example?"

"Probably mine and my husband's. She stated that she was afraid to tell the police. She told them that."

"Have the police questioned you about what kind of mother she is?"

"No, not until last night."

"Last night, they questioned you?"

"Last night."

"That was the first time they asked you what kind of mother your . . ."

"First time they asked me questions like did I ever see bruises or anything like that. The first time was last night. Oh, my gosh, I was in shock, the initial time. I mean, I was in shock because Caylee was missing. At that very moment, I didn't know what to do, and I was bombarded with police officers. And then, when I had my first time alone with Casey, our focus primarily was to tell all of her friends to get the word out. And that's been what I've been trying to do ever since."

When the prosecutor cross-examined Cindy about the smell in the car, she said, "There was a bag of pizza for—what?—twelve days in the back of the car, full of maggots. Stunk so bad. Do you know how hot it's been? That smell was terrible."

Lee Anthony, Casey's older brother, took the stand, too, saying that on July 15, before the police had arrived at the family home, he'd pleaded with Casey to tell him where Caylee was. He said that was when she'd broken down in tears and said she hadn't seen her daughter in thirty-one days.

Casey shed a few tears in court that day while her family members testified, but reverted to her disinterested facial expression when they stepped down.

Baez argued to the judge that a bond of $10,000 would be appropriate. He said that the family can't pay a high bond and that Casey Anthony had the right to freedom while facing lesser charges. He requested that the judge order a sketch artist to draw a depiction of the baby-sitter, Zenaida Fernandez-Gonzalez, who may have had ties to

Miami, Bradenton or Gainesville in Florida, or to Brooklyn, New York, or Charlotte, North Carolina.

But Judge Strickland was not impressed with the integrity of Baez's client. He said that he doubted Casey's alleged intention of aiding investigators and finding Caylee. The testimony heard in court today will "keep me up tonight," he said. "I just heard some fairly compelling evidence as to a body decomposing." He described Casey's past conduct as "strange and difficult to describe."

He added, "Not a bit of useful information has been provided by Ms. Anthony as to the whereabouts of her daughter. And I would add that the truth and Ms. Anthony are strangers."

Nonetheless, he set Casey's bond at $500,000, saying the law did not allow him to hold her without bail. He explained that he'd set the bail at an amount higher than the current charges would indicate after hearing credible evidence of human decomposition found in Casey's car. If released, he recommended electronic monitoring of the accused.

The $500,000 amount required to bail Casey out of the county jail meant that the person posting it was required to pay 10 percent of the bond amount, or $50,000, in cash and possess sufficient collateral to back the remaining balance.

Before Casey was led out of the courtroom, she turned and looked back at her family. Cindy yelled, "Casey, we love you!" Her daughter nodded and sobbed out loud before being led away in chains.

At a news conference after the bond hearing, José Baez expressed indignation at Judge Strickland's ruling. "This is not a capital case, and if it were, they certainly would file it if they had evidence to. There is circumstantial evidence of a possible homicide, I will give them that. But circumstantial evidence has not made them confident enough to charge her with any homicide or kidnapping or any capital offense." He said that Casey was "willing to cooperate fully" with law enforcement, but her assistance should be used to help find Caylee and not to prosecute his client.

When asked why his client had lied to detectives, Baez said, "I am aware and have to save that for her defense. I would love to disclose the reasons, and I'm sure she would, but it certainly creates a disadvantage."

Investigators spent time with the media, too, telling them that they wanted Casey to remain in jail. They also attempted to quash rumors by insisting that Casey's parents were not suspects. Ron Stucker, chief of the Criminal Investigation Division of the Orange County Sheriff's Office, said that the Florida Department of Law Enforcement and the FBI were helping with the investigation. The FBI was doing lab work and making it a priority, as well as working on out-of-state leads. The state agency was following up leads in Florida and also offering lab assistance for processing evidence.

He described the reliability of the cadaver dogs: "In very layman's terms, they can seek out the scent of human decomposition. And from what I understand, they can actually distinguish the difference between human decomposition and animal decomposition."

That night, Greta Van Susteren of Fox News interviewed forensic pathologist Dr. Michael Baden, who said "decomposition of flesh, human flesh, a human body, is different than old pizza and old kitchen garbage. One could confuse a human decaying body odor with a large animal, like a deer or even a big dog, but not with the pizza.

"Cadaver dogs, in particular, are trained to smell the gases that are produced by a decomposing body. So the fact that the cadaver dogs alerted on the car is certainly something to be investigated. Cadaver dogs can be wrong, but they won't alert on pizza. They could alert on a dead mouse on the ground, for example. But there's a uniqueness to the chemicals that are produced as the body deteriorates after a few days."

"If you set a person who's died in a trunk, for instance,

you'd not have the odor, I assume, for some period of time," Van Susteren replied. "And then you would have to, at least, have the body remain there in order for the odor to seep into the materials in the car?"

"No," Baden said. "Depending on the temperature—the higher the temperature, the more smell—within twenty-four hours, one could get considerable decomposition in hot weather. And then the fluids—the decomposition fluids—which seep into the car, they would be there long after the body is removed. And, Greta, it's interesting that the detective, homicide detective, said he saw hairs in the vehicle that looked like, to his naked eye, they could belong to Caylee. And from here, a dead person's hair is very different under the microscope, from hair from a live person. So the crime lab, by looking at that hair, should be able to tell by DNA whether it belongs to Caylee, should be able to tell who the dad is from the DNA, and should also be able to tell if the baby was alive or dead when she was deposited in the vehicle."

In the same show, Baez spoke of another sighting of Caylee—called in directly to Cindy Anthony. "Someone says that they were ninety-nine percent sure that they spotted her at the airport boarding a flight to Atlanta on July second. We don't know what their final destination was. One of the things that seems very encouraging was, they asked her for her name, and she answered her name, and the way she answered her name is exactly as the family knows she would answer her name, but using both her first, middle and last name, and the way she pronounces her last name. She can't say it very well. She says, 'Ant-nee,' and that's one of the things that makes the family very encouraged at this point."

But detectives followed up the lead and discovered a serious flaw in the airport sighting. The same Orlando airport video cameras that had had no difficulty tracking Lisa Nowak's movements in 2006 picked up no sign of Caylee's presence. And at the Hartsfield-Jackson International Airport in Atlanta, where there are even more cameras—almost 400 in all—not one of them picked up her arrival there.

The seemingly related sighting of Caylee at a restaurant in northern Georgia led nowhere, either. White County police interviewed staff and patrons to no avail. No one remembered ever seeing Caylee.

CHAPTER 33

In an interview at the nursing home on July 22, Shirley Cuza shared her insight about her daughter Cindy's family with investigators. When questioned, she also touched on the other big tragedy in her life—her husband Alex's disabling stroke.

"Is there anything your husband might know that you don't? Or are you always with him any time Cindy was here?"

"He can't even remember his aide's name," she said. "If I ask him, 'Who gave you a bath last night?' he doesn't know . . . So, now, he can remember World War II and anything up to before his stroke . . . but he can't . . . tell you what he had for supper last night."

"So he wouldn't be able to tell us if he's seen Caylee? He wouldn't be able to . . . tell us if he's seen Caylee since Father's Day?"

"Oh, I know he hasn't seen her since Father's Day. Now whether he can tell you anything about Father's Day, I don't know."

Detectives interviewed Jesse Grund, Amy Huizenga and Tony Lazzaro on July 23. Tony granted law enforcement permission to set up electronic surveillance on his cell phone. He agreed, as well, to a thorough inspection of his Jeep. In the forensics garage, they searched for signs of blood using a special light, conducting presumptive blood tests on suspicious stains and by spraying the interior of the doors with Blue Star. All results were negative.

The investigation was only a week old, but already Cindy had lost patience with Detective Melich. She left a message on Sergeant John Allen's phone just before 8:30 on the morning of July 23.

"I just had a thought. There's one photo of Caylee . . . in her little blue dress, smiling, and there's some reddish curtains in the background . . . I've been told over and over again, it's Zanny's apartment . . . I'm just wondering if . . . you guys have investigated that or asked any of her friends—if you're looking into that angle. If you don't have any idea, I'm thinking that maybe if the media show this picture and say not just 'Have you seen me?' but 'Do you recognize this room?'

". . . I heard on the radio you guys have contacted the FBI. If that's true, I think this is a very key picture. I think it's something we should be looking at. So if you don't feel comfortable talking to me, please call my son Lee. I know you guys think I'm not cooperating, but you know why I was upset with Yuri yesterday.

"I told you guys that I could clear up that matter between the fifteenth and the eighth with a simple phone call, and I was not afforded that opportunity until early yesterday morning when my mother woke up and I was able to speak with her. And she did confirm it was the fifteenth from an email that her and my aunt had done.

"And he threatened me, sir, with sending a squad car and making a big deal about it . . . I've been working very carefully to protect my parents. They are very, very ill. I don't want them getting stressed out like I am—they already are.

"I'm very sorry if you think I am not cooperating . . . I think I have more . . . than anyone else in this investigation."

* * *

That day, assorted investigators and cadaver dogs descended on a large children's playground surrounded by chain-link fence. The surface of the area consisted of dirt, grass and mulch. In the center, an area of ground showed signs of disturbance as if someone had been digging there.

Gerus sniffed out the suspicious patch, but showed no interest in it. Bones came in for a secondary search, finding nothing to merit an alert. The forensic techs probed and excavated the ground, uncovering a small yellow bucket with the remains of a tiny dead animal inside.

William Rivera, founder of the Never Lose Hope Foundation of Orlando, got the idea of using an automatic telephone system through his telemarketing firm to help in the search for missing children. George Anthony took advantage of the set-up, sending a message about his granddaughter to hundreds of thousands of people in the Central Florida counties of Orange, Seminole, Lake, Osceola and Volusia: "Please help my family to bring her home for her third birthday."

Rivera planned more calls for Thursday, July 24. All the resulting tips, he said, would be turned over to the investigators in the Orange County Sheriff's Office.

Tony Lazzaro met detectives behind Target, where they wired him for sound. He then drove to Subway at the corner of Goldenrod Road and University Boulevard to meet with Lee Anthony. He turned on the radio while he waited for Lee to arrive. Detectives called and asked him to turn it off.

They exchanged pleasantries as Lee slid into Tony's Jeep. Then Lee griped about the release of video of jail visits and the audiotapes of phone conversations, as well as the media chasing him. He told Tony about a highway high-speed escape from pursuers that had caused him to take extra precaution the next time he went to the jail to visit Casey. "I parked two roads over behind these construction guys. I told them what was up and said I'd be back in an hour. And they said, 'I got you.' So, I snuck in   like seriously snuck in—I was hugging the wall, behind the bushes, I had my hat down like this," he said, pulling down his cap over his eyes.

After visitation, he said, he slipped out the side door, thinking he would avoid the media. But there was a reporter and a camera guy, so he took off running.

"I've been wanting to reach out to you since that night," Lee said. "We're not any closer than we were on the fifteenth."

"She's not saying anything else?" Tony asked.

"No. Well, here's the problem. Because I haven't been able to talk to her until this last Saturday," he said, "I'm worried that her attorney is not giving her everything. I mean, he's supposed to protect her." He thought that she wanted to reach out, but her attorney was blocking it.

"I am concerned that the police are not looking at Caylee as a missing person, but trying to build a case against my sister for something else—for a homicide or whatever—and I'm really worried about that. It's not Casey's nature. It's not something she would do—not something she would knowingly do. I don't know if there was ever an accident or what the situation is. You know what I mean?" Lee asked.

When Tony indicated his understanding, Lee continued, "But I'm really worried that they put innocent people away all the time. You know what I mean? And I just feel like I need to be doing more to make sure that doesn't happen to my sister—and when that happens, that people don't stop trying to help us find Caylee."

Lee explained that his parents wanted to meet someone close to the case every two days to talk about their ideas and get updated on what was occurring in the search for Caylee. Yuri Melich's response to that request, Lee said, was that every hour spent talking to the family was an hour they weren't able to follow up leads.

He then asked Tony about his impression of Jesse.

"He seemed all right. He was a quiet guy.

". . . I'm just worried about him in a way. Some of the stuff that he tells me, some of the stuff he doesn't tell me . . . kind of rubs me the wrong way, you know. Like, he used to be engaged to my sister for over a year and, like, for a while there, my sister led us to believe he was the father of Caylee. So there's a lot of history there. And, she's always told my parents, 'Yeah, Jesse's still trying to get with me, but I'm not gonna let that happen.' And Jesse tells his parents, 'Casey's still trying to get with me, and I'm not letting it happen.' When in reality, they're still seeing each other on a semi-regular basis at least a couple of times a month, like it's not anything new."

"It's like a recurring thing that they do?"

"Absolutely. Absolutely. They don't ever really get serious but . . . it seems like he's always the one that's right at the start or right at the end of when a relationship would start or end. He's in the picture there. It's almost like, for whatever reason, Casey will see Jesse." Lee talked about Rico and Jesse both being suspects in the disappearance of Caylee, and his concerns about Casey. He said that he went through Casey's cell phone records and discovered that when she'd said she was staking out the nanny's apartment, there were phone calls to a pizza place after midnight. "But if Casey's telling me she's staking out and she's not staking out— She's lying to me like that."

Tony asked, "Does she really like to lie a lot?"

"My sister, since middle school and high school, she's been— If she's deceitful, she's doing it for— You know, I can't even say that. I'm trying to think: Does she really do it just to better herself, or does she say a white lie just to do it? I'm really trying to think now. 'Cause sometimes it seems she lies just to lie . . . I want to figure out what Casey I'm dealing with, you know. I know there's the Casey that would—that doesn't care about anyone but herself and her daughter. And then there's the Casey that will put her daughter in front of everybody else. And that's the Casey I'm trying to get to open up to me, but, like, I don't know."

Lee ran into the Subway to use the restroom. While he was gone, Tony talked to detectives on his cell and got instructions on where to direct the conversation. "I've got to ask you a question," Tony said. "She talked as if everyone knew this nanny. Have you talked to her?"

"That's the key here. My sister has used 'Yes, she's with the nanny,' or 'Yes, she's with the sitter.' I had never heard my sister say the word 'Zanny' or 'Zenaida' before. Now, that doesn't necessarily mean anything, because I also haven't been living at home for maybe the past three years. You know what I mean, around the time Caylee was born? So I'm not an expert when it comes to that."

Lee brought up the abrupt change in Casey's friends. Lee said that at Casey's birthday party in March, all the attendees were girls. Tony said that he didn't think that Casey had any girlfriends—that all her friends were guys. Then Lee moved to her drug use, saying that he didn't think she'd even smoked pot until she started dating Rico.

Tony said that he didn't think she used anything more serious than pot, but "I don't know if I can believe what Casey tells me."

"Whatever she's telling you about drugs, I think you can take it on face value," said Lee. But he couldn't guarantee the honesty of anything else she said.

CHAPTER 34

Over the next two days, detectives continued to interview Casey's friends, talking to Brittany Schrieber, Rico Morales, Troy Brown and Jeffrey Hopkins. Jeff told officers that the last time he'd seen Casey was a couple of weeks ago at Miller's Ale House at Waterford Lakes. "She was with some other people I recognized from high school. About five or six other guys. She was the only female there." He said it had been at least a year since he'd seen her before that last encounter.

They asked when he'd last seen Caylee. "I don't think I've seen her baby besides in pictures, actually."

"You never met the little girl?"

"No, I don't think I've ever come in contact with the little girl." He also told them that he did not have a son named Zack—he actually had no children.

Cindy met again with a group of Casey's friends, searching desperately for answers that pointed to anyone other than her daughter. Patrick Bourgeois, an acquaintance from high school, was Casey's first visitor when he came to the jail on July 24. He wanted to let her know that he and others from high school were behind her, and would help her in any way they could.

Initially, Casey did not recognize him, and blew him off with a short, uncommunicative exchange. Later she told family members that she'd really appreciated his visit.

The next day, Casey got more visitors—the first visits from Cindy, George and Lee. All their meetings were by video feed, without any face-to-face contact through a screen or a Plexiglas divider. Visitors sat in a different room—a telephone connection provided the audio and the images were relayed on a video monitor.

Lee visited first. He focused on his own investigation in the search for Caylee. He suggested that Casey needed to communicate by letter since everything was recorded. He explained to her that José Baez was not obligated to follow her wishes regarding communication with family or with law enforcement if he believed it was not in her best interest. "I have nothing against him, but you need to know that if you reach out through him, he may not be giving us the same information. He's told us his number-one focus is you, that his secondary focus is Caylee. The truth is—it's a business. The truth is, the most important thing is himself. Then you. Then Caylee."

Lee continued, "My first focus is Caylee. My second focus is you. My third focus is Mom, then Dad, then me . . . I need you to tell me if my focus should be anything different from that—if any of my priorities should be in different order or if anyone else should be in that."

"No," Casey said. "I think your priorities are where they should be, and that's exactly where mine are, so, honestly, I'll sit here as long as I have to. My only concern is Caylee."

He told her that José Baez had not been returning phone calls from the investigators. Lee encouraged her to reach out to law enforcement to correct any mistakes she'd made in her original statement. Casey, however, did not want to speak to them. She wanted to put it in writing so they could not misconstrue what she said. Lee agreed with her and told her to send it by regular mail and to also send a copy to him, and one to her lawyer. When he asked how she'd chosen Baez for her attorney, she explained that another inmate had recommended Baez, and four others had seconded that suggestion.

Lee said, "I need to know who I can trust out here. I'm going to read you some names and give you the opportunity to respond if you want. If I can trust them, don't say anything."

Casey laughed and Lee started his list. "Myself."

There was no response from Casey and Lee realized his set-up wasn't working. "Well, tip me off somehow."

"Yeah," she said with a smile.

Lee listed names one-by-one for Casey's response. She told him he could trust Amy, Ryan, Mom and Dad, but shouldn't even bother with Annie, Melina, Jesse or Jeffrey. She said that she hadn't known Will long enough to be certain, and that Lee would have to decide about Rico on his own. As for Tony, she said, "I'd like to say yes. But I'm kind of on the fence about that one, unfortunately." She complained that he hadn't even attempted to visit her.

When Lee asked where he should start in finding Caylee—should he focus on searching, following tips or talking to people?—Casey said, "Check locally, Lee. In all honesty, places that are familiar to us, our family. Ask Mom for specific places I've mentioned when we've spoke over the last period of time, the last few weeks." Lee asked her if she'd received any letters from him or from her mom. When Casey said she had not, Lee said that they had been writing since July 16 and giving the letters to José, but apparently, he was not passing them along.

Casey hinted that there were clues to the mystery of what happened to Caylee in the passwords for her MySpace and Facebook pages, and said there were a lot of answers in the cell phone that she'd lost. It was all vague, but Lee dutifully took notes. He asked what she wanted him to do.

"If you can speak to the media, directly yourself, coming from me, my concern is Caylee, that's all I want. No one has once said anything for me, voiced that I love my daughter, that I want her safety, that she and my family are my only concern." Casey paused to allow her brother to catch up on his note-taking. Tears glistened in her eyes, she sniffled and her face reddened. "All I want is to see her again," she continued. "To see her laugh, to see her smile and to just be with our family. Nothing else matters to me at this point."

"Understand that we all feel this way—every one of us. Okay?"

"I know, but again, they've been hearing that from you, from her uncle, her grandparents, but not from," Casey paused, sighed and exhaled, "her mother."

George and Cindy made their first visit of the day at 9 A.M. Casey spoke first to her mother, giving her details about Zanny's family and geographical connections. Cindy handed the phone over to George, who said, "Hey, gorgeous, how you doing?"

"I look like hell," she sobbed.

"You really need to keep your spirit high through all of this," her father urged.

"I have. I've not really been crying. I read books and do other things to keep my mind off of stuff."

"You know I want to reach out and hug you—give you the big Papa Joe hug."

Casey sniffled and wiped her eyes.

"You know we gotta get that little girl back. Any way we can, and we're doing everything we can." When her father asked her about the cities she may have visited with Caylee, Casey admitted that the last time she'd been to Jacksonville was in March. The only time she'd left town, she said, was on a day trip to Cocoa Beach in May.

Cindy got back on the line and said, "Listen, I'm in front of the cameras all the time. What message do you want me to give to Zanny and Caylee?"

"Tell Zanny that she needs to return Caylee."

"What do you think her reasons are?" Cindy asked.

"Mom, I don't know."

"Okay."

"I forgive her. My only concern is that Caylee comes back to us and that she's happy and that she's okay."

"What do you want me to tell Caylee?"

Casey's voice strained and shot up an octave as she answered, "That Mommy loves her very much. And that she's the most important thing in this entire world to me. And to be brave." Casey sniffled and sighed as she wiped her eyes and her nose.

"Anything else?"

"Just that I love her. I truly, truly love that little girl, and miss her so much. God, I really miss you guys."

Cindy choked on tears as she said, "We miss you, too."

Casey talked about her agreement with Lee to write letters. When Cindy asked if she was protecting someone, Casey said, "I'm protecting my family, yes, but not from anything I've done."

"Is someone threatening us?"

Casey bent her hand forward and wiped her eyes with the back of her wrist as she sniffled.

"Is someone threatening us?" Cindy repeated.

"Mom, just leave it at that, please. For right now, just leave it at that."

"Okay. I trust you. Just know you don't have to protect this family. This family is tough. We've been through a lot in the last week-and-a-half. We're pretty darned strong. We almost lost it a few times, but we're stronger now than we've ever been. So don't protect Mom, or Dad, or Lee. We have to protect Caylee . . . I've got a question for you: How come you never had a chance to get the car? It doesn't make sense."

"Mom," she said, outlining the syllable with exasperation. "Because this is recorded, they are going to see things and they are going to misconstrue. Like I said, there are things I need to directly say to each of you."

"Okay. I trust that . . . Has someone else been in our house?"

"I don't know, Mom, possibly. A long time ago, she had a key," Casey said, referring to Zenaida.

"How about Jesse? He's been real close. Is there anything you want me to say to Jesse?"

"I would like Jesse to stay as far away from you guys

as possible. I'm saying that wholeheartedly and as calmly as possible . . . In my gut, I don't know if I can trust him."

"I've had that feeling all along," Cindy agreed. "We've got one minute. What do you want to say to us?"

"That I love you and I miss you. You guys stay as strong as possible."

"We are, Casey. Our whole life is turned upside down looking for this little girl."

"I know. Trust me, if I could be out there with you, I would be in a heartbeat."

"We're going to see her little face again," Cindy reassured her.

"I pray to God every day that we do."

At 2 P.M. Casey's parents were back. Casey's morning tears were replaced by subtle traces of anger whenever she felt challenged by her mother.

"I have to ask: Did Caylee ever stay at Tony's?" Cindy asked.

"No."

"Are you sure?"

"Positive. We'd hung out over there, but she never stayed, no."

"Tony admitted to Lee that there's drugs in his home," Cindy said. "Could this be related to anything like that?"

"No. It's not."

In a conciliatory tone, Cindy said, "Just had to ask, sweetheart."

"No. His roommates smoke weed. But no."

Cindy told her that although she was getting a few nasty calls, most callers were sympathetic and supportive. "Everybody that knows you are saying that you're the mom of the group. You're the one that always takes care of everybody else."

"That's how it's always been. That's the truth."

"I know. 'Cause you're a lot like me."

"I'm a lot like you—you're exactly right. And that's what people have said. Like, you know, 'Your mom's a real spitfire.' People have been talking you up like crazy. 'I wouldn't piss her off.' 'No, you wouldn't.' They would respect you more than anyone else," Casey said.

"All I'm trying to do is find Caylee for both of us . . ."

"Oh, I know."

"For all of us, and I'll do whatever it takes."

"I feel the exact same way," Casey assured her. "It's exactly what I've been saying. I don't care what I have to do. When I told them I would lie, I would steal—I would do anything, by any means, to get her back. That's exactly how I feel. That's the truth."

"Casey, we have to find her before her third birthday. That's coming up fast."

"Mom, I know—we have a couple weeks."

"I don't want to wait another minute. Let alone . . ."

Casey cut her off. "I don't want to wait another minute. I want her to be found whether I'm still stuck in here or not. I don't care."

"I think once she's found, then you can tell everyone what you know and you'll be released. Don't you think?"

"Potentially. I don't know. Yuri has it set in his mind that I've done something."

"Well, he thinks you guys did something to Caylee," Cindy said.

When her dad got on the line and told her that he missed her, wanted to take her pain away and wished he could've been a better dad and a better granddad, Casey's tears flowed.

"You've been a great dad and the best grandfather. Don't for a second think otherwise. You and Mom have been the best grandparents. Caylee is so lucky to have both of you. I can't even put into words how glad I am that she's had both of you, and that she still has both of you," she said in a strained voice.

Her mother returned to the phone and said, "We never really got a full description of Zanny. We know she's got brown curly hair."

"It's long—about shoulder length—she wears it

straight." Casey described Zanny. "It's curly, but she also wears it straight, that's what I'm telling you, it's called a straightener, remember? She's the one that gave me my straightener." She elaborated on the baby-sitter whom everyone involved with Casey had yet to meet. Zanny, she said, was 5'6" or 5'7", 140 pounds, brown eyes and no tattoos that she'd seen, even when Zanny was in a bathing suit. She added that her mother's name was Gloria, her stepdad, who'd legally adopted her, was Victor, and her older sister was Samantha, a student at the University of Central Florida. She gave the names of Zanny's roommates, Raquel Farrell and Jennifer Rosa, and provided employment history for both of them.

When Casey complained that detectives had never created a composite drawing and never shown her a photograph of the Zenaida who lived in Kissimmee, Cindy said, "They told us you couldn't pick her out in a line-up."

"They're full of shit."

George asked Casey if she would be willing to talk to the FBI or anyone in law enforcement. She assured her father that she would talk to anyone they sent to her. She did say, though, that she would not be comfortable talking to Detective Melich or Sergeant Allen, but would be willing to talk to Appie Wells. She said she didn't care if she talked to him one-on-one or if the attorney were present.

As they wrapped up the conversation, Cindy asked, "What's your gut telling you right now?"

"My gut is telling me that she's okay."

"And your gut's telling you that she's close or she's hiding?"

"She's not far. I know in my heart she's not far. I can feel it."

CHAPTER 35

Over the weekend, Lee emailed Melich the detailed description of Zanny and other details from the conversations he and his parents had had with Casey at the jail. Law enforcement, however, was convinced that Zenaida did not exist.

George and Cindy prepared for the second Caylee vigil on Sunday, July 27. They planned to hold one every Sunday night until Caylee came home. That afternoon, Richard Grund called George, leaving a message that offered help, and asked one question: Why aren't you doing what ex-cops do?

George must have understood the meaning of that question, that a former law enforcement officer would first focus his suspicions on the person closest to the missing person—his daughter Casey. According to Richard, George called back right away and said, "Here's my answer to your question as to why I'm not doing what you think I should be doing: because my wife doesn't want me to."

Despite the rain that day, more than two hundred people filled the front yard of the Anthony home. A minister delivered a short sermon. Everyone joined hands as he led the group in prayer. "Casey has gotten deceived and we are standing here to ask God to break that bondage off of her."

Cindy led the group in a chant of "Bring Caylee home!"

Outside of the prayer, no one spoke about Casey or her situation in jail. They were encouraged by the news that an anonymous corporation had put up a $225,000 reward for the safe return of Caylee.

Rozzie Franco of Fox News approached Cindy at the end of the service to discuss Detective Yuri Melich. "We asked him about a grid pattern from your home, and why they hadn't done that and why they're not searching actively. What do you think? What are your thoughts on that?"

"I don't know," Cindy said. "I mean, they had receipts that could have traced my daughter's last actions for the last month. They didn't want them. They didn't even want to go through any of her personal things. It's too late now, guys. I've already put her stuff away. So you know, I let it sit out in the bedroom for the last week, and no one's wanted to come through any of the stuff that we took from the apartment . . .

"And I'm frustrated. I just want one of them from the sheriff's department to call me and give me some respect, give my husband some respect, give us a little update. They were so good about coming here every day for the first three days, because they knew we were giving them everything they wanted, and I've given them everything they wanted. I open my home to them. I let them search my backyard without question. I let them take my computers without question . . .

"I feel like I am the one who's being punished for trying to look for my granddaughter. And I can't keep doing this day after day. I've been grabbed by the media. My son gets chased down on his way to see his sister this morning. . . . My son is a tough person, but he called me this morning, he said, 'Mom, this is first time I felt like my life was in danger.' "

Cindy concluded the interview with some venting about the media: ". . . This has to stop. Quit harassing her friends, her friends trying to speak to the authorities. They won't return their phone calls. But they don't need to be on the media. They've already said Casey is a great mom, that she's always taken good care of Caylee; she's always been worried about Caylee, that she's been around cigarette smoke or whatever. This Zenaida person I've known about for the last three years. Do they think that she's been plotting to murder her child for three years now? Come on. Give me a break!"

Lee sat down for an interview with Orange County Detectives Eric Edwards and Michael Erickson that day. He provided the investigators with a handwritten list of receipts containing twenty-two dated entries in chronological order. "I want to make sure that we're on the same page—that these receipts were very organized . . . I saw them that night," Lee said, referring to July 15, "when they were being taken out of the bag." He added that he'd created the list when he visited the attorney on July 28.

"It would have been very nice to have those receipts," Detective Edwards said. "The attorney currently has them?"

"Yes, he does."

"And you can't remember when you took them and gave them to the attorney, but it was some time . . ."

"I want to say it had to be this . . . past Monday. Not yesterday, the week prior. It had to be around that time."

"Like the twenty-first?" Edwards asked.

"Yeah. Within a day or two, one way or the other. And we had offered it up . . . first to the officers on that—at this point, we're early morning into the sixteenth—we offered it to them at that time. We offered it to them again on the evening of the sixteenth and again on the evening of the seventeenth. I was present for every time when that was offered to them," Lee avowed.

The detectives moved on to questions about Casey's relationships with the men in her life. Lee said, "Ricardo and Casey had been seeing each other from February until the month . . . of April on kind of a full-time basis. They decided to break it off, see what they can do as friends. But they were still having, you know, a relationship . . . kind of on a semi-serious level up until Casey started hanging out with Tony—and actually even through the initial part of hanging out with Tony. So, it was in that time that she kind of transitioned . . . from Ricardo to Tony."

"She kind of seems like she may swing from boy-friend to boyfriend to keep a comfort?"

"Sure. Absolutely," Lee said.

"Is that . . . how you look back at her past and . . ."

"Absolutely. That's very accurate. But also to make sure that we're clear on this, Casey—unbeknownst to Jesse's and my parents—Casey and Jesse still maintained a semi-regular relationship, and always have over the past few years. This includes, from what I've been able to find out, at least into May when she started to see Tony."

Lee laughed. "She's always maintained to my mother and father that Jesse is the one pursuing her, and she's trying to get him out of . . . her life, while Jesse maintains that same thing to his parents. When, truth be told, even through phone records, you can see they equally reach out and facilitate the relationship between them-selves. No one person is chasing the other more than the other."

Edwards wanted to clear up a piece of confusing in-formation with Lee: "Now we go to the eighth [of June]. I have highlighted that in red because your Mom origi-nally thought, in her frantic state, that she hadn't seen Caylee from the eighth on. But now that changes. We know that to be the fifteenth. And that's just over stress. There's no finger-pointing going on there."

"Right." Lee nodded.

"It's just that she recalled originally that's the first time. You believe, though, that may have influenced your sister picking the ninth as . . ."

"A hundred percent," Lee interjected.

". . . when the abduction occurs?" Edwards finished.

"Absolutely."

"Okay, which is a red flag as far as what her thought

process may have been—in my mind, anyway. We cruise on through—we get to the fifteenth. You know from talking to Mom that they went and visited Granddad in Mount Dora?"

"Um hum." Lee nodded.

"When they came back, you believe from talking to Mom, that your sister, Casey, was at the house and actually [uploaded] the video and the pictures onto MySpace?"

"Yes."

"Or onto the home computer?"

"And MySpace, yes."

"And MySpace? Okay. And that being the forensics stuff that we know of, the last time any digital recording or any photographs were taken or existed of your niece . . ."

"Exactly."

". . . Was on the fifteenth?" Edwards continued.

"Yes," Lee affirmed.

Judge Strickland's decision to permit audio and video recordings to be admitted into the record earlier that day was on Lee's mind when he talked to his sister on the telephone. "Here's an FYI for you, so you can conduct yourself accordingly," Lee warned. "Everything is public record, including this phone call, including the visitation video, all that stuff is going to end up being released at some point."

"I know it is," Casey said.

"I had no knowledge of that whatsoever," Lee complained.

"They told me about that yesterday."

"They told me after we did that. There are obviously things I may have asked in a different way."

"Yeah, absolutely."

"I don't want you, you know, to feel for any reason we are not on your side about anything, because we are, about everything. We are completely behind you . . ."

"I know."

". . . and being completely behind you, our entire focus,

our entire days—every second of every day is consumed by what we can do to find Caylee."

"Of course," Casey acknowledged.

He then asked her if she had anything she could tell him that would help them find Caylee, but Casey said that nothing came to her mind.

"Do you think Caylee is okay, right now?" Lee asked.

"My gut feeling, as Mom asked me yesterday, and as the psychologist asked me this morning, that I met with through the court: In my gut, she's still okay. And it still feels like she's close to home."

CHAPTER 36

On July 29, Cindy and George came to the jail again to visit their daughter. They sat in the hard, uncomfortable chairs staring at an empty screen, waiting for their daughter's arrival on the other end. Finally, personnel informed them that Casey had been taken to court. They joined her there, and then came back for a visit the next day.

After exchanging greetings and news, Casey sighed, sniffled and wiped her eyes. "I'm being as strong as I can—considering the situation. It's hard—it's just very hard."

"I know. I know," Cindy commiserated.

"I just wanna go home," Casey sobbed. "Every day I wake up, I'm just hoping and praying I get to go home. I just want to be with you guys. I just wanna help find her, because I feel a little hopeless, I feel a little helpless here."

Cindy reassured her that everyone was being supportive and sending love her way. When the conversation turned to Caylee, Cindy said, "I want her home so that we can celebrate her third birthday as a family again."

"Every day I can feel it, Mom. I know I'm going to be home with you guys. I know she's going to be home with us. Everyone just has to keep that faith, because mine's growing stronger every day."

George offered his reassurance, too, and apologized for not being a better dad and grandpa. Casey rebuffed that, saying, "Dad, I can't say this to you enough: You've done everything you possibly can, and you're the best father and by far, the best grandfather I ever met . . . I mean that with all my heart. Don't think otherwise for a minute."

When Cindy returned to the phone, her voice was stretched thin and high from the stress and tears. "I want you both home so bad, Casey. I'm trying to stay so strong for you."

"You're doing such a great job, Mom. I want you to know that . . ."

"I'm trying so hard, but it's getting harder every day . . . She's not going to hurt Caylee, is she, Casey? She's not going to hurt Caylee?"

"I told you, in my gut, I know she is okay. I can feel it, Mom; I know she's still okay. We're going to get our little girl back, and she's going to be just as she was."

"Don't ever let anybody outside the family . . ." Cindy began.

"No. Trust me. I've said the same thing. I'm going to be the crazy, over-protective mom at that point, but I don't care. I think it's well deserved."

"You've always been a protective mommy."

"Well, like I said, 'the crazy . . . ,'" Casey said with a chuckle. "I won't let her out of my sight. So, I'll do whatever I have to. We'll figure it all out when it comes to it. I mean, I've been thinking about jobs and schedules and what I can do . . ."

"You won't have to work. You won't have to work. We'll figure everything out."

Casey said, "I'm kind of glad I haven't been crying every day—inside, of course, yeah, but I'm keeping my wits about me and staying as strong as I possibly can. This is the strongest I've ever been. Because even when I want to break down, I've been able to calm myself quickly, without doing much of that. It's hard, considering where I am, considering the situation, but I just keep thinking about you guys, 'cause that's the thing that makes me feel okay about not crying, and not being so emotionally distraught I can't even think straight."

"I know," her mother said. "It's the same way with me. I mean, I could curl up in a ball and be so absorbed with her not being there, which is— There are moments I'm like that—but I know that's not going to bring her home."

"I know it."

"Someone has to be her little voice out there."

"Exactly. But you aren't a 'little voice' by any means," Casey said with a laugh.

"Well, you know me . . ."

"Exactly. And it's funny. I'm going to say this, and you're going to laugh—I think it's hilarious. Everyone says that—you guys have always said I'm the loudest in the family, then it's you, then it's Lee and then Dad, because Dad is quiet and reserved, we know that. But I've been told by many sources that it is your son that's the loud one," Casey grinned. "Then it's you. Then it's me. So, hah!" Casey laughed.

Cindy was not amused. She answered seriously, "That's okay. I don't want to be the loud one. I don't want to be . . ."

"Oh, you're still the middle one. So, you're still the moderator. We know that Dad will always process things thoroughly before having any reaction or saying anything. He's very choosy about his words. He always has been. Which is good. 'Cause I think within our family, we need someone like that. 'Cause little Caylee is like you and I."

When Cindy asked Casey about the letter to the family that she'd promised Lee, Casey said that she had been too busy to write it. But later in the conversation, Casey contradicted herself when she said that she liked visitors because she had nothing to do but read and take naps. Although she'd said she wanted to talk to Ryan Pasley, she was declining any visits outside of family and her attorney. She said she'd rather see friends after she got out of jail.

When they left the visitation, George told reporters, "You want to reach out and touch them and give them a hug and make her feel the love that we have, to know we love her daughter unconditionally. We want our grand-daughter back."

For his part, Ryan didn't sound as if he were beating down any walls to speak to his childhood friend, when interviewed by law enforcement that day. He said he'd thought about visiting her in the hopes he could get information from her, but decided not to go. He knew she wasn't saying anything, because "she's lawyered up." He added, "I'm sure . . . her lawyer is telling her just shut up, and hopefully they won't find anything . . . I guess that's what I'm going to assume, because he actually called me and asked me questions.

"I answered whatever questions he had and then he ended up asking me, 'Do you think you'd be a good person . . . as a character witness or a reference for Caylee?' And I said, 'To be honest with you, from the truth that I've told you, I'm not going to be . . . I mean, I'm going to be a big detriment to your case.' He's like, 'Yeah, you're probably right,' and he even hung up the phone," Ryan chuckled.

"Really?" Yuri Melich asked. "When was this conversation?"

"Two or three days after . . . the incident got reported . . . José actually called me . . . on his cell phone . . . because Casey had given him my number and said go ahead and give me a call . . . And I told him, 'You know I'll tell you whatever you want to know. I just don't think it's going to help your case.'"

Melich said, "I understand, based on what you're telling me, and not only you, a whole bunch of other people, she's just a pathological liar."

"Yeah," Ryan agreed.

Melich asked what it would take to get Casey to talk.

"It's really going to take the fear of God, to be honest with you. Because that's the type of person she is. She's not going to do anything for anybody unless there's something in it for her . . . And she has to be scared."

He asked about Casey's drug use and Ryan said, "She

started telling me that she was, you know, smoking pot and this and that."

"Well, what other 'this and that? Because I'm trying to make sense of what her friends are telling me down here."

"But that is literally what she would say . . . I would ask her specifically, and she said, 'Well, you know, just pot and, you know, whatever else is around,' is the . . . way she put it."

"Do you know if she was rolling? Was she doing Ex, popping pills?"

"It's a very good possibility, to be honest with you, because, you know, just the fact that she actually released to me that she was smoking pot—she's always known that I've been against it completely . . . She felt very apologetic after she even told me that. She was trying to explain herself over and over again."

The state attorney general sent a message to justices at the Fifth District Court of Appeal in Daytona Beach that morning, informing them that Casey Anthony was a person of interest in the disappearance of Caylee. He argued that the bail was not unreasonably high because Casey was the key to finding the little girl.

The three-judge panel responded by denying José Baez's request to lower Casey's bond to $10,000. Baez announced his intention to file an appeal to the Florida Supreme Court.

Cindy walked into the Orange County Sheriff's Office clutching a black loose-leaf binder for a meeting with the FBI on July 30. There, she launched into a litany of the wrongs committed by local law enforcement and a passionate protestation of her daughter's innocence.

She expressed irritation with investigators for not seriously considering the airport sighting of Caylee. She complained that Yuri Melich had told Lee, "We wasted a lot of time checking out that lead." She griped that an investigator talking to Wanda Weiry, the woman who'd reported the sighting, said, "I don't know why we're doing this, 'cause this little girl is dead."

Cindy wanted the FBI to focus on following the leads to locate Zenaida and recover Caylee, rather than persecuting her innocent daughter. Cindy said she would do anything to get Caylee back, proclaiming that "If someone called and said, 'Ms. Anthony, take a butcher knife and put it in your heart,' I would do it. I would do it without hesitation." She added that Casey would do the same thing.

"I trust my daughter. I still trust my daughter for her decisions for Caylee." She's the "kind of Mom that's just perfect . . . She was a loving mother." Cindy also said that she was certain that Casey would have cracked by now if it were an accident.

Cindy aired her suspicions about Amy and Rico, saying that neither one of them had volunteered to distribute fliers as Casey's other friends had, and that Zanny might really be Amy. She also shared a new version of the abduction scenario that Casey had supposedly told to Lee: "Casey said that she was in Blanchard Park with Zanny and . . . Zanny's sister . . . When they were getting ready to leave, Zanny's sister . . . took Caylee. And Casey said, 'Where are you guys going?' And Zanny pushed Casey to the ground . . . and threatened her. 'Listen, bitch,' this is what she said, 'I'm going to teach you a lesson . . . You're not getting Caylee back.'"

Throughout the interview, she kept returning to her criticism of the investigation conducted by Orange County. The FBI assured her that they thought everything was being done right. Cindy was not mollified by their opinion and carped again on the wasted three days when they'd concentrated on proving Casey's guilt. The agent reminded her, "We lost the first seventy-two hours before we even knew Caylee was missing."

Public perception of Casey had never been great from the moment it was learned that she had not reported her daughter missing for thirty-one days. The emergence of pictures showing Casey partying in a bar on June 20, less than a week after the alleged abduction of Caylee, sent Casey's image plummeting like a rock.

It was hard to believe it could sink any lower. Then along came Travis Nichols. Just released from prison, he claimed that he'd talked briefly with Casey while in the holding cell at court. "I was asking her where the baby was. She said, 'I don't have the baby, Travis, my boyfriend has the baby,' and she started smiling."

Casey demonstrated once again that her worst enemy was not her mother, or the elusive Zanny, or the Orange County detectives—it was Casey herself.

CHAPTER 37

It was George's turn with the FBI the next day, and the tone of the interview was in sharp contrast to Cindy's. George apologized for the previous day: "I'm sorry my wife came off tough."

Although he questioned the course of the investigation, he seemed satisfied with the assurances of the agent, voicing only one complaint about Orange County investigators: He said he'd had to hear about his daughter's arrest on the evening news. George explained that when detectives had taken Casey away on July 16, Melich said, "'Mr. Anthony, if stuff changes and she's not coming back, I will call you. I will give you a heads-up.' But no one ever called."

The agent brought up what appeared to be a sharp difference between Casey before the age of 20 and Casey since. George agreed with him, but could not explain it—could not point to any traumatic event that might have impacted his daughter's mental outlook. And although he said, "She always seemed to be a good mother," he did not insist upon his daughter's innocence.

George mentioned that Baez had invited him and his wife to his house to get away. He said that he didn't feel comfortable going to José's house, because the attorney's first instinct is for Casey at the expense of all else, even Caylee. George said, "I didn't appreciate that. It seems like everything we'd given him, he's not followed up with our daughter."

In response, the agent said, "He's trying to twist it in his way to help him out down the road. There are certain things he doesn't want to know. It puts a tremendous ethical burden on him."

"I understand that, but . . ." George began.

"Believe me, I'm not defending defense attorneys," the agent chuckled.

George laughed, then turned serious. "It all boils down to: My daughter knows something and she won't say anything. And she's been coached—that's a bad thing to say. She's being told, 'These are your rights,' 'This is what you can't do.'" George thought Baez should let her know "the best thing is to recover her daughter, and some of the charges would go away." He added, "There are little threads of truth in all the lies she's telling, and we just can't get it together."

Despite his doubts about his daughter's honesty, he expressed a father's genuine concern. He worried about Casey being in prison and being mistreated by other inmates because a child was involved in the crime.

He repeated the Blanchard Park story that Cindy had related the day before; but, unlike his wife, he delivered it without any conviction in its veracity. He said he'd doubted the existence of Zanny and Jeff's son Zack for quite some time. He said that when he'd asked Caylee, "Did you have a good time with Zanny today?" Caylee had shown no reaction. Similarly, she looked blank when he'd asked, "How's Zack?"

Bringing up Casey's one-time fiancé, George said, "I believe Jesse is very jealous of the relationships Casey has had since their relationship was called off. I've seen him be very angry at different times. I've seen him be angry, not just at me, but especially my wife a couple of different times."

One of the surprises in the interview concerned the family's financial situation. He said he didn't gamble, but had actually lost the money in an email scam. He said that he "saw it as a quick fix. I lied to my wife and told her that it was on-line gambling."

George's day was not yet done. He and Cindy both sat down with Corporals Yuri Melich and Eric Edwards of the Orange County Sheriff's Office to answer their questions. Cindy insisted that although Casey and Caylee had spent the night with Zanny on occasion, the two had never stayed overnight with any of Casey's boyfriends. She also said that she never called her daughter demanding that Casey bring Caylee home.

When asked about the biological father of Caylee, Cindy explained it was Eric, one of Casey's old friends from high school. Caylee was conceived, she said, from a single sexual encounter. Eric had been killed, but Casey had stayed in contact with the widow, the mother of Caylee's half-brother.

The detectives also spoke to Jesse Grund that day, asking his possible explanations of what had happened. Jesse said, "There are two different types of what-if scenarios that have gone through my head in regards to what could have happened to Caylee, because I'll say this for the record . . . I don't believe Casey would have ever hurt Caylee on purpose, and there's no way that I personally could ever foresee her doing that. I believe that there are times where Casey would leave Caylee unattended to do things. Get on the computer, talk on the phone. And at that point . . ."

Edwards interrupted, "And where would she be unattended?"

"Caylee would usually hang out in the living room while Casey was in the computer room, or sometimes Casey would go outside to use the telephone and leave Caylee in the living room. She also went outside and played with Caylee a lot, and then she'd also be playing with the dogs. She let Caylee play in her playpen while she'd go do something. So, there were plenty of times where I could have foreseen, because we both know, with children, something quick can happen. I mean, Caylee was somebody who liked picking up rocks and putting them in her mouth or, you know, dog food was another thing . . . And Caylee, at any point, could have picked one of those things up, asphyxiated and died . . ."

"So you're talking the time frames that Casey would leave her alone from time to time are lengthy?"

"I mean, yeah . . ."

"How about the pool?" Edwards asked.

"I don't know enough about Caylee and the pool . . . I knew that Caylee loved the pool, but I never actually saw Caylee in the pool. Now, I was under the understanding that they actually had to move the ladder, because Caylee kept trying to get into the pool, and things of that nature. I believe, at any point in time, something possibly could have accidentally happened to Caylee. And if something accidentally happened to Caylee, I literally believe that Casey would have an emotional breakdown—a mental breakdown—to the point where I almost believe that she would take Caylee and put her somewhere and then tell herself a new story, a new reality of what happened to her."

"Because she's been living in a false reality for years?"

"Correct," Jesse said with a nod. "So I don't think it's that far out of the spectrum. I think if something happened to Caylee, her one toe that she's had in reality for the last couple of years—her one foot—would be gone, and she would be completely in her own separate world. And I think that's because Casey directly has some issues that, mentally, she's never gotten taken care of. I do believe something accidentally happened to Caylee, which I believe is a what-if scenario that could have happened. Choke on a piece of dog food, eat a rock, slip coming out of the pool together, just fall off of something that she's climbed too high. Caylee was a rambunctious little kid. She liked to climb. She liked to run around. She liked to do things. You know, what three-year-old doesn't?"

"Now Casey actually kind of lives under Mom's thumb. It seems like Mom's very judgmental of her as far as parental capabilities. You think Casey would be more than afraid to say, 'Mom, now look what happened—look what I've done'?" Edwards asked.

"I believe there is the distinct possibility that Casey wouldn't tell Mom if something like this happened. I don't think there's any way. I don't even think that she would have told anyone except herself . . . The only way I think somebody would have known is if she reached out to somebody to help her. But I don't. Casey's been an independent, self-sufficient person, who thrives off the attention of others . . . but she likes to do things on her own."

"Do you think she would have the strength, the inner strength, at that point in time, to take the child and put the child somewhere without help? . . . Because it seems like she has to fall on men or boyfriends to have that crutch for confidence. Faced with that situation, would she have to call upon one of these guys?"

"I believe she would reach out to somebody for help," Jesse affirmed.

"Who would that be?" Edwards asked.

"It would not be me . . . The only person that it would have been with would be her current boyfriend, which would be Tony Lazzaro. That's the only person I could think of that she would have personally reached out to. Because again, they weren't together for very long, and she was already falling in love with him in her mind . . . She wouldn't reach out to me in regards to anything Caylee-related, especially if Caylee got hurt or anything, because she knew what my reaction would be. She also knows I tend to be an honest and righteous individual. I'm going to come right out and tell the correct people if something happened."

On August 1, George and Cindy left their home at 9 A.M. in response to a request to come to the Orange County Sheriff's Office. As soon as they left, crime-scene techs pulled up to the house. And just moments after that, detectives parked in the driveway and a dismayed-looking George stepped out of their vehicle.

He opened the garage door and led the investigators through his home. They left the house, entering the backyard. George unlocked the shed and the techs took possession of a one-gallon red plastic gas can and a black plastic oil pan. They went back inside the house and out into the garage, where George showed them the 2 1/4-gallon red metal gas can. They seized it as evidence, too.

That evening, George, Cindy and Lee were at Speed Park Motorsports in Daytona Beach for a benefit and a candlelight vigil for three missing children—Trenton Ducket, Zachary Bernhardt and Caylee Anthony. Family members of all three were present, as well as Kid Finders Network, with their mobile billboard featuring pictures of missing children. The event started at 4 P.M. and activities included music by a DJ and children's fingerprinting.

When Cindy returned to Orlando, she read an email from her mother:

Dear Cindy, We are sick over this. We are so worried about Caylee. And we are very worried about you.

I've seen so many interviews. Now, they discuss you after you leave. The only one who has remained kind to you is Mike on M and J *[the Mike and Juliette Morning Show* out of Tampa]. Then today, you blew it. For every one's sake—yours, Caylee's, and yes, even Casey's—stay off TV or act like the person you really are, a nice person who has worked for thirty years, making the home and raising a nice family. You are taking the spotlight off Caylee. We know you love Casey, but what about the future?

Be mad at me if you want. It hurts to see Dad plastered on most newscasts in his fragile condition. I still believe Casey's better off in jail, there are a lot of nutcases out there who would like to see her harmed. Think about it. If she gets out on bond, you all really might be in danger.

Cindy wrote back:

I will have no life without Caylee. I will do everything I can to bring her home. I could care less
about Mike and Juliette as long as Caylee's picture
gets out there. That is what I want. I am sorry for
what this is doing to you and Dad, but I cannot stop
doing what I can to get Caylee back.

As for the bond, George and Lee and I agree for
a lot of other reasons that Casey is better where she
is and Caylee is also safer. Casey may have lied but
I know she is not responsible for any harm to Caylee. I will fight for both of my girls. Finding Caylee
will bring Casey home. Please know that I think of
you and Dad every day. I just cannot discuss what I
know at this time. I love you and cannot be mad at
you.

In response, Shirley wrote:

I have a question, you seem to have gotten some of
Casey's things from Tony . . . did you ever get any
of Caylee's clothes back? I can't believe the "nanny"
had all of Caylee's clothes. If you have the answers,
fine. If not, ask Casey where they are.
. . . Personally, I think Casey took Caylee to
hurt you—not that she meant to harm her. She
could have left her with you and then go on with
her lifestyle that she wanted, till she got it out of
her system. She knew she and Caylee would always
have a good home with you . . . I saw George crying last night and it hit me hard. I had another bad
night. You are all grieving and we are grieving for
all of you.

CHAPTER 38

George visited Casey in jail on August 3. He reminded his daughter that it was just six days until Caylee's birthday and he wanted to throw her a big party. He vowed that once Caylee was home, all of the family would volunteer to help find other missing children. Once again, George beat up on himself: "This is destroying your mother. She feels so bad. Maybe we've been all too domineering. Maybe we didn't let you be the best mom—you are the best mom."

"It's nobody's fault. It's nobody's fault," Casey protested.

"Well, I could have opened up more to you. I could have done stuff. But I can't go back. There's times you wanted to talk to me. I wish I woulda listened. But all that's going to change—I'll listen more. I have one question to ask you and I know it's going to be a tough one."

"Yeah?"

"Would you speak to someone about Caylee?"

"I already answered that. I mean, I'll try to the best of my ability," Casey sniffled and rubbed her reddened nose. "Things would be so much easier if I wasn't still here—if I was home. I want you to understand that. I mean, I feel that more each day. I want to be home. I want to be there when Caylee comes home. I want to be there with our family when she comes home. I don't want to have to wait three days, four days, after that happens, to see her."

Still believing Casey's story that lives were in danger, George told her that they could all go into protective custody if she would tell everything. He said that he was meeting with John Walsh of *America's Most Wanted* that week, that a foundation had been established for Caylee, and a website, helpfindcaylee.com, was up and running.

He then reassured her of how much everyone in the family loved her. Casey professed her love for Caylee and her parents—all the while shaking her head back and forth as if she were denying the words she spoke.

As he left the visitation, George spoke to reporters: "She knows who has her daughter. She knows her daughter is safe. And I got to believe her that she knows where—everything is okay." He also said that Casey had given her attorney a letter that might contain clues about Casey's disappearance. The lawyer said no such letter existed. Was this another of Casey's lies to her father? Or was José Baez withholding it from the family?

Cindy's brother Rick sent an email to their mother, Shirley Cuza:

> I am terribly upset about Cindy and George. Casey is the biggest liar in history. She would rather spin lies than find Caylee. She thinks it is a game. She makes them look like the stupidest parents ever in the entire world.
>
> Cindy and George ARE on very thin ice, too. They look like accomplices because nobody can believe they can be THAT stupid to believe Casey. Everyone is frustrated including the media. They have never seen anything like this—ever.
>
> There is no babysitter and there never was. It is all lies, lies and more lies. No one could have a sitter for a year and not know the phone number. No one has ever seen the sitter. No one knows the sitter. The cops aren't stupid. They know there was no sitter and know Casey is stalling.

She will never get out of jail and if and when they find Caylee's body, Casey will get the death penalty. I have no doubt whatsoever. The police will press murder charges even if they can't find a body. They are waiting for the forensic evidence first but even if it is inconclusive, they will still go after suspicion of murder and hold her without bail until the trial.

. . . Casey better change her story to an accidental death and she may cut some time off of her sentence. I know I have her guilty before charged but after she destroyed her family for those worthless people from that club, she more than deserves it.

Cindy agreed to questioning by Detectives Eric Edwards and Mark Hussey at the Orange County Sheriff's Office on August 4. She took a phone call just as she sat in the interview room, and talked sweetly to an FBI agent. But by the time she had completed the call, her fury had been unleashed and lobbed at the investigators: "No one's doing a fucking thing!"

"What do you need?"

"I need someone to pay attention to Caylee, that's missing. I need someone to actually follow up on someone that has called in," she said referring to the sightings of Caylee in the Orlando airport and elsewhere.

Cindy returned to this theme over and over during the hour she spent in the interview room. When Detective Hussey tried to explain the investigative process, Cindy complained that they were trying to build a case against her daughter: "Casey may be a liar, but she didn't murder her daughter."

Later, Cindy said, "You know, everybody can speculate or whatever, I think Casey got mixed up with some bad people."

"Highly possible," Detective Edwards agreed.

"Ricardo, Amy and Tony, who I've just learned are all intertwined. They're all into drugs."

"Sure," said Hussey.

"We talked to another agency. They're all into drugs, they all know each other very well, and for Amy telling me she'd only been to Tony's apartment once has to be a lie, 'cause she knows him. I think she's the one that introduced . . ."

"Uh huh."

"And Tony and Ricardo go way back, and there's some dealings there. So Casey's mixed up somehow, so— And they have the money and means, and Casey's been maintaining all along."

"Uh huh."

"But there are physical threats against this family."

"Uh huh."

"Or harm if she comes clean and tells where Caylee's at . . ."

Edwards asked, "So you think they may be coming from Amy and Ricardo or . . . ?

"I don't know. I mean, my understanding is, these folks have some connections with some people that has money . . . Has a way to make people disappear. Has means to threaten, and Casey's scared. I could see it in her face. She's scared, and I think she's trying to give us clues. I've been saying that from day one for us to figure it out without coming out because—and that's why, I think, I could have Casey out today. I want you to know."

"There's still going to be . . ." Hussey began.

"I could have Casey out today," Cindy insisted. "The bail money is not an issue."

"Uh huh."

"I'm telling you that right now. I have people that help me. I think it's a safety issue for both Casey and Caylee, keeping her ass there for right now until we figure this stuff out. Because if the media and everybody's still pointing fingers at Casey . . ." So if we get off our butt and we keep looking for these people—I'm just saying, me or Lee or whomever, not just you guys—we start looking at these other issues, other possibilities, we're gonna find who these people are, and we're gonna find Caylee."

* * *

The next day, Casey was formally charged with child neglect, a third-degree felony with a maximum sentence of 5 years, and filing a false statement, a misdemeanor with a maximum of 1 year in jail. This delay between arrest and formal charges was typical in Florida.

Cindy was a no-show for her scheduled visit with her daughter that afternoon. She said that she changed her mind because of the videotaping and the public release of their conversations.

Family friend and neighbor Holly Gagne appeared live on *Larry King* that night. He asked, "Holly, you know Casey very well. She used to baby-sit your boys. What do you make of this?"

"There's a lot of confusion, Larry. And, you know, I have answered the question so many times that I just say that the Casey that I knew that baby-sat my children and that has been in my home and we've been friends with for six years would not harm her child, or be a part of her child being harmed in any way."

"So, you're totally shocked?"

"That is putting it lightly, yes. When my husband and I had gotten home from our vacation and we heard the news, we went straight to Cindy and George's home—we were their neighbors for over three years. And I just fell into Cindy's arms and I said, 'What is going on?' And she said, you know, at that time, 'We just don't know.'

"There's been so many twists and turns, Larry, that, you know, and there's so many scenarios. But in my mind, and in my opinion, a scenario that she harmed her child, that she hurt her child, that she knows her child is not alive and she's torturing her parents and putting us all through this, I don't believe that."

Cindy telephoned into that show and the *Nancy Grace* show that evening, pushing the defense's spin: "If they had something to charge her, why wouldn't they do it today, with everything else? So, I mean, hello? We've known this all along. Why else did they go and handcuff her and put her in jail? Because they feel that she needs to be there. And again, once Caylee is found, everybody's going to know that she doesn't need to be there. She doesn't belong there, and she doesn't deserve what everybody's doing to her. No one knows everything. I don't know one hundred percent, but I sure as heck know a lot more, but I can't say a lot of things.

"Today is actually a very hopeful day. You know, I just found out that, you know, they did charge her formally today, which actually is good—because look what they charged her with—they didn't charge her with anything but with voluntary child neglect and withholding evidence. If they had anything concrete on her [for homicide charges], I think they would have used that today. Today was the last day that they had an opportunity to do so. That is, in essence, a victory for us."

CHAPTER 39

Cindy's continued insistence that the horrific odor in the car was nothing but rotting pizza prompted WFTV news to carry out a little experiment of their own. The managing editor, Joel Davis, volunteered the use of his car. Reporters took the leftovers from a Domino's MeatZZa pizza and put it in the trunk under the hot Florida sun. By their own admission, it wasn't the most scientific study, but they hoped it would shed some light on Cindy's story.

Joel said, "About every other day I've taken a look at it. The first day or two, you open the trunk and you have the smell of pizza. But after that, nothing. No smell whatsoever."

A reporter confirmed Joel's observations. "After seven days in the trunk, we decided to see what the pizza was like. Basically, all the moisture is gone. It's got the consistency of shoe leather and you got to get really close to smell anything, and the only smell you can smell is pizza." He added, "Our experiment doesn't support the smelly pizza theory."

The Anthonys advertised on MySpace for two unpaid personal assistants—one to help George, the other for Lee, who were coordinating the search for Caylee:

Need help handling flood of people offering help, donations and tips. Applicants need to be available 24/7 and have a personal cell phone, reliable trans-

portation, a valid driver's license and an ability to
work on his own.

The quiet of the neighborhood around the Anthony
home was now a distant memory. One neighbor even filed
a complaint with the police—he was angry that a TV
truck had scorched his grass.

In the early afternoon of August 6, Detective Yuri Melich,
Sergeant John Allen and two crime-scene investigators
arrived at 4937 Hopespring Drive with a new search warrant. In Casey's bedroom, they asked Cindy about the
clothing Casey had been wearing when Caylee disappeared. She pointed to a pair of charcoal gray pants, but
said, "I washed them because they smelled like the car."
She said the black boots and black shoes that Casey would
have been wearing then had been in the car, which was
still in the forensic garage.

The crime-scene techs covered the windows in Casey's
room with black paper, and turned on the portable alternate light source to illuminate any suspicious stains. They
confiscated the aforementioned pants, along with two pair
of blue jeans, three skirts and five shirts.

After two-and-a-half hours, they were gone. But they
were back again the next day. Cindy had gathered together
a collection of items she claimed were connected to baby-
sitter Zenaida Gonzalez. When the crime techs arrived, it
was all laid out on the living room coffee table. They
took a hair straightener, a soccer ball and a football, a
pink "ready bed," and DVDs of *Bambi*, *Bambi II*, *Blades
of Glory* and a two-disc set of *Transporter*.

On August 8, George blew up at the media gathered
around his home: "I'm not talking to anybody. Stay off
my property! Stay away from me. Stay away from me
right now!"

Still the questions peppered him, and he lashed out
again: "You have no idea what we're going through. You
don't give a— You don't care about me. You don't care

about her," he said pointing to his wife. "You don't care about my granddaughter. You don't care about any of us. Shut up, I'm talking! I am talking! I'm trying to find my granddaughter. You guys don't care about that. All you care about is the sensationalism."

Cindy turned to the media and said, "He's been angry every day. You just haven't seen it, okay? You hear something that finally comes to a head, you know, stuff that festers, okay? Anger has been there since day one. He's been . . ."

"At who, though?" a reporter shouted.

"Anger at the situation. Anger at the fact that Caylee is not home. Anger at a lot of things. Angry that, you know, we are helpless."

George shouted again, "Leave me alone! Leave me alone!"

"Why is he upset?" a reporter asked Cindy.

"This is why he's upset," she said, panning her arm across the media crowd. "Back off, okay? Please, before I lose my husband. Right now!"

George sped off in his car and Cindy turned to the reporters. "You guys see the tough George, the tough Cindy, the tough Lee in front of all you guys. We're not like that all the time, okay? We're falling apart."

The Orange County Sheriff's Office dive team worked in a pond near the Anthony home. Deputy Carlos Padilla said that fortuitously, the training exercise had been planned there before Caylee was reported missing. They found no evidence connected to Caylee's disappearance.

Lee went to the jail visitation site to talk with his sister that day. Casey, however, refused to see him. At a vigil that night, candles were lit; the crowd joined hands and sang "Happy Birthday" to Caylee. Balloons soared from hands into the sky, and tears glistened on every face. George apologized for his outburst that morning and asked everyone to remember the family in their prayers.

Sorrow descended with the sharpness of a scythe on

August 9—the day Caylee should have been celebrating her third birthday.

On August 10, Rick Cuza sent an email addressed to his sister Cindy, nephew Lee and brother-in-law George:

> This is the hardest letter that I ever had to write. My heart is breaking with the passing of Caylee's birthday and she is not home with you guys. You have to be going through hell. I love you guys and my heart is saddened with all that has transpired. I know you guys are right in the middle of it and it has to be a nightmare that is never ending. I have been watching this since it has happened and can see it in its entire perspective. I have a pretty good idea of what really happened. Please don't get angry with me, but listen to what I have to say with an open mind . . . You guys are so close to it, you may not be able to see it the way I see it.
>
> Here goes. You mentioned that the steps of the pool were back after you took them down on the fifteenth of June. The neighbors said that they heard someone in the pool on the afternoon of the sixteenth of June. The cell phone records point out that Casey made a bunch of calls to you and George that you guys did not answer on the sixteenth of June. I think Caylee drowned in the pool and Casey was trying to call you guys. Since she couldn't reach you, she panicked and put Caylee's body in the backyard to hide her.
>
> Then on the eighteenth of June, she returned to either bury her . . . or move the body . . . She put Caylee's body in the trunk and drove away. That is why the dogs hit on your backyard and the car, Cindy . . . She made up the baby sitter a long time ago to cover up for when she said she was going to work. She figured since you "bought in" to that lie a long time ago, she could use the sitter as an alibi.

Not one person has ever seen this sitter. Not one, Cindy. Is this making sense yet?

Casey knows she has to lie to cover everything up. The longer it goes, it will be harder to prove that the cause of death was accidental drowning as the body decomposes. Casey will be charged with murder instead of it being an accident. You must run this scenario past Casey before it is too late. I know you want to believe otherwise, Cindy, but it just don't add up. This is your last chance to get through to Casey. That forensic evidence is due in at anytime now. God bless all of you.

Cindy replied:

Where did you hear that the neighbors heard someone in the pool on the 16th? I have not heard this. The only flaw with that theory is Casey would not cover up an accident and go to prison for it. Sorry. George and I have run through the scenarios. There's a lot you guys don't know and we cannot say. I can assure you I am not mad at you but the facts cannot be released for many reasons. . . . It's tough but we're confident we will have Caylee back with us.

Rick wrote back, explaining the swimming pool story:

Cindy, Greta *[Greta Van Susteren, Fox News]* ran the time line on Friday. No one knows the "ghost sitter." This is a person that Casey made up to fool you about her having a job for two years. She pretended to go to work and said she used this fake sitter to scam you. Can't you see this? There is no sitter.
 . . . Nothing Casey has said is true. I know you want to believe her, but from the pregnancy on, she has lied. I would even bet that the boy that died in the car accident is not the father. 100% guarantee it.
 . . . I am sorry, Cindy, but if you are pinning

your hopes on Casey telling you anything true, you have a big letdown coming . . . She stole from mom and dad, stole THOUSANDS from you and George and stole from her friends. I know she wouldn't purposely hurt Caylee, but she thinks that if they can't find Caylee's body, she won't go to prison. She can and will go just on what they have now . . . Those dogs are highly trained and are not fooled.

. . . I know what is coming next and I hope I am wrong. The forensic evidence will tell the story. Then it will be too late to change her story because no one will believe her. God bless you guys. I am sorry if my candid comments upset you in any way but I had to say what I feel in my heart is true. I hope I am wrong for Caylee's sake but I think she is in Heaven now. My thoughts and prayers are with you guys every day.

In her response, Cindy told Rick that he got the story on Greta wrong, cadaver dogs were unreliable and Brian Burner, the neighbor with the shovel, kept changing his story. Again, she came to her daughter's defense:

Lying does not make someone a murderer. I am not in denial.

. . . The Sheriff's Office thought Casey would crack being in jail this long. She hasn't because she is protecting Caylee. We have a lot of people working to prove Casey's innocence. We cannot come out with evidence until Caylee is safe. You need to keep an open mind. If you don't you are just as bad as the media. Why don't you spend your energy helping us find Caylee. What have you done to put the word out?

. . . I could go on all night, but I refuse to waste my energy justifying any of this to anyone, especially to my own family. I am not mad. I am disappointed. It's bad enough you have little faith in

Casey, but George, Lee and I are busting our asses out here every day to find Caylee. I do not see any support for her from my own family. We get more support from complete strangers. Thank God for all of them.

Frustrated with Cindy's stubborn defense of Casey's lies, Rick gave rein to his anger:

I have seen enough of Casey's actions after the fact to know she is full of crap! . . . You can believe her all you want, but I don't buy it for one second. She lied to you in front of me about being pregnant. She was seven months! It was so obvious, it was ridiculous.

Her own friends said she is a liar and a good, decent person does not steal from their parents and grandparents. If it was you that was in trouble, I would believe YOU. I do not believe anything that Casey says . . . Casey is the only person that really knows where Caylee is and what really happened to her. She is playing you, George and Lee like a bass fiddle and has for years. You need to wake up.

Rick challenged Cindy to prove the sitter existed and question why anyone would not step forward to claim the reward if Caylee was still alive:

This is a made up story by Casey to get the police to take the heat off of her. You have enabled Casey to lie and steal for years. As long as you support her, you won't find out what happened to Caylee.

The "word" is already out. The "word" is Casey is a pathological liar and only she knows what happened to Caylee. No parent would be at a night club every Friday after their daughter is kidnapped . . . She has no remorse or doesn't care about anyone except herself.

Get real, Cindy. This is hard for me but you have to face the facts here. You are so far out in left field on this you have lost touch with reality. There is nothing that anyone can do here or anywhere without Casey coming clean and telling the truth for once in her life . . . I know you want to believe that Caylee is still out there alive, but . . . the reality should have set in after Caylee wasn't home for her third birthday. I would want to choke the life out of Casey.

You have my deepest sympathy. I truly am sorry for you guys and want this to have a happy ending. I am praying for you all.

Cindy was angry now:

This is why I am no longer going to reply to you again. You did not read a word I wrote. I cannot tell you everything that is going on. I am getting real. I know who is in my corner and it is not my family. We do not want or need your sympathy, or even pity. Please do not reach out to me again. Use your contacts to get Caylee's face out there because she is alive. I believe that, as I believe there is a God. You need more faith. Please do not destroy our relationship. I forgive your ignorance at this point.

Rick was now enraged. He responded in all caps:

. . . YOUR IGNORANCE IS INTOLERABLE. I AM YOUR BROTHER AND I DEMAND TO KNOW IF ANYONE OTHER THAN CASEY HAS SEEN THIS STUPID SITTER. IF YOU CAN'T ANSWER THAT SIMPLE REQUEST, THEN YOU ARE ALL BY YOURSELF ON THIS. YOU NEED TO GET SOME PSYCHIATRIC HELP!

For five hours, Rick cooled down while waiting for an email from Cindy. When it didn't come, he wrote to his sister again:

No babysitter. No kidnapping. Case closed. Mom never heard Caylee on her phone. It was a wrong number. Don't bother Mom and Dad anymore. Bother Casey. Put the blame where it goes. It makes me sick to see you guys going through this because of Casey. I won't bother you anymore. You couldn't give me an answer if anyone other than Casey could verify a babysitter. Your silence is very loud and clear. There is nothing I can do for you if you can't see reality. All the faith in the universe won't bring Caylee back. It will take a long time for you to "heal" if you ever can. I know you are grieving, so I will let you have your peace.

All I wanted was a STRAIGHT answer which no one seems to be able to give. I have heard all the BS I can take. I would believe in the tooth fairy or ET or Santa before I trusted and believed in Casey. After I heard what she did to Mom and Dad and you guys, I wouldn't donate a nickel to bond her out if I won the lotto.

That is the disdain that I have for her . . . I know you hate me right now but that is the risk I have to take to get you back to reality. You can hate me, but some day, you will see I was trying to help you.

CHAPTER 40

On August 11, the Fifth District Court of Appeals in Daytona Beach denied Casey Anthony's motion for a rehearing on the bond. The same day, Cindy and George were driving around town, towing a portable billboard with photos of Caylee.

By this point, the public had submitted more than 1,300 leads to the investigators. On this day a forensic unit responded to a site 4 and a half miles by road from 4937 Hopespring Drive. A tip alerted the sheriff's office to a square-shaped spot of dirt in a field next to a wooded area.

The unit found small pieces of bone and hair on its surface. An investigator probed the dirt, finding nothing. Carefully, one inch at a time, they removed the soil searching for bones or any additional evidence. They uncovered a wood beam, but in the surrounding dirt, roots were undisturbed. The hair and bones were not human. Another dead end.

That day, county meter reader David Dean helped new employee Roy Kronk with his route on Hopespring and Suburban. They stopped in a shady area by the swamp on Suburban to take a break. David thought about the close proximity to the Anthony home and said, "You know, Roy, I think that little girl is in the swamp back there."

Roy agreed it was possible, and they talked about Casey's remark to her parents that Caylee was nearby.

Roy got out of the truck and went into the woods a little ways to relieve himself. When he returned to the truck, another meter reader, Chris Gibson, was with David. Roy said, "Hey, guys, I saw a bag down there."

David thought Roy was kidding around because of his earlier comment, and didn't pay any attention. Roy walked away from the truck and along the swamp line. He shouted, "Hey, guys, I see a skull in here."

David still didn't take him seriously, but walked back that way to see what he'd seen. Halfway there, he nearly stepped on the largest rattlesnake he'd ever seen. He let out an involuntary yelp. Then, he realized the snake was dead. They all marveled at it. David picked it up with his shovel, put it in the back of his truck and took it back to the office. The find was a big hit with the other meter readers. They all gathered around, snapping photos with their cell phones.

All but Roy forgot about what else had been seen in the swampy woods.

Roy made his first telephone call to the police. With some difficulty he described the location on Suburban Drive near Hidden Oaks Elementary School and the Anthony home. "There's, like, a big swamp area there, and we found a dead, four-foot eastern diamond rattle back, but that's not the real thing. There's, like, two little 'in' areas you can go and there's a big, long tree laying down and there's a lot of swamp back in there. Well, back behind one of the trees down there was a gray bag and then a little bit further up than that, I saw something white. But after I saw that four-foot eastern diamond rattlesnake, I'm not going in that property."

He called back the next day to report his discovery one more time. The third day, he called again to report that he was at the location waiting for them to dispatch an officer. Deputy Richard Cain responded first. Roy pointed out what he described as "a bag of bones". Cain went into the mucky woods and poked around with his baton, flipping a small piece of a plastic bag, but not seeing anything but leaves and sticks.

While Cain checked out the site, Deputy Keithlin Cutcher arrived on the scene. Roy spoke of his suspicion that he might have found Caylee's remains. "[Casey] said she was very close. She was really close."

Cain walked out of the woods and Cutcher asked, "What's going on?"

Cain said, "Oh, it's nothing. It was just a bag of trash." He turned to Roy and argued that the remains would not be skeletal yet. Then he said, "You're just wasting the county's time."

On August 12, crime-scene investigators were gathered at another location 16 miles from the Anthony home to a brush line bordering a lake. They collected potential evidence—a faded pink baseball cap emblazoned with "V.I.P. Very Important Princess," along with the dirt and debris found with it. The next day, they brought out cadaver dog Gerus to search the scene. He did not alert to anything.

Detective Appie Wells met with Kiomarie Torres Cruz at the wooded area near Hidden Oaks Elementary School. From this interview, another piece of confusion entered the case. Kiomarie told the investigator about hearing a child in the background when she'd had a conversation with Casey Anthony on July 9. It turned out that Kiomarie was mistaken—she'd actually received a call from another Casey, and was confused about the source.

Kiomarie, however, provided new insight into the suspect. She said that Casey was a nice girl except for when she drank, "but I have a very strong feeling she is bipolar . . . She has called me before, back in the day, I remember after she had the baby, when we were actually talking a lot . . .

"She would call, ask me a couple of questions and then call back the next day and I'd have the answers to the questions. She's like, 'I never asked you that.' "

Detective Wells probed further, "She wasn't just trying to trip you up?"

"This is what drives me insane, because Casey was never like this when we were in high school or middle school. She was perfectly fine, and it was after she had the baby when the issue started. I mean, the boyfriends—I don't want to get started on that. I cannot keep track of who she was dating and who she was with."

"Okay."

"I know what she would do in spite of her mother, because her mother did—I don't know how you say it—but push her really, really hard, like, to do the right things."

"Right. She had a lot of high expectations."

"To be the perfect all-American girl." Kiomarie continued, "... her mother does not like Hispanic people, and most of the guys she was with were either Hispanic or of a different race."

Rick sent an email to his mother, describing his exchange with Cindy, and said he'd forward it all to her to read.

I did my best to talk some sense into her but to no avail . . . When the facts are known, Cindy will have to face them. Right now she is in denial.

Shirley wrote back to her son:

I read all the letters. I agree with most of what you said. I know she won't believe any of us until she sees that little body or Casey says where she's at.

I made her upset with the last note that I wrote . . . George told a reporter that he lost his job, so now his job is to drive Caylee's billboard around. I'm asking where he got money for gas.

. . . I'm afraid Cindy will mess around and lose her job. Maybe she will lose her credibility and they might not want her back. She should go back to work and let the police handle it from here. But, she won't.

Rick replied to his mother:

. . . How can they possibly believe a lying snot that has never told the truth? How can they not see that all of Casey's actions are not of someone that cares that Caylee is missing? . . . She is guilty as hell, Mom. Cindy and George . . . need to blame themselves for enabling Casey to steal and lie and get away with it. They created her and bought in to all her lies and excuses for way too long. They are still doing it. It absolutely amazes me. They both need to get counseling before they go off the deep end, but I think they already have lost their minds.

Fired up after communicating with his mother, Rick tried one more time to batter through Cindy's shell of denial:

You guys need to quit making statements on TV. You have both lost your minds. People want to hurt you for being so stupid. Casey could give a rat's ass about Caylee. Her boyfriend can't even stand her for what she did. There was no kidnapping and you know it. This charade has gone on long enough. How could you believe a ridiculous story like this? You guys look like the stupidest people on the planet. The more George opens his mouth, the more asinine he sounds. You guys need counseling right away.

After the police spoke today and said that there is not one speck of evidence that points to a kidnapping, you said something really stupid. You said that since Casey does not have Caylee then she must have been kidnapped.

Cindy, Caylee is dead. Casey will lie to her own grave. Bet on it. She is a sociopath and cannot tell the truth. Caylee may have died in an accident but Casey will lie to the end.

You just need to quit talking to the media. You are not helping your cause. People that used to sympathize with you now hate you for being so ignorant. I have to be blunt because you aren't listening to the facts here. There is no supporting evidence to Casey's story. NONE.

She is going to prison for a long time and there is nothing anyone can do. You probably hate me but deep down you know I am right . . . Please get some counseling before it is too late. I didn't want to meddle in your business, but this is way too important to let go. You guys need help. Mom thinks so, too. Please come back to reality.

Rick did not hear back from his sister for six long days.

CHAPTER 41

Casey cancelled two scheduled visits with her brother Lee, but, on August 14, she agreed to meet with her parents. Reporters jostled George and Cindy Anthony as they approached the jail. The Anthonys were in no mood for the media. George said, "You don't want to be knocked down, get out of my way. I'm done with you guys. Leave me alone. Do not come past here. Please, do not come past here. Out of respect for these other people, for a change. Honor them."

A reporter shouted, "Do you have anything to say about the new theory that Caylee might be dead and it might be an accident?"

Cindy snapped, "Frickin' quit publicizing that stuff! She's out there!"

George screamed, "Shut up! Shut up! Shut up! Leave us alone, please. Do not follow us in the gates. Do not bother us when we're standing in line. Let's go. Let us go. Let's go."

His anger contrasted with the message on the matching tee shirts worn by George and Cindy. The Never Lose Hope Foundation had made them for the couple with a butterfly and the message "Fly Home Baby. We Miss You!"

They entered the visitation area and sat in uncomfortable chairs. On the video monitor, Casey smiled and greeted her parents. "Good morning."

"Good morning, beautiful. I love you."

"Hi. I love you, too," Casey responded.

Cindy threw her hands over her mouth trying to quell her sobs.

"Why is she crying already?" Casey sneered.

"Because we haven't seen you," George said. "How's your day going so far?"

"I was asleep," Casey said rubbing her eyes. "It's okay. I got up at five and stayed awake for about an hour and went to bed for a little bit. So my eyes are red. I'm a little tired."

"So what else is going on with you?" George asked.

"Nothing," Casey said with a laugh. "The usual. Just waiting around." Casey asked about their tee shirts and told her father that she liked them.

George handed the phone to his wife. Cindy choked on her words as she said, "Hi, sweetie."

"Hi, Mom," Casey said and wiped at her eyes. Laughing, she said, "Well I lasted a minute. How are you feeling?"

"Not— We're not doing well, Case," Cindy cried. "None of us. Lee's been sick. Dad's boiling up at the media."

"I heard," Casey snickered.

Cindy's face screwed up with pain. "Someone just said that Caylee was dead this morning—that she drowned in the pool. That's the newest news out there."

"Surprise, surprise."

"It's very hard," Cindy sniffled.

"Yeah, I know," Casey said, her voice turning harsh. "Trust me, I know that. Someone just sent me some of the stuff on line—the comments that people have been leaving, blogs—articles, I guess, that people have been writing. It was very upsetting last night to see that."

"You know, it's terrible, Casey. We get hate mail, threatening letters."

"Well, I haven't gotten anything like that, thankfully. All the letters I've gotten are positive . . ."

"We need to have something to go on," Cindy pleaded.

Casey widened her eyes and flared her nostrils. With a toss of her hair, she snapped, "Mom, I don't have anything. I'm sorry. I've been here a month. I've been here a month today. Do you understand how *I* feel? I mean, do you really understand how *I* feel in this? I'm completely, completely out of the loop with everything. The only information I get is when I see my attorney. That's it. Outside of that, I have nothing to go on. I just have to sit here and wait and wonder. Wonder if something's going on—wonder if something's new."

"Have they asked about which one of us you want to speak to?" Cindy asked, referring to the possibility that Casey could visit privately, in person, with one other person.

"Yeah, I wanna see Dad. You know I wanna see everybody, but I had to choose, and I wanna see Dad."

Cindy's face contorted. "Well, then, here, talk to your Dad." She handed George the phone, wiped her eye and slumped forward, folding her arms tight across her midsection.

"Hey, sweetheart," George said. "I want you to know you are the boss through this whole thing, alright?"

"No, Dad, I'm not," she snapped. "I haven't been since I got here."

George talked over his daughter. "Listen to me for a second. Okay? Listen. Think of you owning this conglomerate—this huge business. José is one of your employees, so is the sheriff's department, so is the FBI, so am I, so is Lee and so is Mom. We're all working with you. And, if for some reason, something's not being said or being done, you can make it change. You're the one that . . ."

"Dad, I've told José. I've given him information to give to you guys. We've given everything to the police. But nobody's helping us—it's obvious. We know their intention. I'm sorry. I've helped in every way that I possibly can since the day I got here."

"Okay," George nodded.

"They didn't even give me twenty-four hours to help them—the police—without putting me here," Casey ranted. "So, it's obvious where everybody's intentions lie.

I know you guys want Caylee. I want Caylee more than anyone can understand, but I can't do anything from where I'm at."

". . . Sweetie, I'm not trying to get you upset."

"I am upset now. I'm completely upset. The media is going to have a freaking field day with this . . ."

George tried to interrupt, but Casey cut him off. "Let me speak for a second, Dad. I have let everybody talk . . ."

"Okay, here's your mom," George said, handing the phone to Cindy.

"Can someone let me . . ." Casey pulled the phone from her ear and clenched both fists in front of her as her face contorted. "Come on."

"Casey, hold on, sweetheart. Settle down," Cindy said.

"Nobody is letting me speak. You want me to talk, then give me three seconds to say something."

"Go ahead, sweetheart."

"I am not in control over any of this, because I do not know what the hell is going on. I do not know what is going on. My entire life has been taken from me. Everything has been taken from me. You don't understand. Everybody wants me to have answers. I do not have any answers because I do not know what is going on.

"I have no one to talk to. Except José when he comes— he's the only person I can talk to right now, because I cannot even say anything to you guys besides telling you that I love you," she said with a sniffle as her nose stuffed up from her tears.

"I want Caylee. Things like that, and that isn't even being put on the air, which it should be. It is everything else, everything that I am not saying. That's why I have not been calling, why I have not been taking calls, because him and I said we're not going to do that. I am trying to make sure that I am not going to give anybody else anything else to throw against me. But even with me giving them nothing, they are still doing it. So how am I . . ."

". . . You'll be fine once Caylee is found," Cindy assured her.

"Mom, I understand that. Do you understand my position on this? You guys expect me to have a thousand answers, and I have nothing. I have been here a month, out of contact with everybody except you guys, on the rare occasion that I get to see you, and my attorney. Do you understand? What am I supposed to learn from that? A month I have been removed from the situation. You guys are not understanding my side on this, and I am sorry."

"No, I understand."

"No, you don't," Casey said with scorn. "Because you are still asking me if there is anything I can tell you that can help, that I am the one that can do this. I can't.

"The opportunity was there that I probably could have helped. I am trying. I was trying. There is nothing more that I can say or do until I'm home, and even then, I do not know what I can do from that point. But I can at least do something other than sit on my butt all day and read or look up stuff for my case, because that has to be my focus right now. That has to be my focus . . ."

"Your focus has to be Caylee."

"Mom, if that is my focus, which it is, I can't do anything from here. I do not have access to the Internet. I can't make phone calls. I can't go anywhere."

". . . I was in Lake County two days ago," Cindy said.

"Okay."

"Is there anything there?"

"Mom! Geez!" Casey pulled the phone away from her ear in anger, clenching her fists and shaking the receiver. A moment later, she brought it back and said, "I'm sorry. I love you guys. I miss you."

"All right, sweetheart. Here's Dad. Hold on."

"No. I'm going to hang up, and just walk away right now, because . . ."

"Please don't," Cindy pleaded.

"I'm frustrated. I'm angry, and I don't want to be angry. This is the first time I've truly been angry this entire time, but I'm so beyond frustrated with all of this. I can't even swallow right now. It hurts."

"Just understand, we're all going in so many directions. We just want to go in the right one."

"Well, I can't point you in that direction when I'm literally at a standstill."

"Okay."

"I'm just as removed from the situation as somebody who has no clue what's going on. At least— Even random people that we've never met have more outlook on this than I do. That's really, really sad. That's really sad. I literally have nothing right now."

"Well, none of us has anything right now, Casey."

"You guys have each other. You're sitting next to Dad. You still have Lee. You have access to our community, to our family and friends, to our house." Anger tightened Casey's eyebrows and creased her forehead. After a bitter laugh, she continued. "You are taking that for granted. I have no one to comfort me but myself and the occasional visit, which has to be business for the sake of finding Caylee. So, yeah, I may look like I'm in charge, but you're wrong. I'm completely pushed away from everybody."

"All we can tell you is they have to honor your wishes when you say something. That's all Dad is trying to tell you."

"And he has been, Mom. He has been with everything— everything," she said defending her attorney José Baez.

". . . Well, I hope he's telling you honestly what you're up against."

A greater stridency entered Casey's voice. "Mom, I know what I'm honestly up against," she snarled. "Do you guys understand what I'm honestly up against? And by keeping me here, you're not helping me help myself. I'm sorry to say that."

"We don't have the means to get you out anyway, sweetheart. We don't."

"I understand that, but the opportunity was there, and it wasn't taken advantage of . . ."

"We didn't have an opportunity. I don't know where you're hearing that."

"Just give Dad the phone," Casey ordered. "I don't want to get frustrated. Just give Dad the phone."

"Hey, sweetie," George said.

"This is seriously the first time I've ever been angry— that I've been this frustrated—that I can't even think straight at this moment. Throughout this entire thing, I was pissed off at the police station. I was mad when all of that happened, but I tried to look at things subjectively, and this entire time, I haven't sat in my room for that entire month and been mad. Not once. Not one time. But right now, this is the most agitated and frustrated that I've been. Even when I sat with José and watched that episode of *Nancy Grace* and stuff that was being said about Mom, and about me and him, and everybody else that I've heard. It frustrates me, but I let it go. Right now, I'm so hurt by everything. I don't even know what to say. And I hate to say that."

"Well," her father said, "I'm not sure I upset you, and neither me or Mom would want to upset you. If we did, I'm sorry for that."

"I know that's not your intention," Casey conceded. "You have to understand where I'm coming from in all of this—and obviously none of you are   while still expecting me, a month literally out of the loop, to have some sort of new insight on all this stuff. I mean, really!" She rubbed a hand across her face as she struggled for words.

"Okay. I realize that this is really hard for you to talk about, especially . . ."

"Because I can't do anything," Casey interrupted, her voice reaching a grating, high pitch. "Because I've done everything. I've said everything. I've thought everything. That's all I can do is sit and think—every day—and that's what I've done."

"Okay. You know, it's hard for you, and it's hard for us because none of us have ever been through this kind of stuff."

"Well, obviously not," Casey said with a rueful laugh.

"You guys still have a crutch or multiple crutches throughout the community with everybody."

"Well, even that is waning at the moment, believe me. Even your mom and I are having our issues every single day, so just realize, it's . . ."

Indifferent, Casey cut him off. "Dad, I know it's going to take a toll on everybody, but understand again where I'm coming from in this. You have to see everybody's side. I've looked at everybody's side in this. I've prayed every single day for insight on everybody's thoughts and everybody's feelings, so I can know where you're standing and where you're coming from. And I know where you're sitting right now, and Mom and Lee and Joe Schmo walking down the block, who's seen this on the media every single day for the last month. I can understand everybody else's side in all this. But the worst part is that nobody can see my side, and I have to keep my mouth shut. I have to keep my mouth shut about how I feel, and with everything else, because all I need to do is give the media more stuff for them and the detectives and whoever else to throw back in my face when this goes to trial."

"Well, all I know is, I'm trying everything I can to get a chance to see you—just you and I. And I know your brother and your mom would like to do that."

"I know that, and when I had that choice, and they told me they were initially setting it up with Lee— God, I would do anything to see one of you right now— absolutely anything. But, I wanna see Lee and I wanna talk to Lee, but I knew most of that would be an interrogation with him. He'd have a whole list of questions he'd ask me . . . Mom will dominate a lot of the conversation, which is how it's been, I mean, you and I, we've been separated for a while," Casey said with a sniffle and a swipe at her eyes. "And we were just— I wanna see all of you, but I want to see the one person who I've been so far disconnected from the longest, and that's been you."

"Well, that's good. I'm glad you made that choice on

your own. Thank you so much—I appreciate that. Thank you."

Casey sighed again.

Next to George, a distressed Cindy laid her head down on the counter and George rubbed lightly on her rounded back. "So how did you get through . . . last Saturday?" George asked, referring to that day that would have been Caylee's third birthday.

"I didn't. I spent the day almost completely by myself, with my head under the covers," Casey said through sniffles as she wiped her eyes. "I read my Bible almost the entire day. I was miserable—just completely and utterly miserable—just as I have been the entire time. It was the first time outside of our visits that I really showed any emotion. And I was open and I didn't care, just because I couldn't hold anything back. I broke down. It was the first time that I truly, truly broke down. And it hurt. I'm still recovering from that. Hearing about the fact that Mom was making chili and there was probably a bunch of people at the house."

"No, there wasn't. There was just your brother and I and your mom. . . . Mom made some of her great chili . . . It was just us. There wasn't no one else . . . Are you eating and stuff?"

"I'm eating so they leave me alone."

"Did you have a chance to enjoy more cold bologna sandwiches and coleslaw?"

"It's a little bit more than that. But yeah, I'm eating so that I'm not being bothered with 'Are you eating?' because if I don't eat, then they'll say something . . . I didn't want to upset Mom. I just—I'm running low on steam, too. If it was not for the fact that I am sitting by myself all day, sleeping, you know, I would probably be—I am getting sick right now. I can feel it. I felt it when I got up. My eyes were still red. It wasn't from sleeping. I'm getting a cold."

"Your mom wants to talk to you," George said and handed the receiver to Cindy.

"Hey," Cindy said.

"Hey, I'm sorry I upset you. I didn't want to upset you . . . That wasn't my intention. I've let everybody talk. I haven't gotten to say anything. I haven't wanted to say anything. I haven't wanted to get frustrated or show that, but I cannot hold that in all of the time. It is getting harder."

"I know," Cindy commiserated.

"I know each day is getting harder on everybody."

"You don't know, Casey, how hard it is."

Casey let out an indignant snort. "Oh, I don't know? Being secluded and I do not know what is going on?"

"But you know what? That is actually a good thing. Because if you were out here . . ."

". . . But you know what, Mom? Again, it's going to blow over. I'm not going to give the media anything when I get out of here—it sucks for them—because I have nothing to say. All I want is my kid back—to be back with my family. That's all I want. That's all I'm asking. But I am not going to ask any of them for it, because they're not going to give that to me. They're not. I will do whatever the hell I have to to get my family back together. That is it. That's all I want to do."

In a heart-breaking and pathetic voice, Cindy asked, "You still think she is okay?"

"I know in my heart, Mom. I know in my gut. She's all right. I can feel it. Every day that gets stronger. I still know she's coming home. I can feel that—she's coming home."

"What can I say to her on the air? What can I tell Zanny that is going to make her bring Caylee back?"

"Tell her that we forgive her. That all we want is our Caylee. That's it."

"I said that yesterday."

"Mom, that's it—that's all I can think of. That's all I can say 'cause that's what I would say. That I forgive her and that I want my baby back. That's it."

"I mean, do you think they actually would do that?"

"I don't know what I can think anymore, Mom. I keep saying it because it's the truth. I want media help as much as we can get it, but they need to help us, too."

"I know."

". . . I'll try to help them any way I can, but if they're coming in here attacking me, they're not getting shit. I'm sorry. I need to be looked at as a victim, because I am just as much of a victim as Caylee."

Time was up, the connection was broken. George and Cindy walked out of the jail clinging to broken promises and shreds of hope.

Keith Williams had grown up in the Anthonys' neighborhood and was drawn to look around the woods near Hidden Oaks Elementary on August 5. He'd talked to a psychic in Texas who told him that Caylee would be found in the woods near the road. He went back on August 18 and scouted the area again. This time, walking the fence line, he found a deflated Father's Day balloon and, a ripped bag of stuffed animals in great condition, along with a few pieces of children's clothing. He picked up the bag and went down to the Anthonys' home.

Cindy answered the door and told him that none of the items looked familiar—and besides, they all knew that Caylee was still alive. Keith tossed the bag back into his trunk, troubled by Cindy's offhand and dismissive manner. He returned to the woods and called the police.

Deputy Richard Cain again responded to cover the tip. Keith pulled the bag from his trunk and pointed out where he'd found it. Cain showed little interest in checking out the location. "This bag is too deteriorated," the deputy said, and, much to Keith's surprise, he tossed the bag back into the woods.

CHAPTER 42

The media ate up the tale voraciously. But who could blame them? A lovely child, a bizarre kidnapping story, a web of lies and an unusual cast of supporting characters—every week, it seemed, new life was breathed into the story. One of the first to arrive on the scene from out of town was author, talk show host and former Los Angeles detective Mark Fuhrman, who'd stepped onto the national stage during the O. J. Simpson trial.

Fuhrman went first to the Anthony family to offer his assistance in locating their missing granddaughter. After talking to them, he visited the Orange County Sheriff's Office. He told investigators about the argument Cindy and Casey had had on June 15, and reported that Cindy wanted to know one way or another if Caylee was dead or alive.

Other out-of-towners joined in the search. Private investigator Jim Hoover drove to town to volunteer his personal services to the Anthony family. He explained, "When you see people on television being harassed and nobody coming to help except for a few people out in front, when you see people being picked on and threatened and hassled and, you know, sometimes you think you just have to go down there and kind of step forward or step in and say, 'Hey, these people don't need this aggravation.' I just thought these people needed some help. I'm going there and offer these people some help as a citizen."

He spotted George doing yard work. "I'm not a reporter," Jim said. "If I can be of any help to you, you know, I'll be more than happy to help you."

George didn't know what to think of this stranger. He simply said, "Thank you."

Jim hung around the street watching the media circus when he saw Cindy come outside. He approached her as well. "I've been seeing what's been going on, on television. I don't think it's fair to you or your family. If I could be of any help to you, I'll be more than happy to help you."

"Wait right here," Cindy said. Fifteen minutes later, she returned. "You're going to get a phone call soon."

Jim's cell rang. It was a private investigator by the name of Dominic Casey. "I checked you out and verified that you are who you say you are. Thanks for offering to help them. Since I've started working this case, I kind of became a pariah. Nobody wants to work with me. So I appreciate any help you can give me."

Dominic Casey of D & A Investigations worked both for José Baez and the Anthony family for a time—then, only for Cindy and George. He claimed that Baez did not pay him as promised.

No high-profile case would be complete, of course, without a psychic on hand. Gale St. John traveled from Toledo, Ohio, to Orlando to provide her insight. But Gale relied on more than just psychic ability. She also traveled with a cadaver dog team. She was not working with the police or with the family, but she claimed to have visions of Caylee's location. She told Nancy Grace, "We have seen a wooded area. This is pretty much agreed upon with the entire time. . . . We've seen . . . a particular-looking building." Following the clues from their visions, the canine teams searched for nine hours, covering an area near Hidden Oaks Elementary School and another on Lee Vista Boulevard. In three months, another psychic's involvement would become even more controversial.

Another man to step into the ring was preceded by his

stellar international reputation. Tim Miller of Texas EquuSearch Mounted Search and Recovery, out of Dickinson, Texas, was best known for his search for Natalee Holloway in Aruba. He had strong enough credentials in the search business that the government of Sri Lanka had called for his assistance in finding missing victims after the tsunami. Much of his work, however, rarely made the front page. Since its founding a decade ago, the organization has participated in more than five hundred searches.

Tim understood, first-hand, what the families of the missing experienced. In 1984, his 16-year-old daughter disappeared. For one-and-a-half years, he knew nothing of her whereabouts. Then kids on dirt bikes found a body. Near their discovery, authorities located the skeletal remains of two other girls. One of them was Laura.

It was the 1997 disappearance of Laura Smither in a nearby town that led Tim to become involved in the search business. He first volunteered for the Laura Recovery Center, founded by Smither's family. The director of that organization encouraged him to combine his love for horses with his passion for the missing, and Texas EquuSearch was born.

Bounty Hunter Leonard Padilla rode into town, wearing a black cowboy hat and chomping on a toothpick. He worked for his family's business, Tony Padilla Bail Bonds in Sacramento, a company with three decades of experience. He believed Casey Anthony was being railroaded and he was determined to get her out of jail. He appeared on the *Nancy Grace* show on August 15 to explain his presence in Orlando.

"The original contact came from a friend of mine in New York, who suggested that there was something that could be done here. And, I—myself and my family— have gotten involved in high-profile cases in the past, and sometimes it required bailing a person out of jail so they could talk to somebody other than law enforcement.

"Obviously, in this particular situation, he put me in contact with the attorney . . . I said to my nephew, 'Look, if we get her out of jail, she's liable to be more pliable as far as talking to somebody. She's sat in there for thirty days. It hasn't done law enforcement any good. Let's take a run at it.'

"I'm looking at it like this: I don't think the three-year old is dead. I think she's alive. I think Casey just handed her off to a baby-sitter. These young ladies, when they're sometimes on drugs and things of that nature, they don't remember from one day to the next what they've done, and I believe that's what's taken place here."

This wasn't Padilla's first quixotic mission. He'd run for mayor several times, most recently losing in a primary in June 2008. He'd run for Sacramento County supervisor and the United States Congress, and aspired to be the replacement for the recalled Governor Gray Davis. He'd never had luck in elections.

But he did succeed in getting Casey out on bond on August 21. In an interview with ABC the next day, he said, "There's a two-hundred-fifty thousand-dollar reward out there right now. And for the next week, if somebody brings her back and deposits her anywhere, in a drugstore or in a hospital, they can claim the reward. They can simply state that they were baby-sitting her for the mother and there will be no law enforcement involvement. I'm not a cop. I'm not out to make a case against them. They have a week in which to bring the baby to a drugstore or a hospital or any place that's open, and then they can claim the reward."

And then there was Biteboy, a pop music boy-band drawn to controversy. The group had made headlines in June of 2006 in Topeka when they staged a concert to protest Westboro Baptist Church. Run by Fred Phelps, the church sponsored anti-homosexual demonstrations, but moved on to stage demonstrations at the funerals of soldiers killed in Iraq. It was the latter that caught the interest of Orlando-based Biteboy.

The band was another discovery of music impresario Lou Parlman, best known for introducing teen heartthrobs the Backstreet Boys and 'N Sync to the world. He now managed Biteboy from his federal prison cell, fifty miles outside of Atlanta, where he sat after conviction in a $300 million Ponzi scheme—at the time, the largest one ever.

Biteboy loaded up their instruments and arrived at 4937 Hopespring Drive on August 24 on the back of a flatbed U-Haul trailer. They came to a near-stop and launched into their Casey Anthony song, "Wine Sick Mind." Before they could run through all the lyrics, Leonard Padilla strode out of his RV command center and approached Richard Namey, the man driving the Chevy Blazer that towed the flatbed. According to Richard, when he rolled down the window, Leonard slammed both hands down on the door frame, making it impossible to roll the window back up. "I'm gonna have you arrested," he threatened. "You are interfering with an active murder investigation."

"You have no such authority," Richard said.

"I'll kick your ass," Leonard snapped.

Richard kept his vehicle rolling slowly forward and Leonard approached the band swinging his fist at Ricky Namey—Richard's son—on the flatbed. His target moved in time to dodge the impact, and Leonard connected with the microphone. The stand fell over, cutting Ricky's hand. As they pulled away, the band left behind a CD of their song for Casey's listening pleasure.

The next week, Ricky filed a criminal complaint against Padilla. Rob Dick, another bounty hunter working with Padilla, filed a complaint against the band. Leonard grew dismayed with Casey after sitting down with her in her home. Casey started to explain the Zenaida Fernandez-Gonzalez story and Leonard cut her off. "If you want to discuss something with me, tell me the truth. I don't want to hear that. That's bunk. I traveled three thousand miles and you're going to start with this?"

"Get out of my house!" Casey shrieked at him. "You're not going to talk to me like a cop. Get outta here." Leonard left. His support for Casey was on a downhill slide.

Add to that mix the experts consulted by the defense. Henry Lee, the forensic scientist who dismayed many of his admirers with his performance on the witness stand during the Michael Peterson trial, came to Orlando to render his opinion on the evidence gathered by the Orange County Sheriff's Office. Kathy Reichs was the forensic anthropologist brought into the case. She was best known to the general public for her Temperance Brennan novels and *Bones*, the Fox television show the books spawned. Larry Koblinsky, of the Forensic Science Department at John Jay College provided advice and opinion in the areas of forensic biology, serology and DNA analysis. In addition, two world-renowned forensic pathologists involved with the defense were Cyril Wecht and Michael Baden.

Perhaps the oddest visitor to the Orlando area was Tropical Storm Fay. She was the first in history to make landfall in Florida four different times and had an impact on the search for Caylee Anthony. She went through Orlando on August 21, dumping twenty-five inches of rain. The heavy downpour flooded a wooded area behind Hidden Oaks Elementary School, near the Anthonys' home, on Suburban Drive.

Casey Anthony was arrested again—this time on three new charges: uttering a false instrument, fraudulent use of personal information and petty theft for stealing from Amy Huizenga. The next day, Padilla revoked her bail.

CHAPTER 43

It was time for the next sideshow in the Casey Anthony drama. Deputy Anthony Rusciano, who'd had a lengthy text flirtation and a few hasty sexual encounters with Casey in the spring, sat down with Detective Yuri Melich and Sergeant John Allen. Allen asked him about his relationship with Casey. "During our initial conversation, where you indicated you'd met her only once at a party, you have since told us that wasn't true, and you lied to us because you were just afraid, right?"

"Yes, sir," Anthony said.

"Okay, you come in here today and you told us another version of those events."

"Yes, sir."

"And that wasn't entirely true either, right?"

"There's a little more to it, yes, sir."

". . . But you are in no way trying to impede our investigation?"

"Absolutely not."

"You don't have some information about this and you're trying to misdirect us in some other direction, right?"

"Absolutely not."

"You're just simply . . . don't want to be associated with this," Allen pressed.

"Yes, sir."

". . . You didn't help in any crime."

"No, sir."

"You didn't help cover up a crime?"

"No, sir."

He may have been innocent in the disappearance of Caylee Anthony, but it did not save Anthony Rusciano's job. He'd lied to fellow law enforcement officers about the breadth of his relationship with Casey. His career with the Orange County Sheriff's Office was over.

On the same day that Fay hit Orlando, Allen and Melich, along with Special Agent Scott Bolin, traveled to the home of Cindy's mother, Shirley Cuza, to question her again about the case. When they arrived, Shirley had no electricity due to the storm.

Detective Melich asked her, "How was Cindy's relationship with Caylee when Casey was around? Was there some jealousy between Cindy and Casey about Caylee, like who was the better mother, or who took better care?"

"Cindy tried not to overstep her, but she was happy, I think, when Casey was gone and she was taking care of her. I think there was. Sometimes in my heart, I says to myself . . . I don't want to think that . . . Caylee isn't alive, but I wondered if she [Casey] hated her mom more than she loved Caylee."

A while later in the interview, Melich asked, "What do you think it's going to take for Casey to tell anyone what happened?"

"She probably needs somebody to threaten her, personally. You know, I hate to think of her being put in a jail with them women that's going to beat the hell out of her, but it might do her some good."

"Do you think she would open up to you?"

"No. I don't think she would open up to me, because she knows I'm mad at her . . . I mean, our last words weren't loving words. I did say, I said, 'Casey, I love you, but I don't like you.' I don't like the stuff she's doing."

Melich also interviewed Cindy's brother Rick that day over speakerphone. Three FBI agents were present during the conversation. When Rick was asked about the relationship between Cindy and Casey, he said, "Casey resented Cindy. She resented Cindy to the point where she could see that Caylee likes Cindy way better than she likes her. And to me, that was normal for a baby to like the grandma, because grandmas always spoil kids."

Cindy received an email informing her that her brother Rick was posting on an on-line forum about the case. Cindy forwarded the message to Rick with a question:

Is this true?

Her brother wrote back:

You are alive. You never responded to any of my last emails. Yes, I was on a blog . . . Yes, I MAY talk to Greta . . . I would not tell Greta anything bad. I would tell her that you are a good person *[who]* loves your daughter very much and absolutely adored Caylee. The people of this country think you and George are wackos. They think Casey is a monster.
. . . You and George are in such denial and no one can reach you anymore. I love you and hate like hell to see you go through this. This is very hard on Mom, too. It is slowly killing her . . . Those people on that blog were ripping you guys apart. I tried to set them straight. I couldn't stand seeing you guys get bashed so bad. Some people were really nice though. They really feel for you and George and Lee. I am not trying to hurt you in any way.

Cindy lashed back at him, criticizing him for spreading lies and pleading with him not to go on Greta Van Susteren's show. Rick agreed to the latter, but objected to her characterization of what he said:

I am trying to reason with you . . . It's not you against the world. We are trying to help you. Have you asked or received any counseling yet? I am real serious about this. Families that go through bad things need to get it . . . I used to be able to talk to you, but you are so involved in this you are lost. We are all hoping for the best. Casey has ALL the answers though.

I am here when you are ready to open up. Okay? I mean it. I am here.

She snapped back saying that the story of George pushing his father through a plate-glass window was a lie, her 401K was gone before Caylee was born and Casey did not steal a checkbook from their Mom's house—all allegations he had made in the chat room.

Casey may be a liar about some things but she is a good kid and a great mother. I've told you, you do not know the facts. You are so fixated on the sitter. Get over the sitter. Just because I have no pictures of her, it doesn't mean she doesn't exist.
. . . You think you are going to open my eyes to something—you have. I have a brother who is only looking for someone to pay attention to him and he has no faith in me or family loyalty . . . My eyes have never been so open. I can certainly see through you. And thank you for saying that you will not waste your time for your niece. That statement proves to me that you have no soul either. I pray to God that you will be forgiven by him because I will never forgive you. You have crossed the line.

Three minutes later, she sent a postscript:

Oh yeah, Greta told me when she was in my house after she interviewed us that she cannot wait to hear me tell everyone "Fuck you" when this is all over and Caylee is home.

Rick was angered by his sister's messages. He wrote:

George did wrestle with his dad and put him through the window. That is why George had to start his own business. Don't lie to me about it. Mom filled me in on Casey so don't lie to me about her.

He ranted that they were stupid for being manipulated by Casey and warned:

If the cops didn't think you were stupid, they would bring charges against you and George for destroying evidence . . . Oh, by the way, everyone on Greta thinks Caylee is dead including Greta. Do you ever watch her show? What a moron you are. Mental Hospital here you come.

On Sunday, August 31, the sheriff's office loaded EquuSearch infrared equipment in their helicopter and lifted off, looking for recently disturbed patches of earth and fresh tire tracks in suspicious places, and mapping out other search possibilities. On the ground, more than 200 volunteers covered an area north of the Orlando International Airport.

A couple of developments in the case eroded away the volunteer numbers. On Monday, the sheriff's office issued a statement that read:

FBI Laboratory evidence, along with additional evidence that has not been made public, leads investigators to the belief there is strong probability that Caylee is deceased. If any evidence to the contrary is provided, it will be vigorously pursued.

On Tuesday, the public learned of the offer of limited immunity extended to Casey Anthony by the state attorney's office. If accepted, prosecutors could not use any of Casey's statements against her, but they could use any evidence obtained from the information she provided. The offer had an expiration date: Time was up at 9 A.M. But there was no response from Casey or her attorney.

Fewer than thirty-five volunteers showed up that morning. Search Director Mandy Albritton said, "We worry that the community has soured on the family and is not keeping Caylee first. It is sad that we've had such a low turnout." She said that typically she expected one thousand volunteers. EquuSearch had already expended $30,000 since they'd begun the search on Friday.

Sheriff Kevin Beary pleaded for more help. "We need to try to find some closure on this case. That's why EquuSearch is here." He pledged a $5,000 contribution to the organization, as well as the use of the department's airboats. "EquuSearch is a reputable operation with expert volunteers. Regardless whether she's alive or passed away, we need to find Caylee." On Wednesday, sixty-five people showed up to struggle through thick undergrowth, slog over swampy ground and avoid a legion of snakes as they looked for duffle bags, bones and rolled-up rugs. Still, nothing turned up.

In a display of ingratitude for the organization's work, Cindy lashed out at EquuSearch for Tim Miller's suggestions that Caylee might be dead. She said that Miller was brought here to look for a living child, not a dead one. In a written release, Cindy said, "It is evident his motives were to obtain publicity for his organization at the expense of exploiting my granddaughter's disappearance."

Tim Miller, who had devoted the past decade to helping others suffering from the pain of a missing loved one, responded simply: "We are holding on to that little bit of hope that Caylee is still alive. But if not, it's important that her little body is found."

Cindy had now alienated two former allies. That week, she said, "Right now, I think [Caylee's] somewhere in Texas or even Puerto Rico."

Leonard Padilla summed up a lot of people's feeling on *Nancy Grace*: "She's living in total denial."

CHAPTER 44

The evidence was piling up in the case against Casey Anthony. Lab results painted a grim picture. Cell phone and computer analysis found no calls, text messages or emails to Zanny the nanny. Tests of the air in the Pontiac Sunfire indicated high levels of chloroform in the trunk as well as the presence of a decomposing body—confirming the anecdotal stories of the odor in the car. Hairs found in the trunk were connected to Caylee—but, more important for the prosecution, the hairs had the distinctive banding only present post-mortem.

Leonard Padilla, who'd previously described Casey as a mother who knew her child was somewhere safe, now believed that Caylee was no longer alive. He was convinced that no one would ever be able to claim the $225,000 reward for the safe return of the little girl. He established a $50,000 reward for the recovery of her body. He told Greta Van Susteren that he hoped someone would claim the reward soon and make life easier for Tim Miller of Texas EquuSearch. "Because he's out there in the swamp being mosquito-bit with a lot of good-hearted volunteers, and the person who has the answer is not saying anything."

Nonetheless, murder charges had not been filed against Casey Anthony. On September 5, two bond companies partnered to put up the half million dollars in bail. Casey was fitted with an ankle bracelet to monitor her movements before she left the correctional facility.

Wearing a Caylee tee shirt and a black baseball cap, she kept her head down as she slipped into her attorney's black SUV. Among the reporters awaiting her arrival at home were a dozen protestors. One toddler held a sign that read, "How could you kill a baby like me?" Other signs proclaimed, "Baby Killer" and "Orlando's O.J.?"

The situation in the Chickasaw Oaks community around the Anthony home went downhill fast. A lawyer for the homeowners' association, a group of 127 families, appealed to a judge to force protestors and reporters out of the neighborhood. The judge, citing the right of free speech, would not banish them.

They filed again, asking for the crowd to be moved to a vacant lot at the end of Hopespring Drive by the intersection with Suburban Drive. That, too, was denied, because the protestors didn't receive notification of the action. They tried a third time, but again were turned down.

Tourists from all over the country flocked to the Anthony home to take snapshots standing in front of the house—grinning as if they were posing on the edge of the Grand Canyon. Even more bizarre, a busload of ten seniors—all Alzheimer's disease patients—made a field trip to the Anthony home. They were disappointed when they arrived; no protestors were present.

At the vigil on September 8, things turned ugly. George told protestor Larry Donovan to get off of his property. Larry said, "I am not on your property, I am standing in the public right of way."

George lunged at the man and, grabbing both of his arms, pushed him back three to four feet into the roadway. George turned to protestor Patricia Young, took hold of her arm, forcing her out onto the pavement, too. Police were dispatched to the scene, where an officer listened to the complaints. Observing no injuries on either battered person, they reviewed a Channel 9 News videotape of the incident. Law enforcement then spoke to George, telling him they were filing a report and wanted to take his statement if he desired to provide one. He provided a mild version of the events and added, "No one was injured."

George's behavior inflamed the crowd. By September 11, the Anthonys and the protestors were cursing at each other every time a family member came out of the house. A man showed up with a three-foot-wide hunk of plastic shaped like a tombstone. On its front, it read, "Caylee Anthony 2005–2008." Lee zoomed into the driveway in a black Mustang, and missed hitting a family by inches. The toddler in the group cried out in fear. Lee told a deputy that he'd honked to warn them before he pulled into the driveway. Someone in the crowd shouted, "You lie like your sister."

Protestors and supporters of the family engaged in shouting matches. George yanked lawn chairs from the patch of grass between the sidewalk and the street, and tossed them into the road. Cindy had a nose-to-nose confrontation with one of her female critics. During the argument, the arm of the woman's small boy was clipped by a car door. The Department of Children and Families began an investigation into that incident. Lee attacked a sign reading, "I wouldn't let my dog go missing for a month without looking," throwing it on the ground and stomping on it.

Casey was arrested again on September 15 on additional charges of petty theft, check forgery and using a false identity. She spent one night in a jail cell and was returned to her home the next day. José Baez objected to law enforcement's actions. "I think we are seeing the games that are being played. I am not intimidated—not in any way, shape or form. If police can do this to her, they can do it to anyone."

The protestors had a different opinion. They thought Casey should be arrested and held behind bars for the rest of her life. Media reports that Casey's phone records showed no telephone calls to the mysterious nanny had fueled the flames of their anger. This quick release from jail made their outrage burn hotter ready for spontaneous combustion.

It soon came. Just before midnight on September 17, George stormed out of his house to confront the protestors throwing things at his home. A woman jerked on George's tee shirt, attempting to drag him out into the street. Cindy raced to his rescue clutching an aluminum baseball bat. She wedged herself in between her husband and the protestors. Law enforcement arrived and created a temporary calm.

At 1:30 A.M., on September 18, Casey Anthony dialed 9-1-1. "There are protestors still outside of the house. We already called about an hour-and-a-half ago, and it took officers thirty minutes to get here. The protestors are now banging on our garage door, and they've still been throwing things at our windows and our garage, and now the media is here. My father is going outside and there is going to be a fight. So, please can you send people down here? There is now a physical altercation. You need to send vehicles immediately."

"It is getting physical?" the operator asked.

"Yes, it's getting physical right now."

"You see them physically fighting?"

"Yes, I see them physically fight. We have surveillance."

"Okay, do you know if there are any weapons?"

"I don't know if there are any weapons," Casey said. "I know that my father is outside and so is my mother. So send as many people as you possibly can."

"And who is this?"

"They need to be arrested, because this can't keep happening. We already had six or seven officers out here for almost forty-five minutes, and they did not do anything. And these are the same punks that were out here all night throwing stuff at our house."

"Okay, stay on the line with me. Okay?"

"I absolutely will, but they need to hurry up. They were— They just left not that long ago."

"The police officers left?"

"The police officers just left at about one o'clock, yes. A media van just pulled up, and that is when all of this started happening," Casey said.

"About how many people are out there?"

"There are at least a dozen people, and now two media vans. And there is actually more people walking in from across the street."

"How many people are actually involved in the alter-cation?"

". . . There are at least a dozen people. My mom is out there now spraying people with the hose. My father is— They are trying to get them off the property. They are also trespassing on our property. Besides, I know . . ."

"Is it still happening?"

"They are still standing on the property. Yes, they are out there recording it."

"So what about the physical altercation? Is it over?"

"It's already over, yes."

"So, it is no longer physical?"

"It is no longer physical. But it was already physical."

"Is this a protestor or is this a resident?"

"It's the protestors."

"No, I'm saying, who are you?" the operator asked again.

"I'm the resident." Casey continued a play-by-play de-scription of the action in her front yard.

"Are they inside now?" the operator asked.

"Yes, my parents are inside right now."

"What happened?"

"Both of my parents were hit by protestors . . . So can we get people out here immediately?" Casey asked.

"There's somebody on their way. I just need you to stay on the line, okay?"

As a result of that night, Orange County officials in-creased patrols in the area. Members of the Guardian Angels, an organization founded three decades ago in New York City to supplement police patrols and bring safety to communities, showed up in their familiar red berets to help law enforcement keep the peace in the Anthonys' neighborhood.

The vigil scheduled for the evening of Sunday, September 21, was cancelled due to fear of disruption. The next day, the trust fund set up to provide money for the Caylee search effort was shut down because of threatening emails and phone calls to SunTrust Bank and the trustee. The threats were the result of rumors spread on the Internet claiming that the Anthonys were using the money for expenses not related to the search. Paul Kelley, one of the fund's administrators, said that there was only $2,500 in the account and just $500 had been spent on tee shirts, bracelets and other small items to promote the search effort. The fund would re-open shortly under a new administrator.

Adding to the chaos of the case that week, Zenaida Fernandez-Gonzalez of nearby Kissimmee, Florida, filed a civil suit against Casey for using her name in her stories to Orange County deputy sheriffs. The complaint read:

> The conduct of defendant, Casey Anthony, exceeds the bounds of decency in a civilized society and was such that a person of normal sensibility upon hearing what she did would exclaim "outrageous."

Zenaida asked the court for $15,000 in damages.

The Anthonys resumed the candlelight vigils on Sunday, September 28. George embraced a new attitude of peace. He was determined not to lash out at the protestors. Thirty people gathered on the lawn to sing and pray to God to help the family endure the hostility of others and to help find Caylee. Despite the shouted taunts of the sign-bearing demonstrators, George's only words to them were, "God bless you."

CHAPTER 45

On October 2, the Orange County Sheriff's Office labeled Casey Anthony as a suspect in the missing person investigation of her daughter. Captain Angelo Nieves, spokesperson for the agency, said, "Her information has been suspect since we began this investigation. This is a person who has been uncooperative since the first day. Over the past two-and-a-half months, we have been diligently working to resolve the case of the missing child. The information she has provided has proven to be false."

In the Orange County Sheriff's Office Forensics Unit, Lee Anthony consented to providing a DNA sample for analysis. The results of that buccal (or mouth) swab would, at last, put a virulent Internet rumor to rest—it would prove that Lee was not Caylee's father.

Casey's high school friend Annie Downing received a phone call from Lee that day warning her to expect a phone call from investigators: "We all know Casey's done bad things, but you need to protect yourself. If they call you, you need to tell them the truth . . . Don't protect Casey."

Another friend of Casey, Melina Calabrese, answered Yuri Melich's questions. He asked her about the photographs of Casey partying in late June and early July. "I would look at my pictures and then I would look at those pictures and it just didn't feel like the Casey that I knew. Basically, didn't look like the Casey I knew. It just looked—I don't know—she was trying too hard to be someone she was not . . . Something about those pictures is just not sitting with me right."

Melich moved to questions about Casey's attitude toward men and dating. Melanie said, "I guess this past year, she would try and do more relationships than just dating . . . She tried again with Jesse. She met that Ricardo guy and she met this Tony guy . . . I heard about her . . . being interested in this guy and being interested in that guy . . . Almost was like a game for her, I think . . . It was kind of fun in high school. You would like a guy, and then you would get his attention and hang out for a bit. And then you'd get bored and go to the next one . . . She just kept doing it since then."

On Friday, October 10, Judge Stan Strickland granted three defense requests ordering that the state provide Casey's attorneys access to the Pontiac, all materials related to investigated tips including the manifest for AirTran Airways flight from Orlando to Atlanta. He held off ruling on the motion allowing Casey to travel to places of interest and on one to preserve forensic evidence, halting all testing, until rules of process could be established by the court.

Knowing that prosecutors would present their case to a grand jury on Tuesday, October 14, 2008, José Baez called a press conference that morning with Casey by his side. "I truly believe that if a prosecutor wanted to walk in there, without calling any testimony, they could ask, 'Does anyone want to indict Casey Anthony?' and they'd all vote 'Yes' by now. She's not running from this. She's never attempted to run from this situation. Casey is going through a nightmare. She's been living a nightmare for the last several months. She has a missing child. She also is someone's child."

The nineteen-member panel heard testimony from six witnesses, including George Anthony and Detective Yuri Melich. Someone forgot to turn off the external audio feed and a portion of the secret proceedings was delivered out to the media trucks. Chief Judge Belvin Perry Jr. warned the reporters that they would be charged with criminal contempt if they revealed anything they overheard.

The grand jury returned an indictment that afternoon charging Casey with first-degree capital murder, writing that she'd violated Florida Statutes with "a premeditated design to effect the death of Casey Marie Anthony." They also charged her with aggravated child abuse, aggravated manslaughter of a child and four counts of providing false information to a law enforcement officer.

As soon as the news was out, Cindy Anthony drove off with Casey. She rendezvoused with a bail bondsman under a bridge. José Baez arrived in another vehicle. Casey left her mother's car and got into the bondsman's SUV. They pulled out into traffic. Casey and her driver, as well as the attorney in another vehicle, thought that the following cars were reporters. José ran one of the vehicles off the road. That's when the lights started flashing. Casey's driver said, "Oh shit! It's the cops," and pulled over to the side.

Casey was arrested. In his car, Detective Eric Edwards spoke to Casey, referring to her lawyer as "Mister Crazy Driver." He asked, "So Mister Baez's intention was to—if it was the press—to keep the press away?"

"Yes," Casey said.

"So, I'm pretty sure the state statute would apply to running press vans off the road, but it just makes it worse when it's unmarked police cars."

"Oh, I completely agree with you," Casey said with a laugh.

During the drive, Casey told Edwards that she would be willing to talk if her attorney were present. As the vehicle exited I-4 heading towards John Young Parkway, Edwards said, "A right-hand turn will take you directly to the jail, and a left-hand turn will take you to an opportunity to assist in the search."

Casey wanted him to make a left-hand turn. He complied, taking her to an interrogation room instead of the jail.

She sat with the detective and called her attorney, who came to the sheriff's central office immediately. He spoke alone with Casey and when he finished, he told the detective to take her to the Orange County Jail.

The next day, Casey appeared in court with José Baez by her side. The judge read her indictment and ordered her held with no bond. On October 28, José Baez entered Casey's plea of not guilty. Judge Strickland set the trial to begin on January 5, 2009.

In the following two weeks, José visited his client in jail seven times. Jailers repeatedly noted him hugging Casey. A corrections official went in on one occasion to separate them. He was told that Orange County Jail policy forbids any kind of touching between visitors and inmates, and agreed not to do it again.

Baez was not the only one chastised in the aftermath of Casey's indictment for murder. Yuri Melich came under the gun, too. He'd logged into a chat room as Dick Tracy Orlando to answer questions about the crutch he was using—he'd broken his leg in three places during a training exercise—and to accept congratulations from well-wishers on the arrest. He never discussed the case, but still his presence was an irritant to others. The Anthonys' attorney, Mark NeJame, complained to the sheriff's office about his posts, and Melich's superiors told him to cut it out.

Sunny Welker reported a conversation with Cindy Anthony. She said the cell phone rang. Cindy was upset with Sunny's website, JusticeforCaylee.com, because it implied that Caylee was dead. According to Sunny, Cindy made derogatory remarks about Texas EquuSearch and told Sunny that she would "kick her ass" when they met face-to-face. Sunny called police. In case anything happened to her, she wanted this incident on the record.

Cindy and George drove up to Mount Dora to visit Cindy's parents. Shirley pulled them aside at the nursing home and said, "I want some answers. I want you to be straight with me. How, after all this evidence, how can you continue to support Casey?"

Cindy immediately came to Casey's defense and launched into the kidnapping story once again.

Shirley stopped her. "Cut the crap. I want the truth."

Cindy grew shrill in her insistence that they would still find Caylee alive.

"Cindy, Casey is a liar and a thief. How can you believe a word she says?" Their exchange grew more heated until a disgusted Shirley turned her back and walked away. She went straight home. Cindy and George followed her there. Shirley was exasperated. It was bad enough that Casey lied, but for Cindy to believe her lies was just too much. Cindy kept arguing on Casey's behalf.

Shirley slammed her hands down hard on the kitchen table. "If you can't tell me the truth, you're not welcome in my house. I hope Casey rots in hell."

On November 5, the defense sent a thick document to the prosecutors urging them to take the death penalty off the table. They argued that if Caylee was dead, then her death must have been an accident. They mentioned Casey's possible depression and her lack of emotion after Caylee's disappearance as proof that she was suffering from some psychological or emotional problem.

In response, Cindy released a statement on Thursday, November 6:

> I feel that a good attorney will plan for the worst case scenario and hope for the best. I know that Casey's attorneys know that she is innocent, but they cannot ignore how the media has already spun the facts and convicted her.
>
> Casey has been severely attacked by the media since she was first arrested and anyone would be a fool to ignore that. All of the negative spin has done her an injustice. Just look at what it has done for

poor Caylee. The media already has given up on looking for this child, when there is simply no credible or concrete evidence to prove that she is dead.

The defense and the family will never give up looking for Caylee. We continue to believe she is alive and so should everyone else who has a conscience. I would ask anyone to ask themselves just how quick would they stop looking for someone that they loved?

Texas EquuSearch had called off their search for Caylee in September, due to high water from Tropical Storm Fay and a lack of cooperation from the Anthonys. But they announced that they were coming back to Orlando to institute a new, massive search effort. On Saturday, November 8, 1,400 volunteers responded to the call. It sounded like a lot, but EquuSearch had hoped for 4,000. It took two hours to divide them into teams of ten people each. Once divided, they were assigned to a square plot of land. Texas EquuSearch had created a grid of the area stretching out 10 miles from the Anthony home. The volunteers boarded buses for transportation to the search sites to seek out the body of a young girl.

They drove down Goldenrod Road past the "command center" that George and Cindy had set up to encourage people to look for a living, breathing Caylee. The Anthonys and their supporters were angered by anyone who operated on the assumption that Caylee was deceased, and the dozen people under the tent shouted, and shook their fists at the volunteers in the buses. Those on the bus responded by yelling out the windows and jeering.

Jackie Mattlin, a volunteer on one of the buses, wondered why the driver didn't take another route and avoid the confrontation al together. Both times she set out for a new location, the driver drove past that spot.

When Jackie arrived at the first search assignment, she and her team members had to jump a fence into a cow pasture and cut across to the adjoining woods. Police and the property owner showed up, and the searchers were ordered to leave.

At the next spot, off of Route 417, the team spent three-and-a-half hours looking through heavy brush, poking into bushes with walking sticks, looking for any bit of debris that could be connected to Caylee Anthony. If they spotted anything, they stood by it until someone trained—usually, a Texas EquuSearch worker, sometimes a police officer—arrived and took custody of the scene. During the search that day, a bag of clothing for a small girl was recovered. But it had no link to Caylee.

On Sunday, November 9, 800 volunteers showed up to search. On Monday, the number was down to 50. That day, bounty hunter Leonard Padilla told Tim Miller that he needed to send divers into the Little Econ River in Blanchard Park. Lisa Hoffman, an EquuSearch team member, found, in a tree by the river, a cross with a beaded chain that resembled beads seen in the Anthony home. Leonard was convinced that Casey had hung the cross there and then thrown Caylee's body into the river.

Tim told Investigation Discovery, "I had my people use side-scan sonar to examine that water . . . and then I went back myself and checked it again. I told Leonard that it only takes an hour to scan it, and that we have put four or five hours into it, just so there would be no question as to whether she was there. I can tell you where every tire is at. I can show you where there is a bucket, where there is an old wheelbarrow and a fender from a car. I can show how deep the water is in every place and what the water temperature is. There is not a body in there."

Nonetheless, Leonard sent the Blackwater Divers into the river on November 10. Cindy and George showed up at this effort to confront Leonard about a memorial service they'd heard he was planning for the next day. "You guys aren't doing any good for Caylee . . . If you want to put divers in there, fine . . . but you're not holding a memorial service for my granddaughter."

Leonard did in the end have his gathering at Blanchard

Park, but he called it a "prayer vigil." Cindy and George still weren't happy. Nearly 100 people arrived, piling up flowers at the base of a cypress tree. Women hung a sign reading, "R.I.P. Caylee Marie. We love you!"

Reverend Richard Grund read scripture and spoke, bringing attendees to tears. "What makes Caylee so different? Nothing. She's like every innocent, she's perfect and she's pure and she's filled with love. And we want to love them back. Don't let your feelings stop with Caylee. There are other Caylees out there . . . Love never gives up, never loses faith and is always hopeful and endures every circumstance. If you love Caylee, then love everyone who loves her."

On November 12, Larry Garrison, spokesperson for the Anthony family, submitted his resignation. In the release, he wrote:

> Due to the erratic behavior over the last several months exhibited by the Anthony family, *[I am]* resigning as their spokesperson. It is my opinion that others have manipulated them into situations that would not dignify the family. I can no longer be part of that behavior. I wish them all the peace and resolution they so deserve. The truth always comes out in the end, and in this case "the truth is better than the spin."

The Anthony family countered, saying they'd fired him, and local TV affiliate WFTV accused him of accepting thousands of dollars for family photographs and pocketing all the money. Dominic Casey of D & A Investigations made the media rounds that day, too. He expressed his belief that Casey Anthony was a "loving and protective mother" and that Caylee was still alive. "You can call me crazy—everyone is calling me crazy. I get death threats on a daily basis."

The next day, divers in the river thought they'd discovered bones along with a child's Gumby toy and a shamrock in a plastic bag held down by bricks. Leonard called the media and then the FBI, irritating the lead investigators at the Orange County Sheriff's Office, who were left out of the loop. The excitement on television and radio was short-lived. The objects found were not human bones. The toy had no connection to Caylee.

Still, two big questions hung in the air: Would the prosecution seek the death penalty? And where was Caylee Marie?

CHAPTER 46

Just as everyone thought the quota for strange had surely been met, more bizarre news piled on the plate. WFTV reported that the city had banished Leonard Padilla and the Blackwater Divers from the park. The truth of the matter, uncovered by the *Orlando Sentinel*, was that the city had requested they suspend their search over the weekend because the park would be filled with families and kids, renting pavilions and playing soccer.

Leonard was, however, in a bit of trouble. Law enforcement wanted him to take a lie detector test to determine if he believed the divers had found real evidence in the river or if it was all a big publicity stunt. From a public relations viewpoint, the worst thing Leonard could have done was leave town—but that's what he did. Everyone said the FBI could administer the test in California as easily as in Florida, and Leonard insisted he was coming back. But still, it didn't look good.

Leonard was not on good terms with Tim Miller of Texas EquuSearch either. Tim's organization had expended nearly $100,000 in their search for Caylee without the cooperation of the little girl's family. Now, Tim was leaving for North Carolina, where families were eager to help him find their loved ones. Leonard had collected funds on his website that Tim claimed were supposed to go to Texas EquuSearch, but never did. To make matters more infuriating, Texas EquuSearch said Leonard Padilla

had come over to their command center signing auto-
graphs, posing for pictures and distracting the focus from
the search for Caylee, where it belonged. One of Leonard's associates said that they were appalled that Tim
would leave Orlando before Caylee was found, and that
he would be refunding all their donations.

On Friday, November 14, Casey filed a counter-suit
against Zenaida Fernandez-Gonzalez. Zenaida, the
woman who'd lost her job and her reputation because of
Casey's kidnapping stories, was now accused by Casey's
family and civil attorney of trying to cash in on a sensa-
tional case with "a frivolous lawsuit, filed for no other
reason but to harass and embarrass" Casey Anthony.

WFTV's Kathi Belich reported on an exclusive that
day that Cindy Anthony was writing a book about her
family's experience, regardless of the outcome. Cindy did
an interview with WESH news and said, "I am not writing a book. I don't know where people get this stuff." On
the other hand, WFTV had a tape of Cindy saying, "I
want to tell my side of things, what happened and how all
of this should not happen to other families." They claimed
that was said in the context of a book discussion. Then a
couple of days later, Cindy and George took WKMG reporter Jessica D'Onofrio on a room-by-room tour of their
home. During the filming, the Anthonys "talked about
a potential book they planned to write in the future." It
seemed the wheels on the Anthony wagon had wobbled
off in opposite directions, and even the most experienced
journalists were having a difficult time determining the
truth.

Saturday, November 15, at Dominic Casey's request,
Private Investigator Jim Hoover came to the offices of D
& A Investigations in Longwood at 8 A.M. and waited
fifteen minutes for Dominic to arrive. They both went
inside and Dominic said, "I've got something to tell you."

"What's up?" Jim asked, wondering about the somber
look on the P.I.'s face.

"I know where Caylee is."

Thinking that meant the little girl was still alive, Jim said, "That's great, let's go get her."

"She's dead," Dominic said, and they both sat silently. Then he added, "We have to go find her."

They both climbed into Jim's car and headed to Orlando. On the way down, he told Jim he wanted his help in finding Caylee. "If we find her, do not touch anything or contact the police." In Orlando, Jim followed directions, turning onto Suburban Drive, driving to the end of the street, making a U-turn and parking on the side of the road opposite from the woods—just feet from where Hopespring intersects Suburban—about two blocks from the Anthony home. It was the same location where meter reader Ray Kronk had seen suspicious items in August, where Kiomarie said she used to play with Casey and where Keith Williams had found a Father's Day balloon and a bag of stuffed animals. Tips from both men had been dismissed by the same deputy—Richard Cain.

Now, three months later, the water from Tropical Storm Fay had subsided and two private investigators were there following yet another tip, though Dominic didn't say from whom. Dominic got out of the car and said, "Just wait here." He crossed the street talking on his cell phone. At different times, Dominic said he was talking to his daughter, or to a psychic or to a friend of Casey's. Jim thought he might have been talking to Lee.

But whoever it was, Dominic knew where to go.

Back at the car, knowing that Dominic wanted documentation, Jim picked up one of his video cameras. He filmed twenty seconds and turned it off to review. The color wasn't right. So he grabbed another camera and got out of the car.

While Dominic walked in and out of the woods, Jim taped and he asked, "What are we doing? Where are we looking?"

"We're looking for three flat stones in a line." Suddenly, Dominic spotted the three 12-inch–by–12-inch pavers just five or six feet from the road. The middle one was broken in half. He pointed to them and Jim video-taped them in place. Dominic turned each one over and then got back on the phone.

When he disconnected, Jim said, "We got another location to go to?"

"Yeah," Dominic said and headed to a pile of black plastic bags at a nearby house. He cut them open with a knife. Finding nothing, they moved to the side of the house and through a partly opened gate. There were two two-by-fours and another three pavers in a row beside an air conditioning unit. Dominic moved the pavers and dug into the earth with a hand spade. On several occasions, Jim asked who'd given him the tip—twice Dominic said it was anonymous, the other times, he walked away without answering. Jim later said under oath that he'd gotten the impression that Dominic was showboating—going through the motions and getting them on tape to demonstrate his hard work to his clients. He certainly wasn't dressed for mucking about in the woods.

When their search turned up nothing, the two men drove off and joined George and Cindy at the meet-and-greet event in the tent, where they were selling Caylee tee shirts and shaking hands.

On Sunday, November 16, Jim met Dominic outside of his office for another search in the same location. Dominic went to his truck, lifted the lid and pulled out a rod for probing. This time, Dominic was dressed more appropriately, in jeans and sturdy footwear. Jim asked, "Why are we going back?"

"I want to search the area a little more." They drove back to Suburban Drive and Dominic probed the ground in the woods, talked on the phone and returned to the house they'd visited the day before. He pushed his stick down in the soft ground where the pavers had been.

Jim didn't understand it all, but he began to doubt it was showboating. Maybe Dominic really had a legitimate tip.

* * *

Dennis Milstead, the man in charge of Kid Finders Network and a big supporter of the Anthonys' contention that Caylee was still alive, reacted badly to questions from reporter Kathi Belich. She asked him about his previous arrest for assault and impersonating a police officer, and why his organization's list of accomplishments didn't include finding any missing children. Dennis lunged at her, grabbing her microphone and pushing away the camera and the cameraman holding it.

Michelle Bart, formerly a spokesperson for Kid Finders Network, was now performing that job for the Anthony family as a replacement for the verbally attacked Larry Garrison. It was her job to explain to the media and public why all the searchers looking for a deceased Caylee were wrong because the Anthonys had proof that she was alive.

The besieged Kid Finders Network now had no spokesperson. George Anthony, however, stepped into the breach and declared himself their spokesman, talking about how helpful the organization had been to him and his wife throughout their ordeal.

The next moment of chaos came from Mark NeJame, George and Cindy's attorney. He quit, citing disagreements with his clients, expressing his frustration at their insistence that Caylee was still alive and saying that he was no use as an advisor when his client would not take his advice. He stated with certainty that only one person knew the truth—the jailed Casey Anthony—and she wasn't talking.

Larry Garrison, former spokesperson for George and Cindy Anthony, sent an email to WFTV in November:

> Cindy has been writing me. I believe she may be on meds. I confronted her in an email asking her why she gave Casey's hairbrush instead of Caylee's to the authorities . . . I believe she is frightened I might speak out. I have gone to authorities with

this . . . That is the real reason I am out of there.
Why would anyone not help the police if they were
looking for their granddaughter?

Below that message was the one he'd received from
Cindy:

I never lied. I just never went to my bathroom to get
the hairbrush that I use only for Caylee.

THE DISCOVERY

"A lie will go 'round the world while truth is pulling its boots on."

—Charles Haddon Spurgeon
(often attributed to Mark Twain)

CHAPTER 47

The first week of December, news reports were peppered with bits of information on the case—a national vigil was held, Cindy claimed that her computer had been hacked, Leonard planned a Christmas Day vigil. The first big news came on December 5, when the state announced its intention not to seek the death penalty.

The morning of December 11, Judge Stan Strickland presided over a status hearing and postponed the start of the trial. A new date would be set at another hearing on January 15.

As everyone was filing out of the courtroom, utility worker Ray Kronk pulled his vehicle over on Suburban Drive. Ray was once again assigned to the route in the Chickasaw Oaks subdivision that had instigated his August calls to 9-1-1. He popped on his yellow lights, grabbed his meter stick, in case another snake wandered across his path, and walked a little ways into the woods to take a leak.

He spotted a black plastic bag with a round, dome-like protrusion. He tapped on the bulge. It thudded like a hollow hunk of plastic. He grabbed the bottom of the bag with the meter-box-pulling tool. A human skull with some hair, wrapped with duct tape, rolled onto the ground.

He called his route supervisor Alex Roberts. "I just found a skull. I need the police." He described his location.

David Dean heard the exchange and remembered the spot where they'd found the large rattler. He pushed in the button and said, "I told you she was in there."

Roy replied, "No. I told you."

Belatedly, David realized it was stupid to say something like that over an open radio channel, and he did not respond.

Two deputies reported to the scene immediately. They went down into the woods with Roy to view his discovery. They secured the area with crime-scene tape and called for homicide investigators.

Detective Yuri Melich reported to the scene. He looked into the opening of the black garbage bag and saw additional bones. Beside it was a tan laundry bag with a wire-enforced rim and additional trash bags inside. Next to the skull, he spotted a garment with white and pink vertical stripes.

He felt pretty certain that these were the remains of Caylee Marie Anthony, but that determination was not his to make.

All the items in the immediate vicinity of the skull were collected and taken to the medical examiner's office. There, pathologist Gary Utz laid out the contents. The skull, bones and clothing obviously belonged to a small child. The Winnie the Pooh blanket matched other items found in Caylee's bedroom.

There were no signs of trauma to the skull, but no hair remained on top of it. The hair on the sides was held in place by layers of duct tape across the mouth. The hair was carefully cut to avoid damaging the tape. In the middle of the piece of tape was the faint shadow of a heart-shape. The bag containing the bones had been open and under water for some time, making it possible that some of the evidence had floated away.

Back in the woods, blue tents popped up surrounding the area to protect recovered evidence from the falling rain. Dozens of reporters and onlookers formed a crowd around the outer perimeter in no time. Hidden Oaks Elementary School released students through a back exit, keeping them as far from the unfolding scene as possible.

Melich sought and received a new search warrant for

the Anthony home. Crime-scene investigators found a laundry bag of the same brand and design as the one found in the woods. The detective spotted a photograph of Caylee wearing a pair of striped shorts that looked just like the ones he'd found at the recovery scene earlier that day. They also found and retained sheets of red-and-white heart-shaped stickers in a shoe box in Casey's room. In the shed, the red gas can with duct tape was confiscated once again.

The tape would prove to be the same brand as was found on the skull.

They also collected garbage bags, pool chemicals, vacuum cleaners, diapers, pull-up pants and recipes and containers for making chloroform. Since Cindy had not provided investigators with the right hairbrush in the summer, they made sure they took custody of every hairbrush and toothbrush in the house.

At the Orange County Jail, Lieutenant Tammy Uncer and Sergeant Billy Richardson escorted Casey Anthony to the medical area to view television and see what was happening before her attorney arrived. They wanted to have her near medical and mental health professionals, should they be needed. She already was a little upset. She'd heard a snippet of news on her personal radio—just enough to know something was going on in her case, but not enough to know what that was.

She entered the area and her eyes went immediately to the television broadcasting Channel 9's coverage of the breaking news. She recognized the location and collapsed into a chair and began hyperventilating. She lost her breath. Lieutenant Uncer told her repeatedly to breathe deep—but her breathing remained shallow and rapid.

Her palms were red, blotchy, warm and sweating profusely. She rubbed them together incessantly. "These chains are getting tighter on me," Casey complained about her cuffs. "Please loosen them." The deputies did not comply. They'd already checked the bracelets and knew that they were close to coming off her wrists.

Her eyes seemed drawn to the television, but at the slightest glimpse of the screen, she'd turn away again. She bent over at the waist. "I'm feeling sick to my stomach. I'm going to throw up." Now red blotches rose on her chest and neck as she listened to an announcer describe the find of a small child less than a quarter of a mile from the Anthony home.

After ten minutes, Lieutenant Uncer decided she'd had enough. She took Casey into a medical room to speak to a psychologist. His main concern was to make sure Casey was not going to do any harm to herself. He warned her not to discuss the case with him, since there was an officer in the room.

"No, no," she said. "I won't hurt myself." She asked for a sedative—the first drug of any kind she'd taken in jail.

"Have you taken drugs outside of the jail, for stress or anything like that?"

"No, the most I've ever taken is a muscle relaxant." When the psychologist left to consult with the doctor about medication, Casey asked Lieutenant Uncer, "Is my attorney coming?"

"We assume he's on his way. I don't know for sure. I'll get one of the C.O.'s to find out."

"Will you sit in the room with me? 'Cause I don't want to be alone," Casey pleaded. Her talking and breathing both ran at a rapid pace. "This is surreal. I can't break down and cry, because this isn't real." She then started to talk about the national football championship.

José Baez arrived and was left alone with his client. Casey now broke down and cried. She held her forehead in her hands. Baez stuck his head out the door to ask for tissues. Medical knocked on the door, bringing her a sedative.

Casey was shaking when she left her attorney. She told Lieutenant Uncer that the sedative had settled her stomach. Back in her cell, officers cleared her area of all belongings except reading material, in compliance with her psychological observation status. Casey asked to take a shower, saying it should make her feel better. She appeared calmer after she'd had ten minutes under the water. A mental health counselor came to talk to her. At the end of shift, Lieutenant Uncer stopped by to let Casey know she was leaving and to gauge her disposition. Although she was still crying as she spoke to the counselor, her breathing had returned to normal.

Casey was a puzzle to Uncer. The Lieutenant had always found it weird to talk to her, because before that day, Casey had to shown no signs of distress, and had always seemed devoid of emotion. Now, she was falling apart because a body had been found—a body that had not yet been identified. To investigators, the meaning of her reaction was clear: It was consciousness of guilt. They believed that when she'd seen where the remains were found, she knew it was Caylee—because she knew that was where she'd left her daughter's body.

José Baez got busy in court, filing an emergency motion:

> If the body found is determined to be that of Caylee Marie Anthony, then the defense would request that their own experts be permitted to be present during any forensic testing done, including but not limited to DNA testing or autopsy.

A hearing was set for Friday.

When the news broke, George and Cindy were flying in from the West Coast, where they had appeared on the *Larry King* show the night before. Their new attorney, Brad Conway, said, "They want to be left alone. They want to grieve and go through the process without the publicity that's been focused on them so long. They are realistic about the possibilities and about the fact that this is likely Caylee, but they continue to pray that likely it's not."

As their plane touched down in Orlando, police rushed them off and into a van. The van and another police vehicle pulled up behind a nearby Bennigan's restaurant, where Jim Hoover sat in his car and a limousine waited.

George, Cindy and their luggage transferred into the limo, and Dominic climbed in with them. Jim followed the luxury car to the Ritz-Carlton hotel, where rooms go for about $300 a night. ABC provided three rooms—one for Cindy and George, an adjoining room for Dominic and Jim and a room on another floor for spokesperson Michelle Bart.

They dined in the restaurant that night—where dinner can cost more than $100 per person. They were also joined by Lee and his girlfriend Mallory, and Caitlyn Folmer, from ABC, who ordered appetizers for the table. Everyone selected their entrees individually, except for Lee, who got nothing for himself, but requested a steak for José Baez, who had not yet arrived. No one had much of an appetite. Caitlyn used her credit card to pick up the tab. Soon, this network-paid getaway would instigate motions and arguments in the courtroom.

After dinner, Dominic asked Jim to meet outside the hotel. Cindy Anthony was with him. She gave Jim the keys to the house and asked him to lock up the house once the FBI and Orange County law enforcement were done with the search.

The next morning, Jim sat with George in the lounge sipping coffee. George was very distressed. He talked about the problems he and Cindy were having in their relationship. He didn't think they'd be together once this was all over. He said that the two of them had thrown each other, and Casey, too, underneath the bus with some of the comments they'd made. He confided that he'd been so depressed in September that he'd contemplated suicide.

CHAPTER 48

José argued his motion that the defense be present at the autopsy on Friday. The medical examiner's office objected to their presence, saying that the procedure was private, not a spectacle for lawyers, and that Florida's public policies didn't allow it.

Baez also argued for immediate access to the crime scene: "Photographs, video and schematic drawings are required, so that the defense will, at the bare minimum, have an idea of what the crime scene might have looked like before it was processed and possibly contaminated."

The Orange County sheriff's department objected to having the defense team on the crime scene while they were processing it. Their attorney said, "It's not an excavation site, it's an active crime scene. We are preserving what needs to be preserved. We are doing the job we are supposed to do."

The judge sided with the state, saying it would be "pure folly" to grant that kind of access to the defense team. "I can't assist you in interfering with a murder investigation."

He added that they could have access to the site as soon as it was cleared by the investigators. "There is no time clock on an investigation, and if law enforcement doesn't do an exhaustive job, defense will argue that it was shoddy and inadequate."

Jim drove George and Cindy to the house to pick up more clothes. Dominic went with them. They drove by Lee's home to pick him up to go to Brad Conway's office for fingerprinting, but Lee refused to go. He said that when he'd given his DNA sample, he'd been held against his will, and he wasn't going to risk that again.

At the attorney's office, Cindy called Lee several times. He finally relented and the whole family gave their fingerprints to the FBI. According to Jim, George sat alone on a small sofa. Dominic and Cindy sat side-by-side, in chairs, holding hands, patting and rubbing each other's arms. Cindy said, "You are my rock. Without you, I couldn't get through this kind of thing."

Jim put himself in George's place and knew he'd be angry and embarrassed if his wife had ever done that to him. It made him question the relationship between the private investigator and his client.

Jim didn't spend Friday night at the hotel, but returned Saturday in time for dinner. During the day, George and Cindy relaxed with Dominic, strolling around the golf course and trying to accept the new, ugly reality they faced.

Lee stopped by his parents' home on Saturday. He found a makeshift memorial to Caylee on the edge of the front yard—a cross with "Rest in Peace" on it, draped with a shirt bearing the words, "Remember me." It was more than he could bear—he swooped down and scooped it all up while reporters shouted questions. He walked toward the garage. "Do not follow me onto my property or I will call law enforcement."

Sunday morning, George and Cindy ordered room service, and Dominic and Jim joined them for breakfast. Then Jim drove them all to Eastside Baptist Church for services. Afterwards, they stopped by the house. Cindy was dismayed at the condition of her home after the search. She walked through, getting more and more distressed. She headed for the garage, where she found the cross Lee had plucked out of the yard. She carried it outside and set it beside Caylee's playhouse. She went back into the garage.

She was wielding a baseball bat when she returned. She used it to whale away on the cross, cursing Sergeant John Allen, Leonard Padilla, Sheriff Beary, José Baez—anyone who came to mind. She broke one arm off the cross, then the other. She kept swinging the bat, obscenities flying from her mouth.

Jim approached her. "Yo, okay, calm down. Calm down."

"Oh, this is therapy," Cindy said, turning to him with a look that made him back away. She kept beating the cross until she wore herself out.

José Baez and assistant counsel Linda Kenney-Baden came to the house. At first there were a lot of overlapping conversations going on at once. Jim said, "Dominic, do they know that we searched that area?"

When Dominic said they did, Jim still wasn't sure. He asked George directly, who said he knew about the search, adding that he'd walked down there once himself.

José spoke up, getting everyone's attention: "George, you have to hear this. This is going to be hard for you to hear. I have to tell you, Quantico [the FBI] wants to de-flesh the bones." Although a gruesome concept for the loved ones of a victim, forensic anthropologists value this technique in helping determine the circumstances of death.

A look of disgust crawled across George's face. Cindy dropped her head. "We can't let them do that," she said. "I want her cremated. I want to keep her ashes."

Linda and José talked about the possibility of getting an injunction.

Shirley Cuza had not spoken to her daughter Cindy since their explosive encounter in early November. When she heard the news of the discovery in the woods near their home, she knew her daughter had to be in pain. She picked up the phone to break the silence. "Cindy, I am so sorry for your loss. And I'm sorry I cut you off. I do want you back in my life."

Cindy agreed to be reunited with her mother on one condition—they would never talk about Casey or Caylee again.

From December 11 through December 20, crime-scene investigators from the Orange County Sheriff's Office, the FBI and the Florida Department of Law Enforcement scoured every inch of the wooded area. They cleared out sections of trees and undergrowth. Out on Suburban Drive, one investigator crawled on her knees examining all the uprooted plants placed on white sheets looking for any possible evidence caught in the foliage or the roots. Other investigators worked at sifting tables, running every bucket of dirt and leaves through screens to catch anything of any significance.

While they worked, groups of people stopped by to watch or to drop off flowers, stuffed animals and other mementoes. Many needed to make the pilgrimage to get a sense of closure. They may not have known Casey, but their hearts still ached.

The crime-scene investigators recovered more of Caylee's bones, along with a lot of others that belonged to animals. They unearthed pieces of plastic bags and fabric, shreds of pull-on pants, discarded soda cans, a busted Winnie the Pooh helium balloon, legs for a Barbie doll, a disposable camera, a piece of the same brand of duct tape found on the skull and the gas can, a tattered book that appeared to be one they'd seen Caylee reading in a video and, most heart-wrenching of all, a small heart-shaped sticker—the same size as the adhesive shape on the duct tape attached to the little girl's face.

A somber Dr. Jan Garavaglia, Orange County medical examiner, stood before a bank of microphones on December 19. "With regret, I'm here to inform you that the skeletal remains found on December eleventh are those of the missing toddler, Caylee Anthony . . . The remains are completely skeletonized, with no visible soft tissue . . . and no trauma to the bones prior to death.

". . . The manner of death in this case is homicide. The cause of death will be listed as homicide by undetermined means."

CHAPTER 49

Yuri Melich returned to the Hopespring house on December 20 with yet another search warrant. George was furious. He raved about the ceaseless intrusion into his life, even referring to the investigators as "fucking flunkies."

Cindy was upset. She felt she'd finally gotten the house cleaned up from the last search and now here they were, ready to mess the place up again. She surprised Melich when she said, "One of Caylee's Winnie the Pooh blankets is missing." He knew she didn't know that they'd found one at the recovery scene.

She told Detective Edwards that she'd had people walk that area a month ago, and there was nothing there. She didn't seem to be considering the possibility that it was overlooked. Her belief was that the remains had been deposited there sometime after mid-November.

In January 2009, the case took some strange turns. There was the recovery of the snake from David Dean's freezer. The autopsy of the diamondback found a clear cause of death: blunt force trauma, in all likelihood caused by being run over by a motor vehicle. Nothing was found to tie the snake to Caylee Anthony's murder.

The Florida Bar, investigating José Baez since October, announced that they were not seeking further disciplinary action regarding faxes sent out by Press Corp Media representative Todd Black on behalf of his public relations client, Attorney Baez. In one, Black alleged that State Attorney "Lawson Lamar is facing tough opposition and having a missing baby is a perfect springboard for free commercial time." Another one claimed that "the prosecution has manipulated and shamelessly used the media in the reporting of false, distorted . . . evidence." Baez denied seeing or approving of the faxes before their dissemination. The bar continued to look into allegations that Baez violated advertising rules.

The state attorney's office also received a complaint about Baez, accusing him of making secret entertainment deals to pay for Casey's defense. The judge had to determine if there were such agreements, including the rumored $200,000 deal with ABC News, and if they did exist, whether or not they created a conflict of interest.

Meanwhile, Todd Black finally admitted to the *Orlando Sentinel* that Todd Black was not his legal name. He declined to say what his real name was. His company sent the newspaper an email: "In general, we can tell you that it's been standard procedure for many years to have our company's story reps utilize abbreviated names for security purposes." Reporters at the *Sentinel* took this bit of news as a challenge. They pursued that story until they uncovered his real identity—a felon who'd tried to extort money from a TV reporter in California.

In what seemed to Orlando court observers to be a tit-for-tat move, Baez filed a motion with the court asking the judge to remove the prosecutors from the case. He also requested that Texas EquuSearch turn over all their records—including the names, addresses and phone numbers of all their volunteers. The judge denied the latter motion, saying that he did not have jurisdiction to order a subpoena and that the defense had failed to show the importance of this information or to prove that the organization worked as an agent of the state.

January also marked the announcement of an "Inspirational Caylee Sunshine Doll." Eighteen inches high and cute as a button, this doll even sang "You Are My Sunshine," just as Caylee did in the bittersweet video shown incessantly on television. This new creation was from Jaime Salcedo of Showbiz Promotions, whose other products included a Michael Vick Dog Chew toy, Sarah Palin red-white-and-blue boxers and a tee shirt proclaiming belief in Bigfoot. The absurdity continued when an even more macabre doll popped up on eBay the next week: the Casey Anthony Voodoo Doll, created by an artist in New Orleans.

This only took the focus off the real human tragedy of the case. The events that unfolded on January 22 brought the spotlight back to the seriousness of the crime and its effect on those involved.

George Anthony spoke off-camera to Fox 35 News at the end of December. He said, "There is a hole in my heart big enough for a truck to drive through. I don't think I'll ever have closure. At this point, I'm just hoping to someday be able to accept that Caylee is gone."

Acceptance came at a very high price. On January 22, just before 11 P.M., Brad Conway called the police to report that George was missing. He told the responding officer that Cindy had last seen her husband that morning when he'd left for a job interview. George did make it to the job fair, but his search was unsuccessful, in part because of the negative publicity he'd received.

Cindy told the officers that George had been depressed and upset about Caylee's death. Throughout the day, George had missed meetings—including one at their home with Brad Conway—and did not respond to her calls or text messages. She said that she'd probably added to her husband's despondency when she'd sent him to go shopping the day before to purchase jewelry for Caylee to wear during her cremation.

She noticed that George's medications were missing, along with a photograph of Cindy and Casey, and another one of Caylee, but none of his clothing or personal belongings were gone.

Around 10:45 P.M., George surfaced. He sent out text messages to friends telling them he wanted to be left alone, he wanted to make sure Caylee was in God's arms and he didn't want to live anymore. He would not provide his location to anyone.

Orange County law enforcement tracked the GPS on George's cell phone to Daytona Beach. Officers filled the area where the pings originated, and spotted George's vehicle in the parking lot of the Hawaii Motel. The motel owner said that George had arrived at 7 P.M. with a pillow and a blanket.

Once in the room, George had washed down sleeping pills with beer and started writing a letter. Daytona Beach Police Chief Mike Chitwood and several officers approached the door of the room and knocked. George answered and told the chief, "Hey. I needed to get away. I needed to think. I needed to clear my head. I'm fine. You guys can leave."

Leaving him in peace was not an option. He needed to be seen by mental health professionals. Chief Chitwood convinced George to come with him to the hospital. At 2 A.M., George checked into Halifax Regional Medical Center, involuntarily committed for psychological observation. A three-day stay was mandatory, but George stayed at the facility for eleven days.

CHAPTER 50

José Baez released a statement from his client on Monday, February 9:

> I miss Caylee every day and every minute of every day. I can't be there for Caylee's funeral, but some day, I want to go visit her grave and tell her how much I miss her. I allowed my parents to be in charge of the funeral for Caylee. I told them I wanted her buried in a casket and I wanted there to be a gravestone so I could go visit her. I asked them if there could only be a private funeral for just the family.
>
> I know they cremated her. I still don't want a public event with cameras and everybody around for Caylee's service, but I can't stop my parents from doing what they want. I truly hope that it will help them.

In the obituary Cindy wrote for the newspaper, she emphasized that the family requested "that those with only the purest of hearts and truly honorable intentions attend the service for their beloved child."

A dark cloud nearly rolled over Orlando. The Westboro Baptist Church in Topeka, Kansas, announced that they were coming to protest at the service. Labeled a hate group by the Southern Poverty Law Center, this was the same organization that had garnered attention for picketing military funerals to communicate their belief that U.S. troops killed in combat are suffering God's punishment for a nation harboring homosexuals. Fortunately for the family, the church demonstration did not happen.

Security for the February 10 event was tight, with private and public security present. They carried a list of people to exclude from the event—including Leonard Padilla, Richard and Jesse Grund, and Amy Huizenga. Mourners had to pass through metal detectors and were not permitted to carry bags into the church. Lines started to form outside of the church two hours before the scheduled service.

More than 1,200 people attended the ceremony. It began with a medley of Caylee's favorite songs, including "Jesus Loves Me" and "You Are My Sunshine."

What should have been a tearful farewell to a lost life turned into yet another controversial episode in the Anthony saga. Cindy made a lot of people uncomfortable with her comment about her daughter: "It breaks my heart that Casey isn't here to honor her child, who she loved so much. Casey, I hope you're able to hear me today. I love you and I wish I could comfort you right now. I wish I could take away all of your pain and wipe away your tears."

But it was Lee who lit up the blogosphere by talking in code. Instead of using his niece's name, he used the initials shared by Caylee Marie Anthony, Cynthia Marie Anthony and Casey Marie Anthony. "C.M.A., I miss you. C.M.A., I am so proud of you. I hope you are proud of me, too." Bloggers judged the message's content and were nearly unanimous in thinking that Lee had directed his comments to his sister.

Casey missed the message, since she did not watch the televised service. José Baez visited with her throughout the two-hour ceremony.

On Suburban Drive at a spontaneous memorial to Caylee, a hundred people gathered for the alternative service. They arrived with flowers, teddy bears and dolls, and placed them on a colorful pile that marked the woods where Caylee's body had been found.

On February 18, the state attorney's office released hundreds of pages of documents, including a page from Casey Anthony's journal. The June 21 date at the top of the page made it explosive:

> I have no regrets, just a bit worried. I just want for everything to work out okay. I completely trust my own judgment & know that I made the right decision. I just hope the ends justifies the means.
>
> I just want to know what the future will hold for me. I guess, I will soon see—This is the happiest that I have been in a very long time.
>
> I hope that my happiness will continue to grow—I've made new friends that I really like. I've surrounded myself with good people—I am finally happy. Let's just hope that doesn't change.

Traditional news sources and bloggers alike grabbed that page and ran as hard and as fast as they could, reporting that Casey had written this passage just days after murdering her daughter. For hours, everyone seemed to overlook the fact that on the opposite page, in the upper left-hand corner, Casey had written " '03"—if that was an indication of the date, it had been written two years before Caylee was even born. With no certainty of the timing of the entry, the story went from blazing hot to frosty cold before the late night news.

While Roy Kronk's attorney was threatening to sue Leonard Padilla over his unfounded speculations about his client, the defamation case pitting Zenaida Gonzalez against Casey Anthony moved into its deposition phase. George, Cindy and Lee were all served with subpoenas. Attorney Brad Conway got a temporary reprieve for Cindy and George on the grounds that his clients weren't mentally or emotionally equipped for questioning at that time. Lee, on the other hand, wanted to be done with it as soon as possible.

He said that he had never heard of Zenaida Gonzalez until the night his mother called 9-1-1, and that the woman who was suing his sister was not the nanny Casey blamed. He laughed a lot during the interview, as if he weren't taking it seriously. Everyone was shocked when Lee contradicted his previous testimony to the police. He'd told law enforcement that Casey was a habitual liar and a thief. During this deposition, though, he said, "To this day, I believe everything my sister tells me." That mistake exposed Lee to the risk of perjury charges.

He didn't answer two questions: whether he believed Casey had anything to do with Caylee's death, and who the father of Caylee was. After the interview, John Morgan asked that a judge force Lee to answer. Lee's attorney, Thomas Luka, responded to the judge that the purpose of those queries was simply to embarrass and annoy the Anthony family.

Morgan wanted Casey for a deposition, too. Because of her status in criminal court, her attorneys objected. As a compromise, he sent twenty-nine written questions. To all but one question, Casey had the same response:

Upon advice and counsel of my attorney, I am invoking my right to remain silent pursuant to the Fifth Amendment of the United States Constitution.

The last question was simple and straightforward:

Were you involved in the death of Caylee?

Casey replied:

The defendant would object to the question and would move to strike it. This question is being sought solely to embarrass, harass and brought in

an attempt to implicate the defendant in an on-
going criminal prosecution for first-degree murder.
The question is without merit and totally improper.

Zenaida's legal team asked the judge to force Casey to
answer the questions. Casey civil attorney Jonathan
Kasen maintained that the deposition should be delayed
until after the criminal trial, because every question was
"inextricably intertwined" with her murder case.

The defense team of eight attorneys and a long list of experts did not come cheap, and the state wanted to know
where Casey Anthony got the money—how she "went
from pauper to princess." The state asked the judge to
force the defense to reveal details on the financial arrangements for all members of the defense team. They were
concerned that if Casey were convicted, she could appeal
on the grounds that her attorney had a conflict of interest
that prevented him from working in her best interests.
   The defense fired back that the state was using tabloid
news rumors to embarrass and harass his client. Casey
submitted a sworn affidavit avowing that her retainer
agreement did not grant rights to her attorney to sell her
story or the story of her daughter. She added a handwritten note:

I believe that Mr. Ashton [assistant state attorney]
is angry because I have refused to take a plea
agreement for a crime I did not commit.

With Casey's statement to the contrary and no proof
to uphold the state's concerns, the judge ruled in favor of
the defense. The public may never know how Casey managed to afford her pricey defense.

The plot of woods where Caylee's remains had been found
went up for sale. The asking price was $89,000. Leonard
Padilla made a $50,000 offer for the land. He wanted to

build a permanent memorial to Caylee to replace the hodgepodge of handmade signs, flowers, stuffed animals and other mementoes. The neighborhood association was not pleased with this idea, nor were the parents who traveled the road to take their children to Hidden Oaks Elementary every day. The owner quietly pulled the lot off the market.

Deputy Richard Cain's lack of action in August led to an Internal Affairs investigation. He lost his badge in December, but still had a job working in an administrative capacity. His position with the county became more precarious when he lied about his performance during questioning in January. By the end of March, he was unemployed.

CHAPTER 51

On April 7, the state made a mistake. In a release of documents to the public, they accidentally included the audiotapes of interviews with the jailers who'd been with Casey when she learned about the discovery in the woods. The judge had not yet ruled on the release of that evidence, but once it was out, there was no taking it back.

Two days later, George Anthony sat down to provide his deposition in the defamation case against his daughter. He bristled early in the interview, accusing attorney Keith Mitnik of putting words in his mouth. Like his son, he said that he'd never heard the name Zenaida Gonzalez before July 8, but had heard the name Zanny for a year before that. He also believed today that there really was a woman named Zanny who'd baby-sat Caylee.

"Were there incidences in the year leading up to the disappearance where your daughter had taken money, to your knowledge, that didn't belong to her?" Mitnik asked.

"Not going to answer that," George said.

Brad Conway added, "That's irrelevant. There are criminal charges pending against her. It's going to affect the ability of her to get a fair trial, so we're not going to answer that question in this forum."

"Just so we're clear, so you can think of the wisdom of taking that position," Mitnik said, "the relevance here is that if she's having to take money from others, then how in the world does she have money to pay for a baby-sitter once a week or every week? And it is highly relevant to this case. So, I am going to ask one more time and see if you want to answer the question, so we don't have to come back on another day, because I know you'd probably rather not on a motion to compel.

"Was your daughter taking money that did not belong to her from others, to your knowledge, in the year leading up to this?"

"I'm not answering that," George said.

"You refuse to answer it?"

"Take it any way you want to take it. Refuse it. I'm not answering it. It's no concern about this lady down here, sitting down here. It's no concern."

Further along, George accused the attorney of flipping him the bird when the lawyer used his middle finger to push his glasses up on the bridge of his nose. Later, George blew up at him over semantics: "If you say 'the remains' one more time, sir, I'm walking out of this room. How dare you say that about my granddaughter? How dare you? How dare you?"

For an hour the contentiousness continued, with George threatening to leave on four separate occasions. Finally it peaked. They took a break and Brad Conway spoke to his client alone. When they returned, George was more cooperative.

That afternoon, Cindy sat in the hot seat, and the level of hostility rose even higher. Pain and anger etched furrows in Cindy's face. Her eyes blazed, her mouth formed a tight horizontal slit. With the first question out of the chute, Cindy was combative: "Explain to me the relevance of the question."

Attorney John Dill asked, "Is there any other person besides your daughter that has told you that they have met or seen Zanny?"

"No, but Caylee talked about Zanny's dog."

"We'll get to that in a second."

"She's another person," she said with a sharp jut of her chin.

"I appreciate that," Dill said. "I just want to be clear."

"If there's a dog that belongs to Zanny, then there must be a Zanny."

"Fair enough," the attorney conceded. "Besides your daughter and Caylee saying that about the dog, okay, is there any other adult that has said to you, 'I have met Zanny' or 'I know who she is'?"

"Not that I'm aware of."

After Dill and Conway had a battle of legal wills over which questions were acceptable, Cindy said, "Listen, bottom line is, I shouldn't be answering any questions that is not relevant to Zenaida Fernandez-Gonzalez that has a civil lawsuit against Casey Marie Anthony. And I am graciously answering these ridiculous questions, that have nothing to do with Mr. Morgan's client that is the Zenaida Gonzalez. Okay?" Cindy seemed to think there were no relevant questions.

"I understand what you want, if I may, Ms. Anthony? I appreciate it and I have a job to do here and I understand that you want to short-circuit the process."

"I'm not trying to short-circuit anything, and I object to that characterization."

Later on in the interview, Cindy complained about the body language of Attorney John Morgan. "He's shaking his head when I'm answering a question. That's exactly what the sheriff's department did to my daughter. They never let her speak. You guys are doing the same thing to me."

When the attorney asked, "Is it fair to say your daughter's lied to you about many things?" Cindy snapped, "It's fair to say the sheriff's department lied to me about many things." Cindy declared questions about her parents and those about Casey stealing from her parents irrelevant. When she was asked about her relationship with her daughter, she balked again.

"I understand you're tired, but let's go back to my question," the attorney said.

"I'm not answering it."

The attorney attempted to explain the law regarding her

obligation to answer any questions that weren't covered by privilege, but Cindy wasn't budging. They all took a break so that she could confer with her lawyer. Cindy was not any more cooperative when they recommenced.

She threatened to walk out or file harassment charges, and she insulted Zenaida, saying she didn't match the description given by Casey. "She doesn't have perfect teeth. She's not a ten. I'm sorry, ma'am, you're cute, but you're not a ten."

Cindy testified that she believed someone else had dumped Caylee's body in the woods near their home after hearing the jail visitation tape where Casey said she thought her daughter was nearby.

Zenaida's attorneys filed a motion to compel, requesting the judge to order Cindy to answer the financial questions that she insisted were irrelevant.

When it was Dominic Casey's turn to be questioned by Zenaida's attorneys, he simply ignored the subpoena, an act that put his private investigator's license in jeopardy.

In April, The Florida Bar was investigating the behavior of José Baez once again. One complaint came from Judge Stan Strickland, the other from Dominic Casey. Both were about the same matter: Jose Baez was accused of telling Dominic not to call 9-1-1 if he found Caylee's remains in the woods. José called the allegations ridiculous.

The promotional announcements were on the air. Oprah would have the first interview with George and Cindy since the discovery of Caylee's body. The show billed it as an exclusive event to air in May. Supporters of the family felt this show was the perfect venue to soften their image. If Oprah loved them, the world would, too.

But then, George and Cindy accepted an invitation to appear on the CBS *Early Show* in April. Oprah responded, "Based on the Anthonys' decision to appear on other programs, we have decided not to move forward with their interview on *The Oprah Winfrey Show* at this time."

Cindy, however, had a different story. She wrote in an email to WKMG news: "I cancelled on Oprah because of integrity." Her reason made no sense to anyone.

George, Cindy and lawyer Brad Conway joined Maggie Rodriquez on the *Early Show* set on April 22. Cindy said, "Sometimes it gets lost that we've lost someone very close to us and we have someone else who's hurting and we miss her dearly, too."

When Maggie asked about the reinstatement of the death penalty earlier in the month, Cindy said that they could not think about that now. George added that he didn't believe there would be a plea deal and that neither of them wanted her to do that. "Casey's not going to admit to something she hasn't done."

"How are you so sure?" Maggie asked. "How do you say with such conviction that she didn't do this?"

"We love our daughter," Cindy said. "We stand behind her. We know what kind of mother she was."

"Is it because you love your daughter that you need to believe this, or is it because you believe unflinchingly that it is not possible that she did this?"

"I don't believe it's possible for my daughter to hurt anyone," George said. "And she definitely wouldn't hurt her own child. I mean, my gosh, I've seen the love she had every single day for her. She had been with us. She wouldn't hurt her."

The interview continued the next day. Maggie asked about Casey: "What kind of young lady did she grow up to be, George?"

"Very sensitive. Very caring. The kind of daughter that any father is proud of, I mean, I'm proud of my daughter. Watching Caylee grow up, you know, it's . . . like watching my daughter grow up again."

The couple talked about their granddaughter, the pain of their loss and the 911 calls in July. Maggie asked about Casey, "What questions would you have for her? What questions has she not answered for you that you need to know?"

"I had time with Casey to ask questions," George said.

"Are you satisfied with the answers she gave you?"

"You know, I'd love to know more."

"Like what?" Maggie prodded.

"I want to know what happened."

"She claimed that the babysitter snatched her?"

"Yes."

"George, shouldn't she have reported her missing?"

"Again, I can't say what my daughter was thinking. We just don't know."

"Do you fault her for anything?"

"How can we?" Cindy asked. We don't know what she's been through. I don't know what that girl has been through. I mean, George and I are living the same nightmare and I can't judge George for certain things that he's done. I understand certain things. I understand his suicide attempt. A lot of people don't know I was there, too. I wrote suicide notes back in the end of July and August."

"You did?"

"Yes, I did. Because I couldn't bear not having Caylee around and not knowing. You know, you get to a point when you miss someone so much that you think life's not worth living."

"And what kept you from going through [with] it?" Maggie asked.

"Casey came home—the first time, Casey came home—the very first night—being able to see her and hug her."

When Maggie asked about jail visitation, Cindy complained about the sunshine laws and the awkwardness of the visits. "What do you say to people who say the evidence is hard to refute?" Maggie asked.

"Well, I guess I could answer in one way," George said. "Has any other case ever gotten all this kind of exposure?"

Brad Conway interjected. "Can I answer that?"

"Sure," Maggie said.

"The evidence is for trial. There's no evidence out there right now. What's out there is discovery. There's reports. There's photos. But that's not evidence."

"What do you say to people who conclude that your daughter is guilty?"

"She's presumed innocent," Cindy said. "You know, the facts have not all come out."

"But people have said some things about her character that she was a liar and that was well documented. Why should people believe her now when her life is at stake?"

"Well, her life *is* at stake."

"Do you feel that although you couldn't save Caylee, you will at least try to save Casey?"

"I don't know what we can do. All we can do is stand behind our daughter. And that's all we can do."

"Unflinching support?"

"Unflinching support," Cindy said. "I believe in her."

"You know," George said, "there's some people that say, Well, we should be done with it . . . We can't. That's our daughter, you know."

"No matter what she may or may not have done."

"No matter what, that's still our daughter. No matter what."

In stark contrast to the position of Cindy and George, the conclusion of the Orange County Sheriff's Office's Investigative Report read:

After several months of investigation, detectives could find no one who has ever met, spoken with or seen any Zenaida Gonzalez who had cared for Caylee Anthony. There has been no factual evidence to suggest that anyone besides Casey Anthony was the last one to be with Caylee when she was last seen alive.

Almost everyone who knows Casey Anthony admits she was prone to lying. Based on statements and eyewitness accounts, it appears that Caylee was last seen alive on June 16, 2008. Evidence obtained from the white 1998 Pontiac Sunfire along with evidence found with the body suggests that Caylee died between June 16 and June 27 2008. Evidence also suggests that Caylee Anthony was in the trunk of the white 1998 Pontiac for a period of time but removed prior to June 27 2008. Evidence on the body suggests that the child's death was not accidental but an intentional act.

As of this writing, there is nothing to suggest that anyone but Casey Anthony is responsible for the death and disposal of Caylee Anthony.

The trial of Casey Anthony for the murder of her daughter is currently expected to begin in June, 2010. José Baez has requested a change of venue, preferably in the Miami–Dade area. The prosecutors are seeking the death penalty.

AFTERWORD

Why?

The death of little Caylee Marie would seem senseless no matter how she died. An innocent child deserves the opportunity to stretch a long shadow into the future. If a toddler dies from illness, we direct our anger at God. When it's by accident, we look for someone to blame. But when a precious one is lost through murder, the natural response is outrage and horror.

Still, we want to know why, because until we do, we cannot do anything to prevent it from happening again to another child. We have to believe there is a way to prevent such a death, or we slide into an endless pit of despair. Our only hope is knowledge, awareness of the red flags that portend disaster and an ability to recognize the warnings in real time.

In initial interviews, many of Casey's friends were convinced that Caylee's death had to have been an accident—something bad happened without any evil intention, causing Casey to panic and dispose of the body. Even Cindy and George contemplated that scenario when they talked to each other about the pool ladder.

Casey's Uncle Rick started there, but quickly reached a different conclusion: "She looks at people like they're objects. They have a shelf life—when she's through with them, they're gone. Caylee was an object, a possession . . . I know in my mind and heart that Casey planned it. Caylee was getting old enough that she could tell on

[Casey], and that was complicated by the tremendous jealousy Casey felt towards Cindy."

Just as Casey's lies made it clear to many that she was involved in her daughter's death, her months of silence made it apparent to many that what happened wasn't an accident. If Caylee had drowned in the pool, or over-dosed from medication intended just to make her sleep, or died from any other mishap, surely Casey would have stepped forward and accepted responsibility, throwing herself on the mercy of the court. But she did not. She clung to her initial story and toyed with the hearts of her family members.

Were her tears during videotaped conversations with her parents born from self-pity, were they manufactured for the purpose of manipulation, or were they the product of genuine regret? Did she come to regret her actions after the fact when she realized that the one person who believed everything she said without question, who looked up to her with adoration and loved her without passing judgment, was now gone?

If Casey did indeed suffer from Narcissistic Personality Disorder, as some have suggested, the death of Caylee wouldn't fit. A young child feeds into a narcissist's need for adulation.

Psychoanalyst Bethany Marshall suggested Casey's actions were the product of a Borderline Personality Disorder, saying, "Casey is a bully. She uses words like weapons. She uses them as objects to control other people . . . There's a ragefulness, impulsivity, lack of empathy toward other people, including her own child, a disregard and violation of the rights of others." But one of the hallmarks of this disorder is self-injury, of which there appears to be no evidence.

Psychologist and author Dr. Juliann Mitchell wrote that

Casey is a sociopathic, superficial sensational-ist . . . She fits the description of someone with an antisocial personality disorder . . . Everything she

DIANE FANNING

does is designed to protect herself by outwitting and outsmarting the legal authorities . . . Others are always expendable . . . Sociopaths are incapable of remaining in love, or even selflessly loving anyone.

That diagnosis seems to track with the last few years of Casey's life, but does not seem compatible with her friends' earlier memories.

Some have turned to Dr. Otto Kernberg's theory of malignant narcissism as the diagnosis that answers the mystery of Casey Anthony's actions in the wake of her daughter's disappearance. He saw that condition as being the mid-point on the spectrum between Narcissistic Personality Disorder and Anti-social Personality Disorder—a place where there are feelings of entitlement, superiority, invincibility and immunity to the laws of others. A disorder that often leads to the destruction of the source of frustration.

There is a lot of overlap in the symptoms of different personality disorders. But no matter where you might place Casey on that continuum, you would have an individual whose self-absorption and insensitivity to others is a destructive force, which damages anything that stands in its way.

It is easy to point to her parents and blame them for creating this monster, but is it fair? Just as model citizens dedicated to helping others can be the product of dreadful parents, perfect parents sometimes nurture hellions. It is impossible to say how much of the blame for Casey's actions derives from the way she was enabled by her parents.

As a close observer of these events and of the Anthony family, I don't know how I'd react if I were in George and Cindy's shoes. I hope that I would be able to embrace reason. But who knows? That acceptance would come with a huge burden of guilt—one that very easily could lead to the suicidal ideation George experienced in January. There is nothing in life that can prepare you for being the family of a victim of such an awful crime, no less its possible perpetrator.

Perhaps the Anthony family could have dealt with their unenviable position better if they had not been trapped in the piercing headlights of national attention, if they had not been constantly besieged by news sources wanting sound bites and headlines, and attention-seekers wanting to be part of the story. Maybe with time for quiet reflection, they could have come to terms with the situation without the hostility and frustration that erupted in the months after Caylee's disappearance.

Could they have acted sooner to prevent this tragedy from happening? You could argue that that was possible. They could have encouraged their daughter to give up her child for adoption. They could have fought for custody of their granddaughter when it seemed that Casey had begun to abandon responsibility. Looking back, it is easy to see other possibilities; but how could they know where their lives were headed?

After the fact, they, like the rest of us, were caught up in a carnival of bright lights, loud voices and the public's ceaseless appetite for entertainment. This story had it all: a young, attractive perpetrator, a resort city locale and an endless supply of interesting side attractions.

Often lost in the sensationalism was the victim, Caylee Marie Anthony—the one little girl who mattered the most.

What of other little children? Is there anything we can do to save future lives? Our only hope is vigilance and empathy. We need to be compassionate and non-judgmental toward women facing an unwanted pregnancy. We need to recognize the warning signs of a parent whose irresponsibility extends to their child. As a society we need to be ever-vigilant about the well-being of our most helpless. With luck and determination, we can protect the little ones who cannot protect themselves—not every time, not in every place. But to save a single child from Caylee Marie's fate is an accomplishment worthy of any sacrifice.

Caylee DOB 8-9-05
last seen by g-parents